BLACK MARRIAGE
AND
FAMILY THERAPY

Contributions in Afro-American and African Studies
Series Advisers: John W. Blassingame and Henry Louis Gates, Jr.

The Afro-Yankees
Providence's Black Community in the Antebellum Era
Robert J. Cottrol

A Case of Black and White:
Northern Volunteers and the Southern Freedom Summers, 1964-1965
Mary Aickin Rothschild

Gatekeepers of Black Culture: Black-Owned Book Publishing in the United
States, 1817-1981
Donald Franklin Joyce

The Craft of an Absolute Winner: Characterization and Narratology in the
Novels of Machado de Assis
Maria Luisa Nunes

BLACK MARRIAGE
AND
FAMILY THERAPY

Edited by
Constance E. Obudho

Contributions in Afro-American and African Studies, Number 72

GREENWOOD PRESS
Westport, Connecticut • London, England

Library of Congress Cataloging in Publication Data
Main entry under title:

Black marriage and family therapy.

(Contributions in Afro-American and African studies,
ISSN 0069-9624 ; no. 72)
  Bibliography: p.
  Includes indexes.
  1. Afro-American families—Addresses, essays,
lectures. 2. Family psychotherapy—United States—
Addresses, essays, lectures. 3. Marriage—United
States—Addresses, essays, lectures. I. Obudho,
Constance E. II. Series.
E185.86.B5257 1983   306.8'08996073   82-20967
ISBN 0-313-22119-7 (lib. bdg.)

Library of Congress Catalog Card Number: 82-20967
ISBN: 0-313-22119-7
ISSN: 0069-9624

First published in 1983

Greenwood Press
A division of Congressional Information Service, Inc.
88 Post Road West
Westport, Connecticut 06881

Printed in the United States of America

10 9 8 7 6 5 4 3 2 1

CONTENTS

84-1537

FIGURES

TABLES

PREFACE

Perhaps someday the behaviors of black people will no longer be thought of as merely deviations from the behaviors of a white majority. Black marriages and family lives, for example, may then receive the legitimacy and respect they deserve from the social science community and from the general public as well.

Much of the past study of marriages and family lives among black people has been replete with negative images. Although some of the myths and misperceptions have been dispelled as a result of some more critical, detailed, and unbiased investigations, old myths die hard. Hopefully, the explorations of those who have been concerned enough to challenge some of the existing myths will continue.

This book, which concerns some of the aspects of the marriages and family lives of black people, provides a look at contemporary behavior. The book is divided into two parts. Part One, entitled "About Marriage and Family," begins with an Introduction which gives a brief overview of the various chapters discussing what was studied and found. The remaining chapters in the first section concern the expression of love among black people, husband-wife relationships, women's feelings about working and being wives and mothers, and some of the styles and processes of parenthood as well as family planning. Part Two, called "Marital and Family Therapy," is composed of four chapters. The research on family therapy with black people is meager compared to other areas of research with blacks. The need for developing and testing techniques is great. The papers in this section present several methods devised by the writer/therapists for their unique clients. These approaches serve as guidelines for further investigations into working with black couples and families. Lastly, there is the chapter "Some Final Comments."

Structurally, the book contains a list of tables, referenced by chapter as well as by table number. Book and article references are included at the end of each individual chapter, and there are subject and author indices.

It is hoped that those who read this book will gain new insights into black family life and that some will be prompted to conduct further critical research into this area.

ACKNOWLEDGMENTS

In the course of preparing any manuscript, there are individuals whose assistance helps make things go more smoothly. Thanks go to Charlotte Nieliwocki who was available for typing and consultation despite her busy schedule and Donna Adamski whose sense of humor often kept me going when things were rough.

PART ONE:

ABOUT MARRIAGE
AND FAMILY

INTRODUCTION—BLACK MARRIAGES AND FAMILY THERAPY: A PERSPECTIVE

Constance E. Obudho

Andrew Billingsley (1968), a noted sociologist, recognized quite some years ago that black marriages have consistently received minimal attention from American scholars. Even though observations of interpersonal relationships among blacks stem from the earliest contact between Africans and whites in this country, looking through textbooks on the American family, one will see references to black relationships on only a few pages and under a limited range of topics. These topics usually include such areas as fertility, illegitimacy, female-headed households, divorce, separation, lower-class status, and child training. Furthermore, when considering black marriages, social scientists have often relied heavily upon stereotypes, myths, invalidated generalizations (English, 1974, p. 39), and unsubstantiated descriptions. As such, black marriages, little understood, have often been viewed as subsystems within and deviations from the forms of the majority white population with inherent troubles and weaknesses. This state of affairs—the lack of substantial information and the distortions of the information that exists—has created much confusion about what black marriages are really like. But, what are black marriages like? Are they indeed different from the marriages of white people? In what ways are they different or the same? What roles do black men and women play in their marriages? What expectations do they have about marriage? Are these marriages indeed fraught with problems? Where are these marriages headed? These are just some of the many questions that may be raised with regard to the condition of black marriages today. Initially, however, a look at the types of issues that have traditionally been studied and what has been reported is in order.

Even before black people could join in legal unions and thus formal marriages could be scrutinized, observations of our relationships were made. During slavery, the descriptive reports of travelers were a major source of information. Rarely were empirical studies done. Furthermore, some of the issues that tended to preoccupy these observers readily lent themselves to value judgments and thus led to distortions and exaggerations of conditions—for example, stable and unstable unions between slaves, the disruption of marital and parental duties and general family ties, the role of the man in the family, intermarriage between blacks and whites, fertility, and mother-child relations, to name but a few (Calhoun, 1917 and Du Bois, 1909). Du Bois (1909, p. 200) noted that it was often difficult to get a clear picture of the lives of slaves with the divergent views presented by the abolitionist who spoke of disrupted lives and the Southern apologist who spoke of idyllic devotion and careless toil. Unfortunately, the stage had been set in terms of the types of issues that were considered important to study, and the early perceptions that were espoused about these issues became steadfast descriptions of black life.

After slavery, observers were concerned with how the new status of blacks affected our lives and how we responded to this new status. The old issues emerged with new emphasis. It was during the Emancipation period and beyond that figures on divorce and separation began to be reported, and the dominant role of the woman and the man's low self-esteem became classic characterizations of black men and women. Blacks were described as having a higher incidence of separation and divorce than whites; black mothers were charged with being more dominant and important than black fathers within the family system; men were judged to have low self-esteem because of the dominance of their wives and mothers; and home environments were report-edly disruptive to the proper upbringing of children (Calhoun, 1917; Dowd, 1926; Frazier, 1939; and Moynihan, 1965).

After observing these problems, social scientists then had to try to explain their occurrence. The use of slavery as an explanation for black behavior has permeated much of the work on black family life. The slavery hypothesis is that the condition of bondage created a certain character among blacks as a group. Because slavery tore families apart, it created a disposition among black men to take their family responsibilities lightly and among black women to be independent of their men. It taught women to make children of utmost importance in their lives because they could not rely upon their men. In addition, it created the disposition among both black men and women to have little concern for sexual restraint. The slavery hypothesis blames the victim for his problems and conveniently ignores the corollaries of slavery that affect the lives of black people, discrimination and segregation. Furthermore, it places an undue value judgment on the behaviors of a group of people without giving regard to individual differences. This latter factor has done a great disservice because it has made others ignorant of the diversity among blacks and has tended to focus research upon certain predictable problem areas. Additional-ly, this notion seems to have blinded researchers to more obvious explana-tions of the behaviors they have observed. For instance, although it was recognized some time ago that there were differences in life-styles among black people differing in socioeconomic backgrounds (Dowd, 1926 and Du

Bois, 1909), this fact seems not to have had as much impact on explanations of the behavior of black people as the effects of slavery which purportedly negated any differences. Even much later, Rainwater (1966) noted that, because of the high degree of role segregation in marriages in lower-class families, both black and white families tended to be matrifocal in comparison to middle-class families. The black as well as the white wife made most of the decisions that kept the family going, and she had the greatest sense of responsibility to the family. The woman tended to turn to female relatives for counsel and support and tended to treat her husband as being uninterested in the day-to-day problems of family life (p. 190). Therefore, in terms of the woman's role in the home, it was not racial differences suggestive of the negative consequences of slavery on blacks, but socioeconomic differences that may produce differing ways of responding in marriage. However, despite such alternative explanations, the idea of the long-reaching consequences of slavery on black behavior remains a topic of discussion.

Another explanation for the behaviors of black people with regard to marriages and life-styles is that many of the behaviors had their origins in the African past (Blackwell, 1975; Dowd, 1917; Du Bois, 1909; Herskovitz, 1958; and Nobles, 1972). In his book *The Myth of the Negro Past*, for instance, Herskovitz (1958) disputed the claim made by some writers that blacks had been stripped of their cultural heritage when they were brought to the plantations (Frazier, 1939 and Johnson, 1934). He felt that there were certain similarities between the past and current behaviors. Herskovitz demonstrated this by investigating the presence of African-like customs among blacks in countries in addition to the United States—Haiti, South America, Nigeria, and the Gold Coast, for example (pp. 6–7). One instance he presented of a behavioral carry-over concerned the practice of common-law marriage. He noted that in Africa and in the other areas where Africanisms supposedly persisted, marriage did not have to be sanctioned by law or any religious body. Consent of relatives was sufficient. The practice of common-law marriage was carried on by blacks in the United States, and according to Herskovitz, it was an extension of the earlier practice in Africa (p. 171). Common-law marriage is still a fact of the black community. Its rate of occurrence is not known. However, whether or not it is a behavioral carry-over from our past in Africa or whether it is due to other more recent variables is debatable. There are other writers who have noted the existence of other so-called Africanisms among certain behaviors displayed by black people (Ladner, 1971); and whether or not these behaviors are also the product of our African past and whether the process of slavery explains contemporary black behavior and life-styles, remain open to discussion.

As indicated before, female-headed households, instances of separation, and instances of divorce are issues that have been repeatedly investigated among black people. While these issues have been used to interpret the condition of black marriages, they only point to limited features of black marriages. In addition, they serve to ignore what is going on in intact situations. Yet, these issues cannot be dismissed because they are factors that impinge on all ethnic groups in this country. Some of the more recent statistics concerning the marriages of black people are reminiscent of past reports and others are more enlightening in that they cover a broader scope. For example, looking at 1975 data and considering the median age at marriage and divorce for black people born 1900 to 1904 and 1950 to 1959,[1] it can be seen that both sexes began marrying and divorcing earlier over time. Men born between 1900 and 1904 tended to marry around age 26.3, while those born 1950–1954 tended to marry around age 20.6. Women born 1900–1904 married around age 20.2, and those born 1955–1959 married around age 17.3 (figures for men born 1955–1959 were reportedly not available because of the number of men available for questioning). In terms of age at which divorced, men born between 1905 and 1909 divorced around age 32.2, while those born 1945–1949 divorced around age 23.6. Women born 1905–1909 divorced around age 27.3, and those born 1945–1949 divorced about age 23.4. The median interval between the first marriage and the end of that marriage in divorce for blacks born 1900–1909 was 6.6 years for men and 7.8 years for women. For individuals born 1940–1949, the statistics were 3.7 years for men and 5.4 years for women. Thus, not only were black people marrying at an earlier age than perhaps their parents and grandparents, we were also divorcing at an earlier age and staying married for shorter periods of time. Values and attitudes within a society change, and black people as well as any other group may become products of this change.

The median interval between divorce after the first marriage and the start of a second marriage is another area of concern. For men born 1900–1909, this interval was 8.6 years, and for women it was 8.7 years. The percentages were also very close for men and women born between 1940 and 1949: 2.9 and 2.7 years, respectively, but a much shorter interval time was incurred. Again, value and attitude changes may play a significant role in the processes of black marriages and associated behaviors.

For cases of remarriage in which the husband married for the first time and the wife was previously married and now a widow, 1.7 percent of the men were in this category, and 6.5 percent of the cases were after the woman's divorce. For women experiencing a first marriage, 3.1 percent of the husbands' marriages had ended owing to widowerhood and 7.7 percent had ended owing to divorce. In cases in which both the man and woman remarried after both had been divorced, the percentage was 9.9. It appears that most black people marrying for the first time choose an individual who has also not been married before. Furthermore, most black people marry only once (69.6 percent).

As far as female-headed families are concerned, more black female family heads are now divorced or single; many now are younger than they were in the early part of this decade; and more now have children than in previous years.[2] The statistics for situations in which children were at home for the years 1970 and 1979 for black women are as follows: 1970, 30.6 percent and 1979, 45.6 percent. In comparison, for white females, the percentages are 7.8 for 1970 and 13.5 for 1979. One-parent families maintained by a black male were 2.4 percent in 1970 and 3.1 percent in 1979. For white males, the percentages were 1.1 in 1970 and 1.7 in 1979. Although the incidence of one-parent families was greater among black people as of 1979, in fact, two-thirds, or 68 percent, of all one-parent families were maintained by whites in that year.

It would be difficult and unfeasible to try to explain in depth the occurrences of separation, divorce, remarriage, and single-parent households within the scope of this introduction. However, the explanations that have been suggested by various writers for some of these issues may be touched upon very briefly. For example, whenever the issues of separation or divorce are considered and blacks and whites with similar income levels are investigated, similar behaviors and family patterns seem to emerge (Herzog, 1966 and Willie, 1970). Furthermore, Willie (1976) suggested that family instability specifically among blacks may be more a function of economic imbalance and racial discrimination than a function of slavery per se (p. 4). Bernard (1966) suggested that divergent levels of education, occupation, and income may account for instability found in black marriages. Lastly, Heiss (1975) made comparisons between blacks and whites in regard to fertility, female dominance, marital status, age at which married, help from relatives, and extended families and concluded that some of the characteristics that have been attributed to blacks are exaggerations of the conditions and that socioeconomic status plays a greater role in the differences than race.

Socioeconomic factors and race may not address the entire matter as far as explaining issues in black marriages is concerned. Individual differences, for example, should be recognized. Nevertheless, whatever the underlying reasons for the behaviors of black people, emphasis must continue to be placed on the strengths of black unions to help correct the distorted picture that has been presented for too long. Fortunately, in contrast to the continued negative trend in the study of black marital life, there has emerged a growing body of literature that has shown a concern for the positive aspects. Many of the more positive studies have been concerned with the differences among black families themselves and not with how the families and marriages deviate from white patterns (Bernard, 1966 and Willie, 1976). Others have tried to dispel some of the negative myths associated with black family life by deliberately focusing upon samples of stably married couples who were above lower-class (Scanzoni, 1971). Still others have tried to emphasize the strengths of the black family by sharing with us a monumental work on a black family spanning several generations (Haley, 1976). Finally, the family therapy literature has attacked the misleading stereotypes about black families which are then wrongly used to form basic hypotheses for treatment (McAdoo, 1977).

In addition to focusing on the more positive aspects of black life, some studies have investigated blacks in greater detail than before. For example, husband-wife relationships including attitudes about the conjugal condition have been brought out more fully (Blood and Wolfe, 1960; Heiss, 1975; Scanzoni, 1971; and Thomas, 1974). Different types of black family structures, extended and nuclear, have been explored and given legitimacy (Heiss, 1975; Martin and Martin, 1978; and Stack, 1975). Finally, more black scholars have become involved in these researches and have brought new interpretations to many of the old topics. It is the aim of this book to carry forth the research on black marriages, to provide some new insights into the various issues that have continued to be studied within the area, and to present some new views which may spark further research.

NOTES

1. *Current Population Reports*, Series P-20, No. 297, Number, Timing, and Duration of Marriages and Divorces in the United States, June 1975, pp. 10, 12, and 16–17.
2. *Current Population Reports*, Series P-20, No. 352, Household and Family Characteristics, March, 1979, p. 3.

REFERENCES

Bernard, J. *Marriage and Family Among Negroes*. Englewood Cliffs, N.J.: Prentice-Hall, 1966.
Billingsley, A. *Black Families in White America*. Englewood Cliffs, N.J.: Prentice-Hall, 1968.
Blackwell, J. E. *The Black Community*. New York: Harper & Row Publishers, 1975.
Blood, R. O., and D. M. Wolfe. *Husbands and Wives: The Dynamics of Married Living*. Glencoe, Ill.: The Free Press of Glencoe, 1960.
Calhoun, A. W. *A Social History of the American Family, Vol. I: Colonial Period*. New York: Barnes & Noble, Inc., 1917.
Dowd, J. *The Negro in American Life*. New York: The Century Co., 1926.
Du Bois, W.E.B. (ed) *The Negro American Family*. Cambridge, Mass.: The M.I.T. Press, 1909.
English, R. H. "Beyond Pathology: Research and Theoretical Perspectives on Black Families." In L. E. Gary (ed) *Social Research and the Black Community: Selected Issues and Priorities*. Washington, D.C.: Howard University Institute for Urban Affairs and Research, 1979.
Frazier, E. F. *The Free Negro Family*. Nashville, Tenn.: Fisk Univeristy Press, 1932.
Haley, A. *Roots*. Garden City, N.Y.: Doubleday & Co., Inc., 1976.
Heiss, J. *The Case of the Black Family: A Sociological Inquiry*. New York: Columbia University Press, 1975.
Herskovitz, M. *The Myth of the Negro Past*. Boston: Beacon Press, 1958.
Herzog, E. "Is There A Breakdown of the Negro Family," *Social Work*, 1966, 11(1), 3–10.
Johnson, C. S. *Shadow of the Plantation*. Chicago: University of Chicago Press, 1934.

Ladner, J. *Tomorrow's Tomorrow: The Black Woman*. New York: Doubleday & Co., Inc. 1971.

Martin, E. O., and J. M. Martin. *The Black Extended Family*. Chicago: The University of Chicago Press, 1978.

McAdoo, H. "Family Therapy in the Black Community," *American Journal of Orthopsychiatry*, 1977, 47(1), 75–79.

Moynihan, D. P. *The Negro Family: The Case for National Action*. Prepared for Office of Policy Planning and Research, 1965.

Rainwater, L. "Crucible of Identity: The Negro Lower Class Family," *Daedalus*, 1966, 95(Winter), 172–217.

Scanzoni, J. H. *The Black Family in Modern Society: Patterns of Stability and Security*. Chicago: The University of Chicago Press, 1971.

Stack, C. B. *All Our Kin: Strategies for Survival in a Black Community*. New York: Harper & Row Publishers, 1975.

Thomas, G. B. *Young Black Adults: Liberation and Family Attitudes*. New York: Friendship Press, 1974.

Willie, C. V. (ed) *The Family Life of Black People*. Columbus, Ohio: Charles V. Merrill, 1970.

————. *A New Look at Black Families*. New York: General Hall, 1976.

2

THE LOVING RELATIONSHIP: IMPETUS FOR BLACK MARRIAGE

Ruth E. G. King and Jean T. Griffin

Love is a prerequisite for marriage. Many would argue the point, for we often hear of people who marry for money, companionship, status, and other reasons that do not include the concept of love. Others would argue that love is the foundation of marriage or the basis on which a happy marriage is built. Love, in general, and black love, in particular, have eluded precise psychological definition. Studies of love tend to generate ambiguous concepts. The term *love* has been defined as styles of interactivity (Lee, 1977), as quantifiable by mathematical formula (Bentler and Hube, 1979), as a social organization (Rosenblatt, 1967), as interpersonal attraction (Berscheid and Walster, 1974), and as interpersonal attitude (Rubin, 1973). Love encompasses elements of all the concepts suggested by the authors and is more than any single one of them.

The operational definition that best applies to the perspective of love to be discussed here is expressed by Erich Fromm. Fromm (1953) has suggested that love has the basic elements of giving the active character of care, responsibility, respect, and knowledge to a relationship. This four letter word L-O-V-E, which has escaped an exact definition over the years, is the basis for forming positive relationships with others and the impetus for marriage.

Recent analyses of social relationships between black people have spanned the perspectives of economics, history, politics, religion, physical and mental health, and marriage and child-bearing (Cade, 1970; Ellis, 1973; Hare, 1979; Hernton, 1965; and Malveaux, 1973). At social gatherings in the black community, discussions often turn into heated debate over "who" or "what" is responsible for difficulties frequently experienced with intimate relationships between black people. Troubled relationships within black romantic couples tend to extend into the marriage, the family, and beyond into employment spheres, educational settings, and social groups.

Concern about these troubled relationships and the possible critical effects on black marriage, family, and community prompted the authors and several colleagues to conduct a study of black love. The results of a survey on black love as well as an intervention to improve black loving relationships will be further discussed.

BLACK LOVE'S HERITAGE

Black Americans are generally regarded as that group of people whose ancestry is primarily African and who for the most part are descendents of slaves transported here from the West African shores. The African concept of love is broader than previous definitions cited. Mbiti (1969) explains the concept in the following way:

African ontology is a recognition that in order to understand the status of an individual at any given time (be it in the area of interpersonal relations, health or disease), attention should be directed at this existential situation in totality. This means that the relationship amongst the interdependent vital forces (life forces), elder, ancestor and God have to be fully appreciated in each individual situation. The primary thrust is on the totality or wholeness, not only of an individual person but that of the existential situation in which he finds himself (p. 34).

Our black heritage is rooted in an existential concept in which love is manifested within the total framework of a "people," a tribe, the family, and the couple in communion with nature. Black people, through the years, have loved each other. Black love has sustained us as a people and has helped us to survive the ills of slavery, segregation, and racism in the United States.

Environmental factors of economics, education, and social attitudes have impacted on the development of black loving relationships and marriage. Ladner (1971) noted the dualism that characterizes the way black women are perceived by the dominant society. Seen as both pillars of strength and immoral persons, black women are forced to accept negative images of self, and the positive image of strength is further diffused into a negative concept. The dualism affects the black male in a somewhat different manner. The larger society regards the man as the primary provider and support for the family, yet job discrimination, unemployment, and limited upward job mobility for black males severely inhibit his ability to provide. Such discrepancies between what society describes as male/female images and the ability for blacks to live up to the images create tension, confusion, and contempt between them, eroding the basis for the development of healthy loving relationships.

Case studies by Kardiner and Ovesey (1951) provide some support for the impact of economic conditions on relationships within the family. The authors provided illustrations of the struggle of families to provide food and shelter to the exclusion of time and energy for mutual showing of affection, attention, and comfort. Thus, blacks are perceived as spending a disproportionate amount of time and energy on economic survival at the expense of fostering personal relationships and are labeled as "failures" owing to an inability to meet their personal and/or economic goals. These negative images presented to blacks by whites have so penetrated the culture that black people often internalize negative self-images and project negative attitudes and behaviors on each other.

Erickson agreed that interaction between the minority and majority cultures allowed little or no basis for blacks to develop positive identities. Fromm indicated it was basic for all men to want to belong to the group he is part of; this allows him to overcome his separateness, be like others in his group, share thoughts, feelings, and try to conform. However, black people in American society cannot become like or fully join in the dominant white culture. Blacks are surrounded by values, economic experiences, and cultural norms of a majority group of which we cannot fully be a part. Hence, the concepts, expectations, and stereotypes of the male and female as held by the majority group in this culture have negatively impacted on the development for blacks of loving relationships, marriage, family, and community.

Despite this situation, black people continue to survive and have hope in face of the overwhelming odds against them. Hill (1971) documented sources of strengths in the black family as strong kinship bonds, strong work orientation, adaptable family roles, high achievement, and religious orientations. Although Hill's documentation occurred only a decade ago, these strengths and others have prevailed since blacks arrived in this country. Gutman (1976) documented the black tradition of long marriages, close family ties, and a majority of two-family households from 1850 to 1925. He also noted that one of the primary causes of many slave uprisings was the separation of families. Documentation by these two authors indicates that many of the dysfunctional images attributed to black families turn out to be myths. Their findings show that the majority of black families do have two parents, black men do earn more than black women, and black women do not dominate or castrate their men. According to Hill (1971), black women work more interdependently and black families do work together to provide support and resources for each other. The heritage of loving relationships between black people and the strength factors within black families are too often over-shadowed by the sensationalism of negative or violent interactions. A tradition of love and strength within black people has served to assure survival in a hostile environment; however, for continued survival blacks must attend to nurturing self-love and the expression of love to others as a basis for marriage.

LEARNING TO LOVE

In some societies, love between two people is not a necessary precondition for marriage. Often the union is arranged by parents or elders of the two families, occasionally when the pair are small children. Some of our black heritage is based on such practices inherent in some African tribes. Customs differ according to accepted societal norms within cultures; however, marriage partners are expected to learn to love each other through their interactions of living together. Examinations of Oriental, East Indian, African, and some South American cultures provide us with evidence that prearranged marriages can be successful and long-lasting. Two assumptions can be made based on successes of prearranged marriages and the critical negative elements that impact loving relationships of black people. These assumptions are that love is a behavior that can be learned and that conditions of the environment can affect the love behavior.

Evidence to support these assumptions are documented in the works of Erich Fromm and Sigmund Freud. According to Fromm (1956), "learning to love like other arts demands practice and concentration" (p. 4). Freud (1922) asserts that as a criterion of health, every person should be able to love and work. Self-esteem, self-image, self-regard, and positive identity can all be regarded as self-love: the practice and ability to love self. Self-love begins with the parent-child relationship as the parents or surrogate parent(s) provide food, warmth, and protection. The child learns "I am loved," and the feeling or emotion is reinforced by nurturing behaviors. The child is loved simply because he/she is, according to Fromm. This love of self is inseparably connected with love for others and makes the parent-child relationship crucial to the extension of loving others. Fromm (1956) considered love (connectedness) as the deepest need humans have; it allows one to overcome the separateness and aloneness of human existence. Absolute failure to achieve this aim, loving self and others, leads to insanity. The importance of parental love is further supported by Erickson's view that parental love perpetuates traditions that keep us connected to past generations. Virtually every theory of personality stresses the importance of a positive self-image, its early formation in the parent-child relationship, and the disastrous effects of negative self-images resulting from lack of self-love (Kelly, Rogers, Maslow, and Coombs, 1962).

Based on the assumption that love is learned behavior, the interaction of love and work coupled with the strengths of black family life, and the concept of love as a developed art, the authors engaged in a study of black love through survey and experiential workshop methods.

BLACK LOVE STUDIED

The Survey

The study of black love included two approaches. A survey was conducted in an attempt to determine what black people think and feel about love and loving relationships in the black community. An experiential workshop was conducted as an intervention to improve loving relationships between black males and females.

The survey instrument was a 17-item questionnaire. Nine items were statements with a five-point Likert response format, three open-ended items elicited descriptive objectives from participants, three items requested biographical data, and there were two open-ended questions.

The items could be categorized into several themes: data about the subject (i.e., age, marital status, and sex); data that defined characteristics of loving and nonloving relationships; data regarding intrapersonal-interpersonal expressions of love; and data regarding the interaction effect of the environment and loving relationships. The data from the scaled questions were computed for frequency, distribution, percentages, and means. Thirty-one variables were determined relevant, based on the frequency distribution and biographical data. The variables were male, female, age, marital status, prospect of aloneness, expression, gender choice, clarity of feelings, love-response, ethnic comparison prediction, environmental effects, self-love prerequisites, and 19 adjectives describing characteristics that enhance or obstruct relationships between people and the environment. The adjectives were arranged alphabetically to determine frequency, reviewed for synonymity, and then selected based on frequency. Adjectives appearing fewer than 10 times were deleted. A statistical analysis (Gamma) was computed to determine the significant correlations between variables.

Subjects volunteered to complete the questionnaire at a professional conference. Sixty-eight surveys were analyzed by the method described above. Subjects were all black; 53 percent female, 47 percent male. The age range was 15–50 years (mean age, 28 years). Fifty-six percent of the respondents were married; 24% single; and 20% divorced, separated, or living with someone.

Results of the questionnaire indicated that black people in the population surveyed describe love in the following terms: trust, respect, compatability, warmth, caring, understanding, and friendship. This rank-order listing encompasses the concept of "active characteristics of love" described by Fromm. The rank-order responses to the question, "What are the obstacles that deter loving relationships?" were as follows: distrust, selfishness, incompatibility, jealousy, insecurity, money, and possessiveness. There were no significant differences in responses in either of the rank-order listings by sex, age, or marital status.

Over 80 percent of the respondents indicated they would rather not live without a significant other person in their life. Two-thirds would prefer to have the "significant other" of the opposite sex, while one-third could allow that significant person to be of the same gender. The latter response may account for the ability of many black women to survive in a culture in which they greatly outnumber black males. All respondents indicated that self-love is a prerequisite for living and loving at least one significant other. A majority indicated that other ethnic groups felt more positive about themselves than black people do. The data also showed that subjects regard the environment as having a negative influence on black relationships.

The segment of the population sampled in this survey indicated that blacks view themselves as capable of loving self and others. Being alone tends not to be a desired state of affairs; rather, living with or having the companionship of significant other(s) is the norm. The study indicates that black people believe in the value of love and perceive the environment as a factor that impacts negatively on loving relationships. Despite the environmental factors, subjects suggested that love between black people has a positive effect on the family and enhances the black community.

Much of the literature has suggested that the economic burdens encountered by black people result in difficulties in loving relationships. The difficulties lie in an implied inability to develop self-love owing to the preoccupation with economic survival and the hostilities within the environment which project negative images on black people. A further implication of such assumptions based on the literature is that black couples, lacking the ability to love, would have a limited basis on which to build a marriage. Outcomes of this limited survey and the workshop interactions dispute the perpetuation of such a negative cycle.

Experiential Workshops

A series of experiential workshops on "black love" have been conducted in the eastern part of the United States, using a sequential learning model developed by the authors and two male colleagues. Based on the rationale that love is a learned behavior, the workshop model was designed to increase awareness of personal affective behaviors and provide opportunities to learn and practice loving behaviors. There are three distinct, progressive phases of the design—cognitive, affective, and spiritual. All phases involve structured, guided exercises to encourage sharing and learning experiences about love.

The number of participants in a given workshop ranged from 20 to 300 persons with an age range from 15 to 50 years. All participants were black and included students, professionals, and blue and white collar workers. An estimated 500 to 700 persons have experienced the workshops in various localities since 1974 when the model was first designed and presented to participants of a professional conference.

The survey described before was included in the first phase of the workshop; however, completion was voluntary, and only a limited number were analyzed. No formal evaluation of the workshop experience has been conducted. Workshop facilitators did receive and record evaluative feedback and summaries from participant discussions. Following is an overview of summaries that relate to love and marriage.

Results of an exercise designed to increase awareness of self-love indicated that participants found it more difficult to share perceptions of personal physical and spiritual strengths than intellectual strengths. Blacks saw themselves as having good minds and liked factors about "intellectual self" such as the ability to reason, having a quick mind, being bright, etc. Love was defined as a feeling, a strong emotion, affection, and a strong attachment to another, as well as by some of the definitions often cited in the literature. The physical expression of showing love for others in the group observed most often was the behavior of hugging or embracing in a rocking motion.

A number of workshops were conducted on the campus of black colleges, and the participants (age 18–22 years) were engaged in a discussion of "living together." While participants regarded living-together situations as experimental for the most part, a majority indicated that a satisfying temporary situation would lead to living together in marriage. Discussions related to black male/female relations in dating situations revealed that young black males feel comfortable receiving telephone calls from the female; however, the male prefers to ask for a date or initiate a personal invitation to get together. Of approximately 100 black males, all but one indicated they desired to have an income greater than the female salary in a marital situation. Black males and females perceived no problems with both partners working and indicated that dual working roles were expected and a part of the growing/sharing experience in a loving relationship.

Simultaneous to the phases of the workshop was the intervention of changing formations from the single individual to couples to family-type groupings to the total group of the entire community. Family grouping occurred on several levels. Participants were sometimes asked to introduce a partner they had been talking with for a half hour to the group as a family member. The participant was asked to use impressions, perceptions, and feelings to assess the other and select to introduce his/her partner the way he/she was impressed by the other, that is, as a wife/husband, mother/father, sister-/brother, aunt/uncle, or cousin. When explaining the rationale for choice of family member, participants most often indicated making choices based on feelings and impressions of intellect based on the conversations with each other. When participants were asked to self-select each other based on interaction and from actual family groupings, similar rationale for choice was given. Workshop leaders also observed and recorded that 90 percent of the family groupings included one, two, or more extended family members such as grandparents, an aunt, uncle, or cousin. These extended family members were always elders in the family who shared love and wisdom in the group.

Informal evaluations of the experiential workshops took the form of comments to leaders immediately following the session as well as weeks and months after the experience. Significant comments include the following:

> I found out things about myself I never knew before.
>
> I never thought about loving another man, but my grandfather really was the first person I can remember loving.
>
> In the group I saw him as a cousin and now I really call him cousin and we still have good feelings about each other.
>
> Really spiritual.

Further evidence concerning participant reactions to the workshop has been shown through an increasing request for such experiences on the part of many black groups and organizations to which past participants belong.

LOVE: AN IMPETUS FOR MARRIAGE

The study of black love, spanning a five-year period and including both the survey and workshop methods, has revealed that love is seen as an active and vital force within the black community. Despite negative forces that suppress and impact on black people in this society, blacks have been able to learn self-love, extend love to others, and build loving relationships as the basis for marriage.

Literature concerning black relationships written by white authors (Moynihan, 1965 and Kardiner and Ovesey, 1951) tends to perpetuate black differences within a deficit model. Implications from their studies tend to portray black people as inferior or less than persons of the majority culture, feeding into a model that assumes that a difference means a deficit.

Black participants of the study did perceive differences in their situation. They acknowledged struggles to develop loving relationships and maintain marriage bonds in some cases. The significant difference that was recognized is knowledge that the struggle to love, to care, and to relate exists within the context of survival. This struggle to survive strengthens the need to love and relate and provides a certain amount of determination to develop and nurture loving relationships.

The workshop model built up to and ended with a focus on the spiritual domain by design. Originators of the model discussed the factors that have contributed to black survival as a method for combining unique elements of the model.

The religious orientation of black people, mentioned by Hill (1972), was regarded as a major significant survival factor. The development of positive loving relationships within black couples can result in marriage, which is consummated in a religious ceremony. The learned loving behavior has the potential to expand into family and communal love. Filmore (1931) states that "love is the purest essence of Being that binds together the human family. Of all the attributes of God, love is undoubtedly the most beautiful" (p. 124). The authors felt it was very important to build on the religious and spiritual aspects of black life.

The results of the study of black love indicate that the youth have positive attitudes about love and marriage. The survey revealed that black persons under 30 felt that communication was essential to a loving relationship, while this factor did not hold statistical significance for persons over 30. The younger group did not regard the environment as a negative factor to the development of loving relationships as did their older counterparts. One might conclude that younger black persons had more hope and enthusiasm or less experience with negative environmental impacts on their personal loving relationships. However, a workshop exercise involving the fantasy of "an ideal mate" produced discussions based on realities of the social and economic environment. The college youth did not focus on the romantic stereotypical ideals of the "tall, dark, and handsome" mate. When sharing fantasies, young women discussed the need for a black male who was a good provider, sensitive to her needs, and could love her and their children. There tended to be minimal discussion of physical attributes in comparison to the importance of moral strength, determination, and reliability. The male wanted his woman to be tender, loving, unselfish, a good companion, and a good mother. The issue of motherhood always surfaced as well as dialogue regarding the female as a worker and partial provider to the household.

While these explorative discussions on perspectives of a marital relationship were based on realities of the environment, there was no exchange of perceived obstacles or barriers. It would appear that black college students regarded communication as basic to establishing positive loving relationships. They regarded factors such as sensitivity to personal needs, moral strength, and the ability to love one another and their children as important to the mating process. The ability to build a trusting relationship between one another was a key factor. There were indicators of this expected trust evidenced in expressed desires for mates who were reliable, dependable, and supportive.

The presence of dual working partners in marriage was regarded as a necessity for survival. This factor tended to be regarded as an expected condition rather than an obstacle. The participants did not regard the expected need for both partners to work as a burden, but a vital part of the sharing experience of a household. Within that context, such attitudes could be viewed as strengths that contribute to successful black marriages.

CONCLUSIONS

The title of this chapter indicates that love is an impetus or moving force for black marriage. An expanded definition of the word *impetus*, according to the *American College Dictionary* (1970), is "the force with which a moving body tends to maintain velocity and overcome resistance" (p. 607). Given the racism in American society, which impacts negatively on the economic and social realities of black people, love, as a moving force, is essential to black marriage.

Black males and females (age 15–50 years) who participated in a study of black love tended to define the phenomenon in ways similar to authors such as Fromm and Erikson. In general, they felt that trust, respect, compatability, caring, and warmth are essential characteristics of a loving relationship. They recognized the negative environmental impacts on the development of loving relationships between black people. Older participants (over 30 years of age) tended to regard environmental factors as significant, while younger participants (under 30) did not. The college students who participated tended to be optimistic about their abilities to develop loving relationships that would culminate in marriage. This particular group also tended to view economic difficulties as realistic conditions of the society that could be overcome.

The concept of love as related to our African heritage encompasses a support system extending from the individual as a vital part of nature into the tribe or group that is the community. With such a heritage, the love that black people have for one another has been a survival factor in this society. Separation of families during slavery times led to supportive behaviors of caring for separated individuals, community care of children, and a tendency to include relatives as an integral part of the basic family. Children were taught to love and respect grandparents, aunts, or uncles who lived with the family and to love, care for, and accept cousins as sister or brother within the family. Certainly, our heritage of developing loving relationships within the nuclear family and the black community has served to sustain love and marriages of black Americans over time.

Black life in America is based on a tradition of working since the total societal work ethic impacts on us all. Black people have been able to engage in self-love, develop positive self-images, and extend love to others. Young black couples in our study regarded love and work as a sharing experience which can help build and maintain marriage. Hence, within the framework of Freud's concept that work and love are basic criteria for viewing or determining the health of individuals, black people with attitudes similar to those of our participants should continue healthy traditions of black love and marriage. Outcomes of our study of black love tend to support indications of a healthy interaction of love and work as well as the retention of traditional strengths of black family life. The strengths and healthy interactions can offset negative forces that erode black loving relationships. Participants of the workshops welcomed the opportunity to surface issues, learn and share loving behaviors, and take the time to relate positively toward each other. The numerous requests for the authors to conduct the experiential workshop by former participants indicates a desire of black people to explore black male/female relationships. Summary reports of workshop participants indicate that love is important to black people. They are cognizant of many troubled relationships within black couples. The most satisfying outcome of our work is the willingness of black people to take time to learn and practice loving behaviors as a mechanism for improving relationships and building the blocks that support and maintain healthy black marriages.

REFERENCES

Bentler, P. M., and G. J. Hubo. "Simple Mini Theories of Love," *Journal of Personality and Social Psychology*, 1979, 37(1), 124-130.

Berscheid, E., and E. Walster, "A Littlebit About Love," In T. L. Houston (ed) *Fundamentals of Interpersonal Attraction*. New York: Academic Press, 1974.

Billingsley, A. *Black Families in White America*. Englewood Cliffs, N.J.: Prentice-Hall, 1968.

Cade, T. *The Black Woman*. New York: New American Library, 1970.

Coombs, W., E. Kelly, A. Maslow, and C. Rodgers. *Perceiving, Behaving and Becoming*. Washington, D.C.: Association for Supervision and Curriculum Development, 1962.

Ellis, W. "A Sexual Crisis," *Essence Magazine*, October 1973, 41, 80-86.

Filmore, C. *The Revealing Word*. Unity Village, MO.: Unity School of Christianity, 1931.

Freud, S. *Beyond the Pleasure Principle*. London, England: International Psycho-analytical Press, 1922.

Fromm, E. *The Art of Loving*. New York: Harper & Row Publishers, 1956.

Gutman, H., and G. Herbert. *The Black Family in Slavery and Freedom: 1750-1925*. New York: Vintage Books, 1976.

Hare, N. "Revolution within Revolution," *Black Scholar*, 1978, 9(7), 38.

Hernton, C. *Sex and Racism in America*. New York: Grove Press, 1965.

Hill, R. B. *The Strength of Black Families*. New York: Emerson Hall Publishers, Inc., 1972.

Idowu, B. E. *African Traditional Religion: A Definition*. Maryknoll, N.Y.: Orbis Books, 1975.

Jones, R. E. *Black Psychology*. New York: Harper & Row Publishers, 1972.

Kardiner, A., and L. Ovesey. *The Mark of Oppression*. Cleveland, Ohio: The World Publishing Co., 1954.

Ladner, J. A. *Tomorrow's Tomorrow: The Black Woman*. Garden City, N.Y.: Anchor Press, 1971.

Lee, J. A. "A Typology of Styles of Loving," *Personality and Social Psychology Bulletin*, 1977, 3(13), 173-182.

Malveaux, J. "Polar Entities Apart," *Essence Magazine*, November 1973, 48.

Mbiti, J. S. *African Religion and Philosophy*. New York: Prokeger Publishing Co., 1969.

Rosenblatt, P. C. "Marital Residence and Function of Love," *Ethnology*, 1967, 6(4), 86-94.

Rubin, Z. *Liking and Loving, An Invitation to Social Psychology*. New York: Holt, Rinehart & Winston, Inc., 1973.

3

BLACK FAMILIES, SOCIAL EVALUATIONS, AND FUTURE MARITAL RELATIONSHIPS

Castellano B. Turner and Barbara F. Turner

Evidence abounds to indicate that marriage as an institution in Western society has, over this century, become increasingly vulnerable. Staples (1978) has pointed out that marriage among Afro-Americans has not escaped this general trend, and may be considered even more fragile than among other groups. Not only is the divorce and separation rate higher for blacks than it is for whites, but the life expectancy of two-thirds of all black marriages is less than 10 years (p. 62).

In any attempt to understand such a distressing state of affairs, a number of distinct (though interrelated) factors must be examined. Primary among these are financial problems. Black families and individual black adults are over-represented among those below the poverty line. Marital conflicts involving financial issues are a major source of stress and subsequent marital dissolution. Moreover, blacks as a group continue to be the largest racial minority in the United States, and as such are subjected to pervasive racism. There has been a great deal of evidence indicating the direct and indirect negative effects of such racism on black marital relationships and black families.

The future character and quality of marital relationships among blacks will likely depend on the same set of interrelated factors—economic, social, and cultural—that are important now. The focus of this paper is on a set of interrelated social-psychological factors: socialization, self-esteem, and social evaluations. Our assumption is that socialization lays the foundation for later adult adjustment and marital relationships. First, we will summarize the current state of knowledge concerning sex-role socialization among blacks. Next, we will briefly review the literature on self-esteem among blacks. We

The data presented in this paper were gathered as part of a research project supported by a faculty research grant, University of Massachusetts, Amherst.

will then relate self-esteem to the results of our own research on social evaluations of "Most Women" and "Most Men." Finally, we will attempt to show how sex-role socialization, self-esteem, and social evaluations together create a developmental sequence that will influence the future marital relationships of present-day black youth.

BLACK FAMILIES AND SOCIALIZATION PROCESSES

Socialization within families must be regarded as a major foundation for the development of both individual self-concepts and evaluations of significant others. Sex-role socialization is especially relevant to an understanding of later adult adjustment and marital relationships. Lewis (1975) has made a convincing case for viewing the content and process of sex-role socialization in Afro-American families, particularly early childhood socialization, as qualitatively different from that found in Euro-American families. Euro-American families, Lewis maintains, are characterized by a dualistic (or dichotomous) mode of sex-role socialization, in which male and female children are taught at an early age to identify gender as the basis for distinct patterns of behavior and sentiments. Afro-American families, on the other hand, do not define appropriateness of behaviors on the basis of gender in early childhood. Unlike white children, both female and male black children are trained to be oriented more toward people rather than to the physical environment. The range of characteristics to which black children are socialized (without regard to gender) imply "expressive" qualities, i.e., affective qualities important in intimate relationships. White female children are socialized in a similar direction, but the characteristics encouraged in white male children may be described as "instrumental," i.e., related to mastery and later to the provider role. We will return to the distinction between expressive and instrumental characteristics later, when considering adult self-concepts.

The early socialization process must, however, be differentiated from *later* socialization within black families. By the time the child reaches puberty, family socialization is largely determined by the realities of the existing social order. At this point, sources of socialization other than the family become important, e.g. peers, school, and the media. The family must then train its youth in ways appropriate to survival within the particular social context in which it finds itself. Because blacks have been subjected to employment discrimination of varying degrees since the end of American slavery, black males have historically had considerable difficulty fulfilling the provider role. It is in the crucial adolescent period, during which black youth are being prepared by direct and indirect encouragement for instrumental behavior in school and work, that gender becomes important. If, as was often the case over many generations of black families in America, the employment opportunities in a particular time and place were greater for black women, emphasis had to be placed upon socializing young females for the provider role. Lewis (1975) summarizes the relevant literature as indicating that many black mothers (who are assumed to be the most important and consistent socializing agents) have had high expectations for daughters and often minimal expectations for sons.

The full significance of this can be understood only when one considers that, in the general social system of the United States, males have been expected to take on the primary provider role within families. If a black male does not, he is likely to experience a strong sense of inadequacy. Yet, more than any other group, black males have been blocked by society itself from fulfilling this role (Merton, 1938 and Clark, 1965). The consequences of this dilemma for developing self-evaluations and evaluations of the opposite sex among black adolescents and adults must be profound. It is this mutual evaluation process that we regard as the bridge to understanding the relationship between family socialization and later marital relationships.

The predictions that we make, however, must take into account that there are several distinct roles in marriage: companion, parent, provider, homemaker, sex partner, and so forth. Early childhood socialization to expressiveness is not particularly relevant to the provider role, but it does relate to the companion, parent, and sex partner roles. Since black females and males are provided equally with early socialization toward expressive qualities, those aspects of marital relationships involving such qualities may not be as great a potential source of tension. On the other hand, if later family socialization to instrumental qualities are differentially provided to the sexes, then expectations and evaluations about the provider role might well be a source of marital tension. We suggest that black males are given the instrumental role of "one-who-will-be-discriminated-against," while black females are given the instrumental role of "one-who-will-hold-together-no-matter-what." How, then are black females and males likely to evaluate themselves and each other?

SELF-ESTEEM AND SOCIAL EVALUATIONS AMONG BLACKS

For decades, it has been a standard assumption in American psychology and sociology that blacks have lower self-esteem than do whites. This assumption persisted despite the findings of numerous studies that failed to support the hypothesis (Baughman and Dahlstrom, 1968; Baughman, 1971; and Harris and Stokes, 1978). It seems likely that the assumption of low black self-esteem has persisted because so many *theoretical* lines support it.

Heiss and Owens (1972) have summarized this line of thinking. Since whites evaluate blacks negatively, it is assumed that blacks will also receive negative evaluations from significant others. Moreover, existing barriers to achievement for blacks and the general conditions of a black person's life are constant reminders of inferiority; therefore, blacks must have low self-esteem. It has generally been argued that the evaluations blacks receive from white society are the primary determinants of low black self-esteem (Kardiner and Ovesey, 1951; Merton, 1938; and Clark, 1965). Rainwater (1966) has suggested, however, that white victimization is only a secondary cause of low self-esteem among blacks. Rainwater maintained that whites, with their greater power, are able to create the circumstances that lead blacks to victimize each other. Thus, in lower-class neighborhoods, individual blacks are presented with negative evaluations from parents and peers. However, the assertion of Rainwater (1966) and Proshansky and Newton (1968) that, in general, blacks receive more negative evaluations from other blacks than whites receive from other whites must also be challenged, because it too is dependent on the unsupported notion that blacks have lower self-esteem than do whites. There is, indeed, considerable evidence that evaluations received from one's primary group are important determinants of self-evaluation (Schafer and Braito, 1979). There has been insufficient evidence, however, to establish that blacks do evaluate other blacks more negatively than whites evaluate other whites.

BLACK-WHITE DIFFERENCES IN CRITERIA
FOR EVALUATING OTHERS

In this section we wish to show that, just as there are multiple aspects to marital roles, there are also various dimensions for self-evaluation and evaluation of others. Our presentation is based on the assumption that the body of theory and research bearing on self-evaluations among blacks is also relevant to research on evaluation of others (Schafer and Braito, 1979).

In contrast to the more traditional theoretical lines suggesting that blacks have lower self-esteem than whites, McCarthy and Yancey (1971) presented a fresh theoretical tack which could account for the finding that blacks have *higher* self-esteem than whites. They suggested that (a) the assumption that blacks use whites as significant others is incorrect and that evaluations blacks receive from other blacks are similar to evaluations whites receive from other whites; (b) the evaluative criteria blacks use may be subcultural ones, not the "unachievable" ones of white society; and (c) rampant discrimination against blacks makes it possible for blacks to rationalize any failure by "blaming the system."

Heiss and Owens (1972) expanded McCarthy and Yancey's formulation by specifying criteria for the traits that fit the formulation. These are traits that are (a) of little concern to the whites with whom a black person interacts; (b) relatively irrelevant for success in the larger society; and (c) thought to be influenced by general social factors. Heiss and Owens suggest that traits meeting these criteria and ones that "relate to intimate interactions are primary group activities. Such matters may be influenced by external forces, but they are 'none of the business' of the larger society" (p. 362). These are, we suggest, "expressive" traits. The formulation of Heiss and Owens suggests the hypothesis that blacks' evaluations of other blacks on expressive traits should not differ from whites' evaulations of other whites. If we recall Lewis's (1975) description of early black socialization as focusing mainly on such expressive qualities, we are led to expect that blacks would rate other blacks even *higher* on such traits than whites would rate other whites. On the other hand, according to Heiss and Owens:

the evaluation of some traits may be importantly affected by persons outside the black community. These are traits which are subject to frequent evaluation by whites and those less subject to the development of subcultural norms. They are those in instrumental areas in which whites have important control over the black man's fate and can therefore impose his [sic] norms. Thus, for those traits that operate in the worlds of school and work the opinions of whites are going to weigh heavily for most blacks. (p. 363)

Gordon's (1971) study of black and white ninth graders lends support to this formulation. The results indicated that on a measure of self-worth *as students* black working and middle-class youngsters rated themselves more negatively. For instrumental traits that reflect primarily adequacy in areas related to the provider role, we would predict that blacks' evaluations of other blacks should be more negative than whites' evaluations of other whites. If Lewis's formulation concerning differential adolescent socialization of black females and males for the provider role is correct, we would expect black men in particular to be seen negatively on such traits by black women.

Thus far, our predictions have been derived from the theoretical frameworks focusing on race differences in social evaluation. An important second focus of this chapter, however, concerns differences between black women and men in social evaluations of women. A voluminous literature indicates that males in our culture have more positive self-concepts than do females (Dinitz et al., 1954; Lynn, 1959; and Sherriffs and McKee, 1957), suggesting that males receive more positive evaluations from both women and men than do females. There is evidence from large-scale surveys, however, that black females do not have as low self-esteem compared to black males as do white females compared to white males (Crain and Weisman, 1972). For that matter, there is evidence that would lead to a prediction that black females should have higher self-esteem than black males. Proshansky and Newton (1968), for example, summarized the literature on the marginal employment situation of low–self-esteem black males with the comment that the unemployed black male "is told that he is 'no good' and 'irresponsible'" (p. 205). Such accusations may come from mothers, girlfriends, and wives; they may also have been heard directed at other men—most importantly, at one's father. To the extent that self-concepts reflect internalized evaluations received from others (Sarbin, 1954), black males can be expected to share such negative views of men. That is, both black females and males are expected to have negative evaluations of "most men" on instrumental traits. On the other hand, black women and men should tend to have equally positive evaluations of "most women" on instrumental traits.

Method

Choice of evaluative traits. It is possible that part of the reason for the frequent finding that blacks have higher self-esteem than whites has to do with the content of the self-esteem measures. Scales heavily weighted with items related to expressive characteristics may well tap the most positive aspects of black self-concepts. Scales focusing largely on instrumental (i.e., mastery and performance) characteristics may fit more closely the values and self-concepts of white society. Hence, we included items intended to tap both instrumental and expressive traits. Of the 15 semantic differential items we used, the following seem to indicate expressive traits: Warm-Cold, Happy-Sad, Calm-Excited, Giving-Taking, Changing-Unchanging, and Quick-Slow. The instrumental dimensions included: Responsible-Irresponsible, Useful-Useless, Trustworthy-Untrustworthy, Reliable-Unreliable, Smart-Dumb, Strong-Weak, and Good-Bad. The remaining two dimensions could be related to either of the two types of traits: Healthy-Sick and Active-Passive. Our plan of analysis, however, depended on the use of empirical scales (i.e., determined by factor analysis) rather than on face-valid combinations of traits.

Subjects. The sample included 28 black females, 31 black males, 45 white females and 37 white males in their first year at a large state university in the Northeast. Most black students entering this university at the time were participants in a special admission program for low-income minority students; therefore, only 20 percent of the 59 blacks were from middle-class families. In order to obtain an *N* comparable to the lower status blacks, lower status whites were oversampled.

Procedure. Interviewers were matched with the respondents for race and self-esteem. The hour-long interview included two self-administered 15-item semantic differential scales (Osgood et al., 1957)—one for the concept "Most men are . . . " and the other for the concept "Most women are . . . ." Each item was scored on a six-point scale.

We assume that in making their ratings, blacks had in mind black women and men and that whites had in mind white women and men. This assumption was supported in a large sample survey by Crain and Weisman (1972) who reported that when an item referred to "most people," associations with other items indicated that respondents assumed "most people" to be members of their own race. Further, several of the black students in our study spontaneously commented, while completing the semantic differential scales, that they had blacks in mind.

Each of the 15 items was scored on a positive-negative dimension such that the higher the score, the more positive the evaluation. Adjective pairs with the "positive" and "negative" adjectives presented first were randomly varied.

The ratings of the 15 items for all respondents were submitted to a principal component factor analysis with orthogonal varimax rotations separately for "most women" and "most men." Five social evaluation factors emerged for ratings of "most women", four for ratings of "most men." Tables 3:1 and 3:2 present the results of this process for the "most women" and "most men" ratings, respectively. In order to ascertain the meaning of each factor, items that loaded high on one given factor were inspected for commonality. All items were assigned to at least one factor even when the highest primary loading of an item was relatively small. Finally, tentative names were assigned to and interpretive descriptions provided for each factor.

Of the "most women" factors (Table 3:1), factors I, III, and V seem to capture expressive characteristics relevant to intimate interactions. It is noteworthy that a trustworthy, reliable woman is also seen as a good and giving one; the image of the nurturant, self-sacrificing mother comes to mind. Factors II and IV seem to capture instrumental characteristics.

The "most men" factors (Table 3:2) that relate clearly to the instrumental or provider role are factors I and III. Note that a responsible man is also viewed as a happy one; hence, the concept Happy-Sad may not be as closely related to intimate interactions as it is to adequacy in the provider role. Factors II and IV seem to capture, respectively, expressive and "he-man" characteristics that are more closely associated with primary group norms.

The 15 evaluative traits cluster differently for ratings of "most women" and "most men," indicating that, for this sample, trait connotations were different when applied to women than when applied to men.

Results

In this section, we will limit our presentation, for the most part, to those results that bear upon the predictions made about black women and men. In an earlier paper (Turner and Turner, 1974), we reported two major findings regarding whites. First, white males were consistently more negative in rating "most women" than were white females, although the difference was significant only for the factors defined by instrumental traits. Second, white females were consistently more positive in rating "most men" than were white males, although the difference was significant only for the factors defined by expressive traits.

The mean factor scores for each race-sex group are shown in Table 3:3. Tests of mean differences between scores on each of the "most women" factors indicated no difference between black females and males on any of the five

TABLE 3:1

"Most Women" Factors

Factor	Primary Loadings		Salient Characteristics	Percent Variance
I. Supportive, Giving Female	Trustworthy-Untrustworthy	.78	High scores view women as more trustworthy, reliable, good, responsible, and giving	52.8
	Reliable-Unreliable	.64		
	Good-Bad	.63		
	Responsible-Irresponsible	.46		
	Giving-Taking	.44		
II. Physically and Mentally Robust Female	Healthy-Sick	.57	High scores view women as more healthy, smart, and strong	16.0
	Smart-Dumb	.54		
	Strong-Weak	.46		
III. Warm Female	Warm-Cold	.81	High scores view women as warmer	11.4
IV. Effective, Efficient Female	Quick-Slow	.65	High scores view women as more quick, useful, responsible, strong, and good	10.6
	Useful-Useless	.54		
	Responsible-Irresponsible	.45		
	Strong-Weak	.44		
	Good-Bad	.35		
V. Active, Expressive Female	Active-Passive	.70	High scores view women as more active, changing, excited, and happy	10.1
	Changing-Unchanging	.41		
	Calm-Excited	-.30		
	Happy-Sad	.23		

TABLE 3:2

"Most Men Factors"

Factor	Primary Loadings		Salient Characteristics	Percent Variance
I. Responsible Male	Responsible-Irresponsible Reliable-Unreliable Trustworthy-Untrustworthy Happy-Sad	.69 .67 .46 .42	High scores view men as more responsible, reliable, trust-worthy, and happy	62.6
II. Lively, Gregari-ous Male	Quick-Slow Smart-Dumb Warm-Cold Giving-Taking Changing-Unchanging	.62 .55 .53 .43 .37	High scores view men as quick, smart, warm, giving, and changing	15.5
III. Good Male	Good-Bad Trustworthy-Untrustworthy Healthy-Sick Useful-Useless	.80 .56 .40 .38	High scores view men as good trustworthy, healthy, and useful	12.4
IV. Vigorous Male	Active-Passive Strong-Weak Calm-Excited	.61 .50 -.18	High scores view men as active, strong, and excited	9.5

31

"most women" factors. This finding is consistent with our prediction. It is further worth noting that blacks as a group were not significantly different from whites on any of these factors.

The "most men" factors present an entirely different picture. On the first factor, "Responsible Male," which is clearly an instrumental factor, tests of differences showed that black females viewed men as significantly less responsible than did black males. The black females also viewed men more negatively on this factor than did the white group. On the other instrumental factor, the "Good Male" factor, the black females and males were not significantly different from each other. They were both significantly more negative in their ratings on this factor, however, than were the whites.

When we examine the two expressive factors for "most men," the pattern changes sharply. On factor II, "Lively, Gregarious Male," the black females rated men more positively than any of the other three groups; white males were the most negative. The difference between the black females and males on this factor did not reach significance at the .05 level, but the difference between the means of black females and males is substantial and approaches significance. On factor IV, "Vigorous Male," the means of the black females

TABLE 3:3

Mean Scores on 9 Social Evaluation

Factors For 4 Race-Sex Groups

Factor	Blacks		Whites	
	Females	Males	Females	Males
"Most Women"				
I. Supportive, Giving Female	-.10	-.14	.15	-.04
II. Physically/Mentally Robust Female	-.14	-.05	.16	-.18
III. Warm Female	-.28	.15	.04	-.09
IV. Effective, Efficient Female	.14	.00	.11	-.36
V. Active, Expressive Female	.12	-.08	-.01	-.03
"Most Men"				
I Responsible Male	-.60	.11	.17	.12
II. Lively, Gregarious Male	.46	.05	.03	-.46
III. Good Male	-.34	-.28	.40	.01
IV. Vigorous Male	.16	.06	.14	-.31

and black males were not significantly different. Again, the main thing that stands out is the very negative ratings of men made by the white males.

Discussion

For the purpose of this chapter, the most provocative finding of our study was that black females and males were significantly different on their "Responsible Male" ratings. To further explore the meaning of this finding, we correlated the ratings of each group with demographic, family, and attitudinal characteristics of the respondents. These additional data were available from both the interview that accompanied the semantic differential and from the questionnaire administered six months earlier, during the orientation sessions preceding the respondents' entrance into the university. The most striking finding was the relationship between "Responsible Male" ratings and ratings of occupational discrimination against black people. Of the 21 occupations (rated on a four-point scale from "open on an equal basis to blacks" to "Not open to blacks"), 17 were significantly correlated with "Responsible Male" scores among black females. For each of the 17 occupations, the more occupational discrimination the respondent perceived against black people, the more unfavorably she rated "most men" on the "Responsible Male" factor.

What, then, is the meaning of these black females' unfavorable evaluations of "most men" as relatively less responsible, less reliable, less trustworthy, and less happy? One possibility, suggested by the astounding correlations with the variables tapping perceived discrimination against blacks, is that "most men" to these respondents are not black, but are white. Is it, perhaps, *white* men, who inflict the evils of occupational discrimination upon black people, who are evaluated by black women as irresponsible? This tempting interpretation is unlikely to account for our findings for two main reasons. First, scores of black male respondents on the "Responsible Male" factor are uncorrelated with their ratings of occupational discrimination on all 21 occupations. It seems highly unlikely that, in rating the characteristics of "most men," black women and black men would have distinctively different groups in mind. Second, we suggest that, if white males as the perpetrators of occupations discrimination are to be denigrated in social evaluations of "most men," their devaluation should most likely appear on the "Good Male" factor. We suggest that "Good-Bad" represents a pure evaluative dimension (Osgood et al., 1957) and that white racists—those who discriminate against blacks—are more likely to be perceived as "bad" than they are to be seen as irresponsible or unreliable. Black females' scores on the "Good Male" factor, however, are significantly correlated with only two of the 21 occupational discrimination items, a result that could occur by chance.

The dictionary definitions of *responsible*, *reliable*, and *trustworthy* are helpful in clarifying the meaning of black females' unfavorable evaluation of men. *Responsible* is defined as "answerable or accountable, as for something within one's power, control or mangement" (*American College Dictionary*, p. 1034). *Reliable* is defined as "can be depended on with certainty. Satisfactory performance may be expected with complete confidence" (p. 1023). *Trust-worthy* is defined as "worthy of trust," which means "reliance on the integrity, justice, etc. of a person," implying "instinctive unquestioning belief" in something or someone (p. 1303). Both *responsible* and *reliable*, then, require *satisfactory performance*, while *trustworthy* is more an inherent trait than one that must be demonstrated in performance. *Responsible*, further, suggests that something is indeed under one's control, power, or management.

We suggest that the black females in our study did, indeed, have black men in mind when they rated "most men." First, ratings of men as less responsible and reliable are highly related to perceptions of occupational discrimination against blacks. A person who is the object of occupational discrimination is not in control and has little power; thus, he cannot be accountable, and is certainly at a disadvantage in demonstrating satisfactory performance. In this predicament, a person may well be sad, rather than happy. The evaluation being made may, in some cases, be that black men are "*not* responsible" rather than that they are "*ir*responsible."

CONCLUSIONS AND IMPLICATIONS

In the research reported here, findings include: (a) black women rated men as less responsible and reliable than did black men; (b) relative to white respondents, black females and males were equally inclined to rate men as less good and more untrustworthy; (c) black women rated black men as less responsible and less reliable than they rated black women; and (d) black women and men did not differ in their ratings of women nor in their ratings of the expressive characteristics of men.

These findings provide support for several of the formulations and predictions presented earlier in this chapter. The findings provide indirect support for Lewis's (1975) proposition that there are two distinct processes of sex-role socialization—one taking place primarily during early childhood, and the other dominating in later childhood and adolescence. This distinction in developmental periods clarifies sex differences in the content of sex-role socialization. Lewis suggested that Afro-American culture gives emphasis in early childhood socialization to expressive traits, undifferentiated by gender. Later, however, training for sex roles is differentiated by gender even among Afro-Americans because of the pressures on families of the existing social order and the increasing variety in socializing agents. During this later process, black males are given two conflicting messages: they are expected to develop instrumental traits appropriate to the provider role, but they are also told that they will be inadequate providers because of racial discrimination.

Our data provide convincing support for Lewis's (1975) distinction between expressive and instrumental traits. Not only did the factor analysis reveal clusters of traits that fit together on these dimensions, but the black-white and female-male differences on these factors were consistent with our formulations concerning the manner in which the race-sex groups probably incorporate each.

We must conclude that the data support the notion that blacks do have some negative perceptions of black men. Contrary to previous theoretical literature, however, we have shown that perceptions of black men are not generally negative; rather, negative perceptions are limited to instrumental traits relevant to adequacy in the provider role. It is important to note that these young black women are highly positive toward the expressive characteristics of men. Most important, we have shown that black females' view of men as less responsible, reliable, and trustworthy is strongly related to perceptions of occupational discrimination against blacks.

Still, these young black women maintained psychological sets that may well have negative consequences for later relationships with black men. A sense of basic trust is the fulcrum of gratifying and mutually fulfilling interpersonal relationships, particularly in marriage. Our findings suggest that, although the young black males studied regarded black women as trustworthy, the black females' views of relationships with black men were laced with the anticipation of disappointment.

On the other hand, we suggest that black females' perception of men as unreliable may foster *self*-reliance, which, in turn, may be a crucial determinant, as well as a result of, the more equalitarian position held by women in the black family as compared to the white family (Blood and Wolfe, 1960 and Scanzoni, 1971).

With the exception of the "Responsible Male" factor, the similarity of the social evaluations held by the black women and black men in our study was striking. Compared to the distinctive differences between the white females and males in evaluations of women and men, differential evaluations of the sexes would seem less likely to be a source of conflict and misunderstanding between black women and men.

The character and quality of relationships between black marital partners in the future seem to have some quite promising aspects. They should be at least as positive as they have been in the past. The foundations for mutual evaluation have slowly swung in a direction that should allow for subcultural as well as general societal improvements in sentiments. First of all, black women must be seen in increasingly positive terms, since rates of labor force participation among white women now match those of black women (U.S. Department of Labor, 1975). Independence and autonomy can no longer be regarded as aberrant sex-role behavior.

Moreover, black women and men are gradually (though all too slowly) gaining access to equal opportunity in education and occupations. If the barriers that have made it difficult for blacks to accept fully themselves and each other are reduced, there should be increased self-esteem in all spheres of life as well as more positive evaluations of other black people. We have provided evidence that the tensions between the sexes among blacks are tied closely to the pressures that society has created for each. Black women's negative views of black men were limited to the realm of instrumental performance, in which society has often stripped the black man of the capacity to perform adequately.

REFERENCES

Baughman, E. E., and W. G. Dahlstrom. *Negro and White Children*. New York: Academic Press, 1968.
———— . *Black Americans*. New York: Academic Press, 1971.
Blood, R., and D. Wolfe. *Husbands and Wives*. New York: The Free Press, 1960.
———— . "Negro-white Differences in Blue-Collar Marriages in a Northern Metropolis," *Social Forces*, 1969, 48, 59–63.
Clark, K. B. *Dark Ghetto: Dilemmas of Social Power*. New York: Harper & Row Publishers, 1965.
Crain, R. L., and C. S. Weisman. *Discrimination, Personality, and Achievement*. New York: Seminar Press, 1972.
Dinitz, S., R. Dykes, and A. Clarke. "Preference for Male or Female Children: Traditional or Affectional," *Marriage and Family Living*, 1954, 16, 128–130.
Gordon, C. *Looking Ahead: Self Conceptions, Race, and Family as Determinants of Adolescent Orientations to Achievement*. Rose Monograph. Washington, D.C.: American Sociological Association, 1971.
Harris, A. R., and R. Stokes. "Race, Self-Evaluation and the Protestant Ethic," *Social Problems*, 1978, 26, 71–85.
Heiss, P., and S. Owens. "Self-Evaluations of Blacks and Whites," *American Journal of Sociology*, 1972, 78, 360–370.
Kardiner, A., and L. Ovesey. *The Mark of Oppression*. New York: World Publishing Co., Inc. 1951.
Lewis, D. K. "The Black Family: Socialization and Sex Roles," *Phylon*, 1975, 36, 221–237.
Lynn, D. B. "A Note on Sex Differences in the Development of Masculine and Feminine Identification," *Psychological Review*, 1959, 66, 126–135.
McCarthy, J. D., and W. L. Yancey. "Uncle Tom and Mr. Charlie: Metaphysical Pathos in the Study of Racism and Personal Disorganization," *American Journal of Sociology*, 1971, 76, 648–672.
Merton, R. K. "Social Structure and Anomie," *American Sociological Review*, 1938, 672–682.
Osgood, E. E., G. J. Suci, and P. H. Tannenbaum. *The Measurement of Meaning*. Urbana: University of Illinois, 1957.
Proshansky, H., and P. Newton. "The Nature and Meaning of Negro Self-Identity," In M. I. Katz, and A. Jensen (eds) *Social Class, Race, and Psychological Development*. New York: Holt, Rinehart & Winston, Inc., 1968.

Rainwater, L. "Crucible of Identity: The Negro Lower Class Family," *Daedalus*, 1966, 95(Winter), 172–217.

Sarbin, G. G. "Role Theory," In G. Lindzey (ed) *The Handbook of Social Psychology*. Reading, Mass.: Addison-Wesley, 1954.

Scanzoni, J. *The Black Family in Modern Society*. Boston: Allyn & Bacon, 1971.

Schafer, R. B., and R. Braito. "Self-concept and Role Performance Evaluation among Marriage Partners," *Journal of Marriage and the Family*, 1979, 41, 801–810.

Sheriffs, A. C., and J. P. McKee. "Qualitative Aspects of Beliefs about Men and Women," *Journal of Personality*, 1957, 25, 451–464.

Staples, R. (ed) *The Black Family: Essays and Studies*, 2nd edition, Belmont, Calif.: Wadsworth Publishing Co., Inc., 1978.

Turner, B. F., and C. B. Turner. "Evaluations of Women and Men among College Students," *Sociological Quarterly*, 1974, 15, 442–456.

U.S. Department of Labor. *1975 Handbook on Women Workers*, Bulletin 297. *The American College Dictionary*. New York: Harper & Brothers, 1951.

4

HUSBAND AND WIFE RELATIONSHIPS OF BLACK MEN AND WOMEN

Essie Manuel Rutledge

The purpose of this chapter is to describe the marital relations of black men and women, using a comparative, descriptive approach. Since we know very little about the nature of black marriages, this analysis should enhance our knowledge in this area, although such an analysis is limited to its descriptive function. It does not lend itself to any causal or relational interpretations. Therefore, it is exploratory. Nevertheless, it provides some insights into some possibilities for pursuing inferential statistical analyses.

Research on this subject is very sparse, and most of it includes only women as respondents. Such research about black or white marriages is one-sided. In other words, it does not provide a complete view of married life. Moreover, such limitation may continue to lead to unfounded generalizations and speculations. Hence, this analysis is an addition to the limited research, and includes both men and women with the hope of adding to a more complete understanding of the nature of black marriages.

Furthermore, the range of knowledge about husband-wife relations is limited. Most of what we know about marital relations is in the areas of marital adjustment (variously referred to as marital happiness or marital satisfaction) and decision making; but most of the research generated has pertained to the former. This paper provides a more varied and informed analysis of the black marital relation than any known study. This is in spite of the fact that these data were collected in 1968 and 1969. No study of marital interaction goals which is a part of this research, to my knowledge, has been reported.

The data on which this study is based were collected in 1968 and 1969 by the Program for Urban Health Research, Department of Psychology, at the University of Michigan.

REVIEW OF PREVIOUS RESEARCH

The review that follows focuses on the marital interaction goals that are classified as "primary relations" or "expressive gratifications," marital happiness/marital satisfaction, and marital disagreement. The study by Scanzoni (1971) is one that analyzes primary relations or expressive gratifications as one aspect of the marital relationship of black couples. His study reveals that of the three forms of husband-wife primary relations—companionship, physical affection, and empathy—husbands perceive them in more positive terms than wives, although a greater proportion of both spouses perceive these relations more positively than negatively.

A number of studies have attempted to ferret out the relationship between marital adjustment and other variables, such as marital happiness and number of children. Two studies conducted during pre-World War II found that couples who had one or two children were happier than those who had more children (cited in Leslie, 1967, pp. 514–515). A study by Reed (1941) reported that twice as many couples who had no children reported happy marriages than those who had four or more living children. Additionally, the proportion of couples reporting happy marriages declined with each additional child (cited in Leslie, 1967, pp. 514–515).

Perhaps the most surprising finding regarding marital satisfaction in the 1960s is that children tend to detract from, rather than contribute to, marital happiness. This was surprising in spite of the fact that earlier studies had revealed the same finding. Nevertheless, it should be pointed out that the findings pertaining to marital satisfaction and children are contradictory. Paris and Luckey (1965) showed that the number of children made no significant difference between wives who increased or decreased their level of marital satisfaction, nor did they find any reliable association between number of children and marital satisfaction. Christensen (1950) found a positive relationship between the number of children and marital happiness, while others found negative relationships in which the greatest adjustment was found in the smallest families. Blood and Wolfe (1960) found a curvilinear relationship whereby marital satisfaction was greatest when there were three children in the family but less with fewer or more children. It has been suggested that contradictory and negative findings may be accounted for, not so much by presence or actual number of children, but by the attitudes of couples regarding children (cited in Paris and Luckey, 1965–1966, pp. 216–217).

Recent studies have also tested the relationship between marital satisfaction and children. Rollins and Feldman (1970) have noted that the marital satisfaction of wives decreases substantially during the childbearing and childrearing phases until the children are getting ready to leave home. A study by Renne

(1970) shows that black parents, and especially those presently raising children, were definitely less likely to be satisfied with their marriages. The number of children was found to have no consistent effect on the proportion of marital dissatisfaction. The author suggests that parenthood for black people is even more difficult than it is for white parents. This is explained by the fact that race, despite the level of income, has a strong impact on the amount of protection that parents can give to their children. Even with an adequate income, blacks can do little in the way of protecting their "children from the irrational restrictions, insults, and degradation black people encounter in this society" (p. 62). The essence of this explanation is that the devastating conditions encountered by black people in the American white-dominated society place additional pressures of child-rearing on parents which further detract from their marital relations. These pressures exceed those faced by white parents. Therefore, it is understandable that children have a greater effect on the marital happiness of black parents than they do on the marital happiness of white parents.

Another variable that has been correlated with marital satisfaction is wife employment status. A study by Paris and Luckey (1965) has shown that there is a relationship between the wife who was employed (or who planned to be employed in the near future) and marital satisfaction; dissatisfied wives were more often working outside the home than were satisfied wives (p. 221). A similar finding by Gover (1963) was that unemployed wives had higher adjustment scores than employed wives (p. 457). Blood and Wolfe (1960) found the average satisfaction scores of working and nonworking wives to be similar (4.68 and 4.72, respectively). Despite these similarities in marital satisfaction, it was further found that when economic necessity is related to wife employment, a differential pattern of marital satisfaction emerged. Thus, women who are in the labor market because of need are more satisfied than those there by choice (Blood and Wolfe, 1960, pp. 101–102). This finding contradicts one by Orden and Bradburn (1969) who made a distinction between need and choice of wives who work. Thus, they found that when married women are in the labor market because of economic needs rather than by choice, there is a significant reduction in marital happiness (Orden and Bradburn, 1969, p. 405).

Research results have confirmed the common sense notion that consensus is related to marital satisfaction. Terman showed that the degree of disagreement between spouses is related to marital happiness. It is substantially related to husband's happiness, but is even more closely related to wife's happiness or unhappiness, as an expression of happiness or unhappiness (Udry, 1971, p. 254).

Length of marriage is another factor found to affect marital satisfaction. Blood and Wolfe (1960) noted that wives were significantly less satisfied with their marriages in later years than at the beginning of marriage. This finding is suggested by the fact that 52 percent of wives were very satisfied with their marriages during the first two years and none was very dissatisfied. In contrast, only 6 percent of the wives were very satisfied with their marriages after 20 years, while 21 percent were conspicuously dissatisfied (p. 264).

Marital satisfaction has been found to correlate with background variables such as age, education, occupation, and income. The findings of Blood and Wolfe (1960) reveal that similarity of age and education produces the greatest satisfaction for wives, whereas husband-superiority and husband-inferiority depress marital satisfaction—husband-superiority lessens satisfaction and husband-inferiority gives the least satisfaction (p. 256). On the other hand, Gurin et al. (1960) found no difference between the young, middle-aged, and old respondents in regard to marital happiness (pp. 112–113). This finding was not completely confirmed by Renne (1970) who tested the same relationship. She found that all persons over 45 years of age were more likely to express marital happiness than younger persons (p. 59). Gurin et al. also showed that for all age groups, marital happiness increases as the educational level of the respondent increases (pp. 112–113). Similar results were found by Blood and Wolfe (1960) and Renne (1970). Renne also found that older blacks (those 45 years and over) who did not go beyond the eighth grade were less likely to be dissatisfied than those who went beyond this grade level (p. 59). This finding suggests that for those blacks, age has an effect on marital happiness that transcends the educational level.

An additional finding by Renne (1970) revealed that for black women, neither education nor affluence compensates for being black. Put another way, race has an impact on black women that exceeds that of education or affluence. In regard to this point, it was reported that younger black women, especially, were much more likely to express marital dissatisfaction than their white counterparts (pp. 56–57). Based on these findings, one could expect similarity among black women with regard to marital happiness, especially for the younger women (those under 45 years); this is regardless of education or income levels. This suggestion corresponds to a finding by Bell (1971). He found that lower status black wives (9 years or less of education) reject both marriage as an institution as well as their own particular marriage, while higher status wives (college graduates) were more accepting of marriage as an institution, but they, too, rejected their own particular marriage.

Another aspect of the marital relation to which research applies is marital disagreement. In an attempt to find out the frequency of disagreements and arguments, Bell (1971) asked his respondents to estimate the amount of arguing in their marriages. Hence, the results indicate that the majority of the couples argue or disagree at some time, with a few arguing frequently (p. 313).

A study by Pineo, which was a 20-year follow-up of the Burgess-Wallin couples, discovered a substantial loss of consensus, including loss of consensus on finances, recreation, religious matters, philosophy of life, demonstration of affection, etc. (cited in Udry, 1966, p. 253). Numerous cross-sectional studies add support to this longitudinal study (e.g., Kirkpatrick and Hobart, 1954 and Udry et al., 1966). Hence, it is concluded, based on known research, that married couples do not agree more with increasing years of marriage; "if anything, couples have less consensus after many years of marriage than they did in the beginning" (cited in Udry, 1966). To state it differently, disagreement among couples is directly related to number of years married.

Blood and Wolfe (1960) investigated marital disagreements by ascertaining the main things about which their respondents disagreed, as well as testing relationships. The areas of disagreement listed were money, children, recreation, personality, in-laws, roles, religion, and politics. Financial problems were found to be the most common category of disagreement, while sex was the least common (p. 241).

They found that both education and age were related to disagreements. Education was related to reporting disagreements as well as to the number of disagreements. All college-educated wives reported at least one area of disagreement, and higher education was associated with fewer reports of no problem areas (p. 244).

In regard to age, all women over 50 years reported fewer disagreements than women of other ages. This finding was attributed to longevity of marriage. Thus, it is believed that by this time disagreements have been settled or forgotten, or else communication between the couple has reached such a level that the danger of disagreement about anything is reduced (Blood and Wolfe, 1960, p. 245). This finding contradicts earlier findings which showed that marital disagreement increases with increasing number of years married (cited in Udry, 1966).

The Blood and Wolfe (1960) study also reveals a relationship between money disagreements and education and income. It was reported that money disagreements were more pronounced for women with high school education than for those with grade school education. This difference is thought to be a function of income, in that women with only a grade school education are usually married to men whose incomes are too low to offer any choice in spending it. In addition, it was found that only 19 percent of city couples, with below-average incomes, could recall disagreement about money. Thus, it was assumed that such disagreements were few. Thirty-seven percent of the disagreements, among couples whose income was six to seven thousand dollars, were financial. On the other hand, it was revealed that only those above the 10 thousand dollar income had enough to reduce disagreements to a low of 9 percent (p. 245).

This review represents the general evidence to which this study relates. It is limited. However, it gives some insights into past research and provides us an opportunity to compare previous research findings with those presented here.

SAMPLE AND METHODS

The data reported in this paper were collected in 1968 and 1969 for a study to investigate the role of stress and heredity in black and white blood pressure differences. The study was based on a sample of 1,000 adults living in Detroit, Michigan. The respondents consisted of married adults between the ages of 25 and 60 years, living with their spouses. A sample of 256 black women was taken from this study for the author's dissertation (1974).

The data for this paper are based on the dissertation study in addition to analysis of data based on the husbands (252) of the 256 wives. This makes a total of 508 respondents.

The sample selected by the Program for Urban Health Research was taken from residence areas which varied in extremes of high and low stress conditions, relative to the city. This was done by a factor analytical technique. The technique resulted in the final selection of high and low stress areas. These areas were in the extreme quartiles of factor scores. The rates showed sharp differences between high and low stress across median income, median education, crime rates, and marital instability. This pattern was also revealed in other rates such as school truancy, "dropouts," welfare registration, etc. (Harburg et al., 1973). Thus, from the standpoint of this study, a high-stress area is a group of two census areas that is low on socioeconomic factors and high in crime rates, marital instability, etc. The reverse of these factors characterizes a low-stress area.

Categorical variables were constructed from questions that seem to fit together in describing certain facets of marital relationships. This resulted in the following variables: importance of marital interaction goals, opportunities for fulfilling marital interaction, marital happiness, and marital disagreements. The data are analyzed by using percentage analysis which resulted in both a description and comparison of the marital relations of black men and women.

A DESCRIPTIVE ANALYSIS

We turn now to a categorical description of the marital relations of black husbands and wives. The following categories have been developed for describing these relations: marital interaction, marital happiness, and marital disagreements. Marital interaction is measured by the importance of marital interaction goals and opportunities for fulfilling these goals (each of these variables is analyzed separately). Marital interaction is a concept that denotes some sort of social exchange between spouses; it is an action-reaction process. Table 4:1 represents a distribution of responses regarding "The Importance of Marital Interaction Goals." The table is intended to show how important it is

TABLE 4:1

Importance of Marital Interaction Goals

Measures of Importance of Interaction	Husbands' Rated Responses %					Wives' Rated Responses %				
	Highly Important	Moderately Important	Not Important	Total %	N	Highly Important	Moderate Important	Not Important	Total %	N
How important is it to spend time with spouse and do things together?	75.0	23.0	2.0	100	252	81.3	17.1	1.6	100	256
How important is it to help make big decisions for the family?	91.0	8.0	1.0	100	252	88.7	10.9	0.4	100	256
How important is it to have the kind of sex life you desire?	83.7	15.5	0.8	100	252	77.4	19.6	3.0	100	256
How important is it to understand how your spouse thinks and feels?	84.5	15.1	0.4	100	252	89.1	9.0	1.5	100	256
How important is it to do well or be successful at handling disagreements?	87.7	11.9	0.4	100	252	87.5	12.5	0.0	100	256
How important is it to be a good husband/wife to your spouse?	92.1	7.5	0.4	100	252	94.9	4.7	0.4	100	256
How important is to to be appreciated by your spouse?	83.3	15.5	1.2	100	252	88.2	9.8	2.0	100	256

for the husbands and wives to interact with each other in varied ways. Three of the interaction goals listed in Table 4:1 can be classified as primary relations or expressive gratifications. It is a fact that black and white Americans seek these gratifications in marriage: companionship, as measured by "How important is it to spend time with spouse and do things together?"; physical affection, as measured by "How important is it to have the kind of sex life you desire?"; and empathy, as measured by "How important is it to understand how your spouse thinks and feels?" Of these three goals, all except one are more important to the wives than the husbands. The exception is physical affection. This goal is expressed as highly important by 83.7 percent of the husbands and by 77.4 percent of the wives. On the other hand, 3 percent of the wives, while less than 1 percent (.8 percent) of the husbands indicated that sex is not important. Also, Table 4:1 shows that all of the interaction goals are highly important for 77 percent or more of wives and for 75 percent or more of the husbands. Additionally, of the seven goals listed, only three are more highly important to the husbands than to the wives. These exceptions include "importance of making big decisions for the family," "importance of having the kind of sex life desired (physical affection)," and "importance of handling disagreements" (which is about equal for both sexes: 87.7 percent for husbands and 87.5 percent for wives). Of the three interaction goals that appear somewhat more important to the husbands than the wives, the one that varies the most from the wives' responses is "the importance of having the kind of sex life desired" (a 6.4 percent difference).

These data suggest that the men value those marital goals that have been traditionally associated with male roles, decision making and sex gratification. On the other hand, the women seem to value those marital interaction goals that are most related to the expressive roles females have been socialized to perform (companionship, item 1; empathy, item 4; to be a good wife, item 6; and to be appreciated by spouse, item 7).

Since the majority of husbands and wives seem to place high importance/value on marital interaction goals, the next step is to analyze how important are their chances for fulfilling certain goals. These were determined by asking the respondents, "How much actual chance do you have to spend time with your spouse and do things together, to help make big decisions for the family, or to have the kind of sex life you desire?" Table 4:2 shows the results. Chances for fulfilling marital interaction goals appear to be better for the husbands than for the wives, although the husbands' chances for companionship (item 1) and sex (item 3) are not significantly different from their wives' chances. These results correspond to the findings by Scanzoni (1971). The husbands tended to evaluate the primary relations more positively than the wives, while the husbands view their opportunities for fulfilling these relations better than the wives do. The greatest difference between husbands and wives is in regard to making family decisions (a 13.1 percent difference), with the husbands having the greatest opportunities in helping to make big family decisions. This

TABLE 4:2

Opportunities for Fulfilling Marital Interaction Goals

Measures of Opportunities for Interaction	Husbands' Rated Responses %					Wives' Rated Responses %				
	Very Good	Moderately Good	Not Good At All	Total %	N	Very Good	Moderately Good	Not Good At All	Total %	N
How much actual chance to spend time with spouse and do things together?	45.2	42.1	12.7	100	252	42.2	44.2	13.6	100	256
How much actual chance to help make big decisions for the family?	86.2	12.6	1.2	100	252	73.1	24.3	2.6	100	256
How much actual chance to have the kind of sex life you desire?	66.3	28.9	4.8	100	252	62.1	32.4	5.5	100	256

47

finding is contrary to the notion of a black matriarchy, which implicates black women as the decision makers of the family. But it corresponds to research that shows that black women do not make the important family decisions alone (Middleton and Putney, 1960; Mack, 1971; and Hyman and Reed, 1969).

In comparing the goals that are common to Tables 4:1 and 4:2, we find that both husbands and wives get less than they desire from their marital relations, even though the wives get somewhat less than their husbands. In other words, their opportunites for fulfilling the marital interaction goals were fewer than the importance or value they placed on them. Discrepancies such as these have the potential for creating psychological dissonance. However, people are capable of reducing or managing dissonance so as to minimize its effect. Therefore, these discrepancies are not likely to cause any serious marital problems.

Of the three goals common to Tables 4:1 and 4:2, the "chance to make big family decisions" comes closest to the value that the couples place on it. Ninety-one percent of the husbands consider it highly important and 86.2 percent of them indicate that their chances for doing it are very good. Eighty-eight percent (88.7 percent) of the wives consider it highly important, while 73.1 percent of them feel that their chances for doing it are very good.

Marital happiness is another variable to be analyzed. It is used in this chapter the way it has been defined by Renne (1970) which takes into account both happiness and unhappiness. The ordinary, not completely satisfactory marriage is considered "happy," while the term *unhappy* is usually reserved for the acute case of dissatisfaction (p. 54). This definition is used with the understanding that theoretically, one could have a completely "happy" marriage, but in reality this seems highly improbable; therefore, a definition closer to reality has been chosen. On the basis of the above conceptualization of "happiness," several measures of it have been chosen. They are found in Table 4:3, which represents a distribution of the responses on several variables considered to be indicators of marital happiness. This is not to imply that the list is exhaustive. It is simply to suggest that these are indirect measures that appear to be indicative of marital happiness. They are indirect in that the respondents were not asked to evaluate their marital happiness or satisfaction, but they were asked questions that seem to be indicative of "happiness." The indirect approach is not unique nor methodologically unsound. It was used by Locke and Burgess and Terman, who conducted some of the pioneer research in marital adjustment, and was found to be a valid measure (cited in Udry, 1966). Paris and Luckey (1956–1966) found very little relationship between direct questions of marital happiness and Locke-Terman marital adjustment scores which led them to conclude "that because of the cultural value placed on 'happy' marriage it is very difficult for subjects to admit their own marriages are less than 'happy'" (p. 221). Therefore, the indirect approach for measuring marital happiness seems to be as effective as the direct approach,

TABLE 4:3

Marital Happiness

Measures of Happiness	Husbands' Rated Responses %a					Wives' Rated Responses %				
	Positive	Moderately Positive	Negative	Total %	N	Positive	Moderately Positive	Negative	Total %	N
How often angry or irritated with spouse?	24.6	52.7	22.7	100	252	16.0	53.5	30.5	100	256
How often you and your husband/wife get on each other's nerves?	35.7	49.6	14.7	100	252	29.3	49.7	21.0	100	256
How much you and your husband/wife see eye to eye and agree on things?	71.4	17.1	11.5	100	252	62.5	19.5	18.0	100	256
How often are you pleased with the things your spouse does?	84.1	14.3	1.6	100	252	74.2	20.3	5.5	100	256
How often have you wished that you never got married?	69.8	22.2	8.0	100	252	64.5	22.2	13.3	100	256
If you had your life to live over again, would you marry the same person?	69.0	18.7	12.3	100	252	66.8	12.5	20.7	100	256

aThe positive ratings imply the greatest amount of happiness; moderate implies less, but not unhappiness; negative implies unhappiness.

even if not better, especially when happiness is measured for a group without any attempt to predict marital success of a given individual. Hence, it should be added that the measures of marital happiness here are not used to predict marital success, but they are used to help describe the marital relations of black men and women.

The data in Table 4:3 show that a majority of husbands and wives express satisfaction on four of the six items, as indicated by the positive-rated responses. On the remaining measures—"How often angry or irritated with spouse?" and "How often you and your husband/wife get on each other's nerves?"—more than 49 percent of both husbands and wives responses are rated as moderately positive.

The measures that appear to contribute most to the marital happiness of husbands are "How often are you pleased with the things your spouse does (84.1 percent)?" and "How much you and your wife see eye-to-eye and agree on things (71.4 percent)?" For the wives the measures are "How often are you pleased with the things your spouse does (74.2 percent)?" and "If you had your life to live over again, would you marry the same person (66.8 percent)?" As shown, "to be pleased with the things spouse does" seems to be an important factor in the marital happiness of both husbands and wives.

When observing the data further, we find that there are certain factors that may contribute to the dissatisfaction or unhappiness of married persons. This is suggested on the basis of the rated responses designated "negative." On the basis of these responses, for husbands and wives frequency of anger and irritation with spouse (22.7 percent and 30.5 percent, respectively) and frequency with which spouses get on each other's nerves (14.7 percent and 21.0 percent, respectively) have the most negative effects on their marital happiness. The effect seems to be somewhat greater for the wives than for the husbands, since a larger proportion of the wives' responses are rated "negative."

Furthermore, it should be noted that the wives express more marital unhappiness than the husbands. This finding corresponds to other research on marital relations (Renne, 1970 and Scanzoni, 1971). It is suggested that women, evidently, expect more out of the marital relation than men; therefore, it seems plausible that women would be more critical of their marriages than their husbands. It is reasonable for wives to expect more out of the marital relationship than their husbands. Females more than males are socialized to perform an expressive role which is in contrast to the instrumental roles learned by men. Thus, women are more likely than men to be sensitive to the socio-emotional aspect of marriage.

The final aspect of the marital relation to be analyzed and discussed is marital disagreement. Discord or disagreement is inevitable within intimate interpersonal relations, such as marriage, even when the rewards exceed the cost. Discord is not necessarily dysfunctional to the relationship. In some cases it might be rather functional to it. Arguments or disagreements have a functional nature; they serve to "clear the air" and to release tensions and emotions that might otherwise remain dangerously suppressed (Hodges, 1971, p. 115). Moreover, disagreements for some married couples are stimulating and enjoyable; they add a positive dimension to marital interaction for those who enjoy a give-and-take relationship (Bell, 1971, p. 314).

Some other function of disagreements in marriage are implied from the dysfunctions that result from not arguing or disagreeing. It has been suggested that for couples who never argue it may mean they lack individuality, that one of the persons in the relationship does not recognize the other as being important enough to disagree with, or that one spouse may fail to disagree with the other because of fear. Thus, reasons for not arguing or disagreeing may be more adverse for a marital relationship than arguing or disagreeing (Bell, 1971, p. 314).

Table 4:4 presents the distribution of responses on marital disagreements. According to the husbands, the issue over which they disagree with their spouses most often is leisure time (27.1 percent), followed by sex (21.0 percent), and money (20.2 percent). On the basis of wives' perceptions, the issue over which they disagree the most is money (30.8 percent), followed by leisure (28.2 percent), and sex (28.9 percent). The issue over which husbands and wives have the least disagreement is drinking (41.7 percent and 44.1 percent, respectively). It should be noted that Blood and Wolfe (1960) found that money and leisure were among the top areas of disagreement in their study of married women.

In sum, these data show that a majority of the respondents disagree with their spouses over all the issues analyzed. This is observed from the rated responses designated "Frequent Disagreements" and "Average Disagreements." Taken positively, frequency of disagreement is suggestive of frequent interaction which may be a sign of a healthy marriage.

SUMMARY AND CONCLUSION

A majority of respondents in our sample considered certain marital interaction goals to be highly important. This corresponds to what one expects of most marriages. Common sense dictates that there should be some marital goals, whether they be ideal and/or real, or even unique to a particular marriage. Such is verified by our respondents. The data also indicate that the spouses did not have the necessary opportunities for fulfilling the valued goals; hence, this created discrepancies between the ideal and the real.

Furthermore, we found that most of our respondents experienced some level of marital happiness, with the husbands experiencing somewhat more happiness than the wives. A greater proportion of wives than husbands seemed to be dissatisfied with their marriages, a finding verified by Renne (1970) and Scanzoni (1971). Finally, most of the husbands and wives expe-

TABLE 4:4

Marital Disagreements

Disagreements	Husbands' Rated Responses %					Wives' Rated Responses %				
	Frequent	Average	Never	Total %	N	Frequent	Average	Never	Total %	N
1. Disagree with spouse about money	20.2	65.1	14.7	100	252	30.8	52.8	16.4	100	256
2. Disagree with spouse on leisure	27.1	60.6	12.3	100	252	28.2	59.7	12.1	100	256
3. Disagree with spouse about sex	21.0	54.8	24.2	100	252	28.9	51.0	20.1	100	256
4. Disagree with spouse about drinking	16.2	42.1	41.7	100	252	20.7	35.2	44.1	100	256

rienced marital disagreements even though their perceptions of the frequency of disagreements varied.

Despite the varying views, we conclude that, in general, the marital relationships of our respondents, as shown by the data presented, are more indicative of solidarity and cohesiveness than instability and weakness. As noted in the introduction, this work was exploratory, and the results speak only to the responses of a relatively small number of black husbands and wives. Nevertheless, they provide some insights into the attitudes and perceptions these men and women have about their marriages. Expanded research is needed to develop a greater understanding of black marriage partners.

REFERENCES

Bell, R. *Marriage and Family Interaction*. Homewood, Ill.: The Dorsey Press, 1971.

Blood, R. O., Jr., and D. M. Wolfe. *Husbands and Wives*. Glencoe, Ill.: The Free Press of Glencoe, 1960.

Christensen, H. (ed) *Handbook of Marriage and Family*. Chicago: Rand McNally, 1964.

Cuber, J., and P. Harroff. "The More Total View: Relationship among Men and Women of the Upper Middle Class," *Journal of Marriage and the Family*, 1963, 25, 140–145.

Gover, D. "Socio-Economic Differential in the Relationship between Marital Adjustment and Wife's Employment Status," *Journal of Marriage and the Family*, 1963, 25, 452–459.

Gurin, G., J. Veroff, and S. Feld. *Americans View Their Mental Health*. New York: Basic Books, Inc., 1960.

Harburg, E. et al. "Socio-Ecological Stress, Suppressed Hostility, Skin Color, and Black-White Male Blood Pressure: Detroit," *Psychosomatic Medicine*, 1973(July–August), 35, 276–296.

Hicks, M. C., and M. Platt. "Marital Happiness and Stability: A Review of the Research in the Sixties," *Journal of Marriage and Family*, 1970, 35, 553–574.

Hodges, H. M., Jr. *Conflict and Consensus: An Introduction to Sociology*. New York: Harper & Row Publishers, 1971.

Leslie, G. R. *The Family in Social Context*. New York: Oxford University Press, 1967.

Luckey, E. B., and J. Bain. "Children: A Factor in Marital Satisfaction," *Journal of Marriage and the Family*, 1970, 32, 43–44.

Orden, S. et al. "Dimensions of Marital Happiness," *American Journal of Sociology*, 1968, 73(May), 715–731.

———, and N. Bradburn. "Working Wives and Marriage Happiness," *American Journal of Sociology*, 1969, 74, 392–407.

Paris, B. L., and E. B. Luckey. "A Longitudinal Study in Marital Satisfaction," *Sociology and Social Research*, 1965–1966, 50, 212–221.

Renne, K. R. "Correlates of Dissatisfaction in Marriage," *Journal of Marriage and the Family*, 1970, 32, 54–67.

Rollins, B. C., and H. Feldman. "Marital Satisfaction over the Family Life Cycle," *Journal of Marriage and Family*, 1970, 32, 20–28.

Rutledge, E. M. *Marital and Family Relations of Black Women.* Ann Arbor, Mich.:
    University Microfilm, 1974(diss.).
Scanzoni, J. *The Black Family in Modern Society.* Boston: Allyn & Bacon, 1971.
Staples, R. (ed) *The Black Family: Essay and Studies.* Belmont, Calif.: Wadsworth
    Publishing Co., 1971.
Udry, R. *The Social Context of Marriage.* Philadelphia: J. P. Lippincott Co., 1966.

5

BLACK HUSBANDS AND WIVES: AN ASSESSMENT OF MARITAL ROLES IN A MIDDLE-CLASS NEIGHBORHOOD

Annie S. Barnes

Studies of the black family have primarily focused on the low-income and working-class communities. Matrifocality, conceptualized as "close affective ties, domestic units dominated by females, and high frequencies of households" (Otterbein, 1966, p. vii), is one type of family structure found in the lower-class family (Frazier, 1939, pp. 102–113; Hippler, 1974, p. 47; Moynihan, 1967, pp. 30–31; and Powdermaker, 1962, p. 204). In the Hunter's Point study by Hippler, such households were described as headed either by a grandmother whose daughters and grandchildren lived with her or by a mother whose children lived with her (Hippler, 1974, p. 21). The female heads were the central figures and the only financial, emotional, and authority leaders in the household; in fact, the men were described as unsuited to steady employment (Hippler, 1974, pp. 43 and 47). Similarly, the men in a Syracuse, New York, low-rent housing project experienced a high rate of unemployment (Willie, 1976, pp. 137–138). The economic marginality of men in such settings as those described by Hippler and Willie tends to foster the maintenance of a black matriarchy. Moreover, it has been found that the black matriarchy in the lower class is a consequence of slavery (Frazier, 1939, p. 102) and more recently of the economic insecurity of Afro-American males (Hippler, 1974, p. 217; King, 1945, p. 103; Powdermaker, 1962, p. 205; and Smith, 1956, p. 22). The prevalence of a matriarchy, however, has been challenged by a number of writers. The Cromwells (1978, pp. 754–756), on the basis of their inner-city neighborhood sample in Kansas City, and Staples (1977, pp. 174–183), using a historical perspective, concluded that the concept of the black matriarchy must be rejected, for it is not the dominant relationship in the black family.

Patriarchy, another type of family structure associated with the black family, is seldom found in Afro-American lower-class communities. Patriarchy, however, has been seen in black working-class communities in Rivertown County, Missouri, and Pulpwood County, Florida, (Martin and

Martin, 1978, p. 20). Furthermore, Scanzoni (1971, p. 241) found that in the American black family, the higher the husband's occupational status, the more likely he will resolve conflict in his favor.

The third type of family structure in the black community is equalitarianism. It was found to be the norm in working-class marriages in an inner-city neighborhood in Kansas City (Cromwell and Cromwell, 1978, p. 757) and in Rivertown and Pulpwood counties (Martin and Martin, 1978, p. 20). It was also a feature of family life in Texas (Bullock, 1941, pp. 29–30) and among middle-class spouses, "especially when both are employed" (Frazier, 1957, p. 331).

Varied types of interaction, including cooperation in the performance of house-related tasks, also characterize the family in the black community. When roles were performed in Rivertown and Pulpwood counties, a rigid division of labor occurred (Martin and Martin, 1978, p. 20), but men in Hunter's Point, it was found, did not usually help their wives (Hippler, 1974, p. 47).

Affective behavior comprises another type of family interaction in the black community. Although black spouses desire companionship, physical affection, and empathy from marriage (Scanzoni, 1971, p. 201), it was impossible for women in Hunter's Point to obtain deep emotional relations; instead, females denigrated male sexuality, and the men were sullenly indifferent to the women or resorted to bragging (Hippler, 1974, pp. 42 and 49). Furthermore, Bernard (1966, p. 98) has suggested that "the Negro wife suffers deprivation in all areas, but it is relatively less marked in the area of companionship and love than in those of income and understanding." The achievement of a strong marital bond has been described as difficult, because blacks on the same social level as whites receive fewer dollars and less job satisfaction (Scanzoni, 1971, pp. 205–209). Moreover, money, extramarital sex, and family problems result in the dissolution of some black marriages (Holloman and Lewis, 1978, p. 223). However, when the occupational, educational, and income status increases, marital cohesiveness does not improve in a corresponding manner (Scanzoni, 1971, p. 201). In addition, it is suggested that large numbers of black women are alienated from black men primarily because of the "acquisition of the colonizer's cultural values" (Staples, 1979, p. 25).

As can be seen from this review of the literature, there are "serious gaps in our knowledge of marriage and family among Negroes" (Bernard, 1966, p. ix). An even greater void exists in the literature of the black middle-class family, which may be a consequence of several factors, including the difficulty of studying middle-class blacks. It may also result from the phenomenon of lumping all blacks together and sometimes comparing them with the white middle-class. This chapter, however, will focus on family structure, cooperation, and affection in a black middle-class neighborhood, and a number of concepts previously employed to describe the lower-class black family will be applied to the black middle-class family. A related purpose of this chapter is to determine the influence of sex, education, occupation, and income on family structure, spousal cooperation, and spousal affective relations.

METHODOLOGY AND SAMPLE

This research was part of a larger study on the black family in Atlanta, Georgia. It was conducted between September, 1969, and August, 1970, in Golden Towers, a northwest Atlanta neighborhood. The subjects were interviewed in their homes and on their jobs by the author concerning family structure, spousal cooperation, and spousal affection. To determine family authority patterns, several questions were asked, including who lived in each household; what the relationship of each person was to the household head; what kinds of decisions each spouse made; which spouse made a majority of the decisions; why women made most of the decisions in some households; and how female spouses reacted to the decision-making process. Similarly, to understand spousal cooperation, the author asked what were the duties of the husband and wife in the home and to its related activities? To obtain the data on affective relations, the respondents were asked to list and describe the religious, social, and cultural activities shared with their spouses and describe the strength (strong, moderate, weak) of their own marital bond. When it was not described, the author then asked the respondents to describe the black middle-class marital bond as they had observed it among their black middle-class friends and acquaintances. Thirty-nine women and 13 men in 41 households participated in the interview. It usually took from three to six hours (divided into two to four visits) to conduct the interview; but when both spouses participated, it was likely to be completed in one session. The demographic data were obtained by mailing a questionnaire and self-addressed envelope to the respondents which netted a 50 percent return. To obtain data on the remainder of the households, the questionnaire was completed on the telephone, in their homes, or on their jobs. It determined the sex of adults, their migration and neighborhood settlement patterns, age, education, occupation, annual income, and church and political affiliations and frequency of participation. Participant observation was engaged in with the entire family in approximately half of the households. To observe routine activities in the home, appointments were made, and I arrived shortly after the residents returned home from work or after their dinner and visited two to four hours. Visitation on Saturday evening in one household lasted several hours, and shorter periods were spent on a few Sunday afternoons in several households. During the visits, I played games with the family or the children, ate, talked, listened to music, and watched television. On other occasions, I became involved in other family activities. Participant observation outside the home included attendance at church services and dinners, a family reunion, restaurant dining, and car rides.

The Golden Towers neighborhood was comprised of 163 residents, 44 percent male and 56 percent female. Of this group, 49 percent of the males and 34 percent of the females were native to Atlanta; and a majority of the migrants were part of the sizable migration movement to Atlanta in recent decades. These residents occupied households with an average membership of approximately four; moreover, extended family members lived in 14 of the 41 households. Besides spouses, extended family members, related guests (2), unrelated guests (8), and 94 children belonged to 35 of the households and six households were childless. This means that the average number of children per family was approximately 2.7, but when the entire neighborhood was considered, the average number of children per household was approximately 2.3.

The demographic characteristics of the spouses and widows were also varied. The 80 residents ranged in age from 30 to over 80 years of age. As can be seen from Table 5:1, 7.5 percent of the population had attended elementary school only; 12.5 percent had attended high school; 50.0 percent had attended college; and 30.0 percent had been enrolled in postgraduate programs. Similarly, as shown in Table 5:2, the residents were employed in service (2.5

TABLE 5:1

Educational Distribution by Sex of Household Heads in Golden Towers, 1970

Amount of Education Completed	Total Na	%	Male N	%	Female N	%
Graduate School						
Ph.D, M.D., D.D.S., J.D., Pharmaceutical, Science	8	10.0	6	15.4	2	4.9
Master's Degree	16	20.0	3	7.7	13	31.7[a]
College						
Four years	22	27.5	7	17.9	15	36.6
One to three years	18	22.5	11	28.2	7	17.1
High School						
Four years	8	10.0	7	17.9	1	2.4
One to three years	2	2.5	1	2.6	1	2.4
Grammar School						
First to eighth grade	6	7.5	4	10.3	2	4.9
Total	80		39		41	

a
  Two of the females listed in the Master's Degree category have completed
  course requirements for the Ph.D. and several in the same category have
  six-year teaching certificates.

TABLE 5:2

Occupational Distribution by Sex of Household Heads in Golden Towers, 1970

Occupation	Husbands N	%	Wives Na	%	Total N	%
Professional						
Physicians, Dentists, Pharmicist	4	100.0	0	0.0	4	
Educators	5	17.9	23	82.1	28	35.0[a]
Clergymen	4	100.0	0	0.0	4	5.0
Nursing	0	0.0	1	100.0	1	1.2
White Collar						
Proprietors	6	66.7	3	33.3	9	11.3
Managers and Officials	4	66.7	2	33.3	6	7.5[a]
Salesmen	1	100.0	0	0.0	1	1.2
Clerks	2	40.0	3	60.0	5	6.3
Blue Collar						
Letter Carriers	3	100.0	0	0.0	3	3.8
Foremen	2	100.0	0	0.0	2	2.5
Craftsmen	6	100.0	0	0.0	6	7.5
Truck drivers	1	100.0	0	0.0	1	1.2
Service Workers						
Domestic Workers	0	0.0	2	100.0	2	2.5[a]
Retired Chauffer	1	100.0	0	0.0	1	1.2
Housewives	0	0.0	7	100.0	7	8.7
Total	39	48.8	41	51.2	80	100.0

[a]
 Three of the employed females (manager, educator, domestic) work parttime.

percent), blue collar (15.0 percent), white collar (26.3 percent), and professional (46.2 percent) occupations. Professional occupations are distinguished
from white collar occupations by the amount of training required; hence, in
this sample, college training was a prerequisite for the professional occupations. Moreover, 8.7 percent of the women were housewives, and 1.2 percent
of the men were retired. In addition, one of the housewives was a retired
domestic worker, and three of the employed females—a manager of her
family's service station, a substitute teacher, and a domestic—only worked
part-time. From their work, the spouses and widows received a combined
annual income that ranged from the $10,000–$13,999 category to over $50,000
(Table 5:3), but the most frequently earned combined income was between
$14,000 and $21,999; and the average household income was $25,207.90.

FINDINGS

Authority Patterns

Matriarchy. The data show that matriarchy was the decision-making pattern in 16 of the 41 Golden Towers households. Both spouses, however,
occupied each of the 16 households, two excepted because of widowhood. The
women made a majority of the decisions concerning their children, including
discipline, health care, clothing, and food needs, and concerning economic
matters, including payment of bills and savings. Another area of female
domination was family activities, such as religious behavior. They decided
when and where the family went to church—of course, a few husbands

TABLE 5:3

Combined Annual Income of Families in Golden Towers, 1970

Class Intervals ($)	x Midpoints ($)	f Frequency	fx Calculations ($)
10,000 to 13,999	11,999.50	4	47,998.00
14,000 to 17,999	15,999.50	7	111,996.50
18,000 to 21,999	19,999.50	7	139,996.50
22,000 to 25,999	23,999.50	2	47,999.00
30,000 to 33,999	31,999.50	1	31,999.50
50,000 to 100,000	75,000.00	3	225,989.50
Total		24	604,989.50

belonged to a different church from their wives. Similarly, the women directed the family's social life; they planned the social occasions in the home, accepted invitations to dinners, parties, dances, and fashion shows, and selected their family friends. Some of these women met their friends prior to marriage, while others were met later on their jobs, in their churches, and in other organizations. At least one woman, however, was tired of associating only with friends she had known more than 20 years and wanted her husband to initiate new friendships. The men made friends on their jobs, but often they were not acceptable for joint social life (a consequence of their marital, social, or sex status). Of course, a few men made friends for their family.

Although the women were leaders in the matriarchal households, the men were not completely outside the decision-making process. They had greater authority than their wives concerning the upkeep of their homes and lawns, spending large sums of money, purchase of cars, and vacation and recreational time schedules. However, as a rule, their authority was only exercised after the situation had been discussed with their spouses.

To set the matriarchal households in their proper perspective, the 16 women's views of the decision-making process was sought. It was not by choice that the women made decisions; in fact, they complained and argued with their spouses, because they did not think ahead for the family, take care of legal and financial business, and assume more household responsibility.

Another measurement utilized to determine the proper perspective of the matriarchal family was the influence of socioeconomic factors, including education, on decision making. As can be seen from Table 5:4, these women were more highly educated than their spouses. Similar to education, as shown in Table 5:5, the women held more prestigious occupations than men, but the men earned more annual income than the women, a consequence of male employment in relatively good paying blue collar jobs as opposed to their wives' employment in lower-paying white collar and professional occupations (Table 5:6).

Another reason given for wife domination was that the men had experienced more job discrimination than women. This was seen in the length of time it took for them to prepare for their career. The women who were school teachers and school administrators utilized the usual training period, while a few of the men either did not receive all the training desired or spent twice as long preparing for their career. For example, one man was trained in cabinet making in the 1940s. Unable to obtain a job in cabinet making, he returned to college and earned a teaching degree. Although both sexes experienced difficulty getting promotions, the men had more problems than the women. The men, for example, were assigned a lower rating or position in government and private industry than their work level, and their promotion was usually delayed. The women have reaped the consequences of their husbands' job experiences. They created, the women say, men who often refuse to discuss their marital difficulties and/or demand an unrestrained and independent

TABLE 5:4

Type of Household Authority by Education of Spouses in Golden Towers, 1970

Type of Authority

Education	Female						Male					
	Matriarchy		Patriarchy		Equalitarianism		Matriarchy		Patriarchy		Equalitarianism	
	N	%	N	%	N	%	N	%	N	%	N	%
Doctoral	0	0.0	2	22.2	0	0.0	0	0.0	3	33.3	3	18.7
Masters	7	43.7	0	0.0	6	37.5	1	7.1	1	11.1	1	6.3
College	6	37.5	6	66.7	10	62.5	8	57.1	2	22.2	8	50.0
High School	1	6.3	1	11.1	0	0.0	2	14.3	3	33.3	3	18.7
Elem. School	2	12.5	0	0.0	0	0.0	3	21.4	0	0.0	1	6.3
Total	16	100.0	9	100.0	16	100.0	14	99.9	9	99.9	16	100.0

TABLE 5:5

Type of Household Authority by Occupation of Spouses in Golden Towers, 1970

Type of Authority

Occupation	Female						Male					
	Matriarchy		Patriarchy		Equalitarianism		Matriarchy		Patriarchy		Equalitarianism	
	N	%	N	%	N	%	N	%	N	%	N	%
Professional	8	50.0	5	55.6	11	68.8	2	14.3	3	33.3	7	43.7
White Collar	5	31.2	0	0.0	3	18.7	6	42.8	3	33.3	4	25.0
Blue Collar	0	0.0	0	0.0	0	0.0	6	42.8	3	33.3	5	31.3
Service Worker	1	6.3	1	11.1	0	0.0	0	0.0	0	0.0	0	0.0
Housewife	2	12.5	3	33.3	2	12.5	0	0.0	0	0.0	0	0.0
Total	16	100.0	9	100.0	16	100.0	14	99.9	9	99.9	16	100.0

TABLE 5:6

Type of Household Authority by Income of Spouses in Golden Towers, 1970

	Type of Authority											
	Female						Male					
Income	Matriarchy		Patriarchy		Equalitarianism		Matriarchy		Patriarchy		Equalitarianism	
	N	%	N	%	N	%	N	%	N	%	N	%
2,000– 5,999	1	16.7	1	50.0	3	23.1	0	0.0	0	0.0	1	8.3
6,000– 9,999	1	16.7	0	0.0	3	23.1	1	14.3	0	0.0	4	33.3
10,000–13,999	4	66.6	0	0.0	7	53.8	6	85.7	3	50.0	6	50.0
14,000–17,999	0	0.0	0	0.0	0	0.0	0	0.0	0	0.0	0	0.0
22,000–25,999	0	0.0	1	50.0	0	0.0	0	0.0	0	0.0	1	8.3
30,000–49,999	0	0.0	0	0.0	0	0.0	0	0.0	1	16.7	0	0.0
50,000–100,000	0	0.0	0	0.0	0	0.0	0	0.0	2	33.3	0	0.0
Total	6	100.0	2	100.0	13	100.0	7	100.0	6	100.0	12	99.9

position in the home which frees them from particular household responsibilities and domination by their wives. This sense of independence, however, decreases the men's prestige in the family, a likely source of male insecurity. These findings suggest yet another dimension of matriarchy, namely, control of household is not synonymous with domination of male spouse. In fact, the personal independence of the husband in some wife-dominated households puts him in a unique position in the black family—he has more personal autonomy than other men in the black family complex.

Although racial discrimination and the relatively low educational and occupational attainment levels of husbands in wife-dominated households are related to matriarchy, they do not adequately account for it since husbands in equalitarian and patriarchal households share the same experiences.It is likely that spouses develop during childhood, to varying degrees, the ability to receive and give love, ambition, leadership skills, and effective decision making. When parents, especially mothers, fail to teach these skills—here called the benign male socialization process—sons will be underprepared to contribute significantly to the family decision-making process. Additionally, perhaps the extent to which childhood skills reach maturity is influenced by the socialization process experienced by the men's wives; a domineering wife could impede the man's development.

Patriarchy. Husband domination, another household relationship, is similar to matriarchal authority. In nine Golden Towers households, the men decided their schedule, approved the activities of their wives and children, and determined the use of household finances, but the women implemented a majority of their decisions and were responsible for the performance of household chores.

An attempt was also made to set patriarchy in its proper perspective by asking the women in these households their reactions. A few of them were subservient, while others desired to utilize their leadership potential; but those who adjusted best to their subservient roles experienced less stress and strain than women who showed dislike for them. Consequently, male domination may be related to female insecurity. The influence of socioeconomic factors was also utilized to set male dominance in its proper perspective. It was found that education (Table 5:4) was significantly related to it. The highest percentage of men in the husband-dominated households had doctorate degrees and high school training, and decision making was not controlled by men who only had elementary training; but the women in husband-dominated households were more highly educated than the men. The men, however, had more prestigious occupations than their wives; hence, 66.6 percent were in white collar and professional positions, 33.0 percent were in blue collar positions, and there were no service work men in male-dominated households (Table 5:5). On the other hand, 55.6 percent of their wives were in professional occupations, 11.1 percent were in service work, and 33.3 percent were house-wives. A smaller percentage of women in husband-dominated than wife-dominated and equalitarian households worked. Additionally, it was found that all husbands who earned $30,000 or more per annum dominated their households, but there were three men who dominated their homes and earned between $10,000 and $13,999 annually (Table 5:6). These findings suggest that childhood socialization, personal training, and a satisfactory self-concept enabled the men in the middle income range to control their households. Moreover, education, prestigious occupations, and enough income to support family were often basic to patriarchy.

Equalitarianism. This was the third type of husband and wife decision-making pattern in Golden Towers. Sixteen couples manifested equal control over household decisions. There was a lot of give and take, and the best suggestions were accepted. Sometimes, however, a spouse made decisions independently, but at times it had severe consequences. A husband, for example, surprised his working wife by giving her a new car for her birthday; she became ill and remained home from work three days.

An attempt was also made to set the equalitarian households in their proper perspective by asking the couples their reaction to the joint decision-making process. In varying degrees, their marriage relations were relaxed and satisfy-ing. In fact, these couples were happier than the patriarchal and matriarchal couples. Moreover, not only did they make joint decisions, but there was no rigid division of labor in their implementation. To understand equalitarian-ism more fully, we correlated the socioeconomic characteristics of the spouses with the decision-making pattern. As can be seen from Table 5:1, the women in these households had bachelors and masters degrees, while their spouses were represented unequally among elementary, high school, college, and graduate training. Nevertheless, 75 percent of the men had at least some college training. This seems to give additional support to the proposition that education is significant to effective participation in the household. It was also found that the women had more prestigious occupations than their spouses. Hence, 87.5 percent were in professional and white collar positions, while 68.7 percent of their spouses were in the same occupations (Table 5:2), and each spouse earned up to $13,999 annually, although one male exception earned up to $25,999 per annum (Table 5:3). Since the women were ahead of their spouses educationally and occupationally and earned about the same income, it is likely that the male spouses' equal contribution to the household also resulted from a nonbenign socialization process during childhood. On the other hand, they may have taught themselves how to participate effectively in the household. Of course, some women say they taught their spouses the necessary household skills and knowledge. Moreover, equal earnings may sometimes help establish spousal equality in the home.

Cooperative Relations

Although all the men may not dominate or participate on an equal basis with their wives in the decision-making process, some of them assist with house-related tasks, including shopping for groceries, cooking, setting the table, washing dishes, and housecleaning. To understand men's performance of household tasks, each chore was cross-tabulated with the education, occupation, and income status of the men. It was consistently found that men who either had some college training or a college degree, blue collar occupations, and earned an annual income between $10,000 and $13,999 performed household tasks more often than the other men. Since six blue collar husbands were married to women in professional occupations, and three were married to women in white collar positions, assistance with household chores may be one way they enhanced their status in the home. Moreover, it is likely that men who occupy the highest and lowest educational, occupation, and income status consider housework demeaning to their manhood. Another index employed to provide understanding of men's domestic chores was the employment of their spouse. The husbands whose spouses were either full or part-time housewives were excerpted to determine whether or not the husbands performed household chores less frequently than husbands whose wives worked. All husbands of the seven full-time and three part-time wives performed at least one of the household tasks, but less frequently and for varied reasons. Thus, husbands shopped for groceries and cooked for such reasons as they had flexible schedules and their wives had not developed their culinary skills. This analysis, therefore, suggests that the husbands of housewives may do fewer house-related tasks than men whose wives work. Interestingly, husbands of these women were 40 to 69 years old, had an educational level that ranged from fourth grade to doctorate degrees, worked in professional, white collar, and blue collar occupations, and earned from $10,000 to approximately $100,000 annually. On the other hand, they were married to women who were 30 to 69 years of age and had either a college degree or some college or elementary school education.

Expressive Relations

Expressive behavior, conceptualized as congenial conversation, companionship, use of names to address spouse, and emotional satisfaction, is another type of spousal behavior. The couples' conversation spanned varied topics, one being previous employment. A college-educated man recounted to his wife his earlier life when he worked hard on the farm for a small amount of money, clothing, or animal manure which he later sold. Perhaps, this is one way he reinforced the extent of his social mobility. Conversation also focused on their contact with whites at professional, civic, and political meetings, and in graduate schools and about racial discrimination, segregation, job experiences, card playing, their children, and their antebellum ancestors. Moreover, the women talked about what they had taught white women and what they had learned from them. Of course, some of the women said they had not learned anything from whites they planned to use.

Companionship, the next type of expressive behavior between spouses, included giving parties, visiting their kinsmen, riding, fishing, playing bridge and other games, watching television, dancing, and attending social and religious activities. Occasionally, a few spouses attended the opera and symphony.

The names spouses used to address one another provide a closer view of their emotional relationship. The men employed a larger number (9) of term categories than the women (7) to address their spouses. However, the largest number addressed their spouses by their first name and, unlike the women, there were no men who called their wives by their last name. Furthermore, almost as many men (9) as women (10) utilized an endearing term to address their spouses; five used only an endearing concept, while four alternated between the use of an endearing concept and a first name or nickname. The men's endearing concepts for their wives were Sweetheart, Sugar, Darling, Darling Dear, Sweetie Face, Baby, Big Angel, and Hon. On the other hand, eight of the women called their spouse by his first name and four by his last name. It was the custom in the 1930s and early 1940s in some sections of the South for black women to be introduced to a man by his last name which they used until marriage. Once they were married, some of the spouses started calling each other by endearing concepts. When they began their family, they changed to Daddy, and when the children were grown, the women reverted to calling them by their last name. Some other women addressed their husbands by nicknames (5), and nickname and Daddy alternately (1), and Daddy (2). The latter was employed to teach young children what to call their father, but it also suggests a certain degree of closeness in the marital relationship. In addition, there were women who addressed their husband by alternating between their first name and an endearing term (5) and by only an endearing term (5). The terms of endearment employed by women for their spouses were Hon, Honey, Sweetie, Sweetie Pie, Baby, Sweetheart, and Sweets and were associated with the total marital complex. Hence, some women employed them to denote a strong emotional bond, while others utilized endearing terms for emphasis in conversation and to get and maintain their husband's attention. Moreover, when spouses were getting along, the women called their husbands by endearing terms, and when tensions existed they addressed them by their first names. Another consideration concerning the use of endearing terms relates to the location of the couple; thus, endearing concepts were usually employed in privacy, while the first name was utilized in situations external to the family. Moreover, terms of address between marriage partners were somewhat reciprocal, but more men (9) than women (6) called their spouses by a nickname.

Another area of expressive husband and wife behavior was emotional satisfaction viewed as respect, warmth, tenderness, and physical affection. As mentioned in the methodology, when only three of the Golden Towers spouses were willing to discuss their own marital bond, it was necessary to obtain their opinions about the strength of all middle-class marriages. A minority of the Golden Towers residents viewed black middle-class marriages as a strong relationship. A white collar husband, for example, believed that wives are lovely and must be caressed and treated sweetly and tenderly and should not be on an equal footing with men, especially when it comes to participation in the military and exposure to harsh language. In addition, a blue collar man, a professional woman, and a part-time housewife held that black middle-class spouses love each other.

Alternatively, a majority of the residents viewed black middle-class marriages as weak. One housewife related that the marital link is weak because the women are responsible for the household, and the children do not receive enough attention. Another professional wife attributed it to the status of the husband; he has been deprived of a good education and forced to work for less money than he needs to support his family. This becomes a source of marital stress. On the other hand, a professional man provided another dimension of marital problems. To him, marriages are weak because spouses are pulled in different directions; for example, variation in spousal occupational interests, religious dedication, and friendship types are a source of frustration for the women and their children. Moreover, in the opinion of blue collar wife, the preceding marital problems are compounded by yet another dimension of marital behavior—extramarital relations. After a man achieves, she said, with the help of his wife, he gets outside interests and forgets about his home. Thus, although a wife may be in dire need of sex, some husbands leave their needs unfulfilled. Yet, an adequate sex life, she also said, was crucial to husband and wife warmth.

That women in Golden Towers value warmth is evident. One woman, for example, related that "It is better to be able to show warmth toward another than to have a million dollars." Similarly, another wife related, "Warmth, love, or whatever you call it, keeps a life from being empty." Furthermore, all women would like their sons to demonstrate respect and kindness to black women, qualities that seem missing in some of their marriages. It appears, however, that some of the women who were either housewives, part-time housewives, or worked in nonauthority-bearing positions had the greatest need for a strong marital bond, but I hastily add that there were indeed women in authority-bearing and prestigious positions who were intensely interested in more love in their marriage. Additionally, these women often talked incessantly about their jobs and children's achievements which, in part, may have been an unconscious effort to compensate for the emotional insecurity in their marriage relationship. It, therefore, seems safe to conclude that the intensity of need for more love and affection in marriage is related to individual needs and personality.

Of course, the extent of affection the women receive in marriage is likely to be related to their husband type. Judging by the women's comments and my own observations in Golden Towers, there seems to be three types of black men who become husbands. Type One is the insecure husband who needs to feel important to everybody, including his family and, therefore, centers his affections on himself. On the other hand, Type Two is the secure husband who has learned either during childhood or adulthood how to contribute effectively to the household and participate comfortably in its related activities. Moreover, he centers his affections on his family and himself and speaks kindly, a great deal of the time, to them. Type Three, however, is the split personality husband who almost demands that his wife work; talks with her in a stiff, unsatisfying, and sometimes argumentative tone; yet is sometimes apologetic for his unkind behavior; expects his wife to forgive him quickly; and may or may not effectively assist with running the household. The types, however, are not rigid. Some black middle-class husbands exhibit characteristics of each type. Perhaps Type Two, though, is the most desirable spouse; and from this analysis it appears that the safest way to develop Type Two is to start at birth. This requires women to train their sons in decision making, cooperation, and receiving and giving love in kin relations. It requires fathers and mothers to daily demonstrate these virtues. In addition, this training should be accompanied by educational and occupational preparation for earning a good living. Lastly, since black women have the major responsibility for rearing children, including their sons, it is their privilege with whatever assistance they can get from their spouses to equip their sons fully for effective family living. In turn, it would enhance the race and the American society.

CONCLUSIONS

An attempt has been made to examine the influence of age, sex, education, occupation, and income on authority, cooperative, and expressive family relations in a black Atlanta neighborhood, known here as Golden Towers. Several conclusions are suggested. First, this black middle-class neighborhood supports the finding that matriarchy characterizes some black families (Frazier, 1939; Hippler, 1974; Moynihan, 1967; and Powdermaker, 1962) and disagrees with the thesis that black matriarchy must be rejected as an insignificant family type (Cromwell and Cromwell, 1978 and Staples, 1977). Second, this study shows that matriarchal, patriarchal, and equalitarian family structures may be found in the black community. Third, the findings suggest elements that relate to each authority pattern. Fourth, a related finding is that the men in matriarchal households possess a relatively high degree of personal autonomy; hence, female control is not synonymous with control of spouse, although this may indeed occur. Fifth, several indices to matriarchy were found, including the extent of women's satisfaction with this type of family structure. It is by necessity rather than by preference that they make and implement most of the household decisions. Utilizing socioeconomic factors, it was shown that women who controlled decision making had more education and more prestigious occupations, but earned less money than their husbands. The economic role of husbands, therefore, did not support the finding in Hunter's Point that the men were often absent from the household and unsuited to steady employment (Hippler, 1974) and in Syracuse that men experienced a high rate of unemployment (Willie, 1976).

The sixth finding is that in the patriarchal households, the men make a majority of the decisions against their spouses' desires, but the women implement some of them and are responsible for household tasks. Seventh, the relatively high educational achievement of men is significantly related to patriarchy, and there are no men in those households with only elementary schooling. The eighth finding is that the men hold more prestigious jobs than their wives and usually earn more money.

Ninth, equalitarianism, the third type of family structure, is the most satisfying in the marriage complex and is related to socioeconomic factors. The women have achieved more education than their spouses, but 75 percent of the men had at least some college training. The women had more prestigious occupations, but less income than their husbands.

The tenth finding is that the elements related to the patterns of decision making in the black family suggest several implications. One is that a high level of education is an essential element to making a significant contribution to the family decision-making process in each family type. Furthermore, prestigious occupations are another key to the men's participation in either a patriarchal or equalitarian household, while income is basic in each type of household. To prevent matriarchy, income must be coupled with a relatively high level of education. It is also suggested here that a benign male socialization process, that is, inadequate training in decisiveness, good reasoning ability, and mechanical skills may lead to male ineffectiveness in the family decision-making process. Moreover, the extent to which skills learned during childhood and adulthood reach maturity is likely to be influenced by the wife's childhood socialization in attitudes toward black men and effective decision making.

The eleventh finding is that the men cooperate in the performance of house-related tasks; hence, this study does not support the finding in Newtown and Pulpwood counties that a rigid division of labor occurs between spouses (Martin and Martin, 1978). Twelve socioeconomic factors are related to men's performance of household tasks. The highest percentage who perform household chores has either a college degree or college schooling, a blue collar occupation, and a $10,000–$13,999 annual income. Additionally, the husbands of housewives do fewer house-related tasks than men whose wives work; and they are an occupationally heterogeneous group.

Thirteen, it was found that couples participate in expressive relations; nevertheless, it appears that only a minority of them experience a strong emotional bond. Hence, the women in Golden Towers do not completely support Bernard's (1966) finding that black women suffer less in the area of companionship and love than income and understanding. Although the women desire warmth and love, a finding supported by Scanzoni (1971), I did not find that they were alienated from their spouses (Staples, 1979) or denigrated male sexuality as found in Hunter's Point (Hippler, 1974). Furthermore, several reasons explain the weak emotional link among some black spouses: men may lack sufficient income to support their family (a finding supported by Scanzoni, 1971) and the men engage in extramarital sex (a finding supported by Holloman and Lewis, 1978). Moreover, sometimes couples lack a strong emotional link because only one spouse assumes major responsibility for running the house; the spouses emphasize material things instead of personal relations in the childrearing process; and spouses are unequally interested in church participation and each other's friends. In addition, they experience inequality in education, occupation, and income. Finally, the ability and willingness to receive and give love to close kin and the personality type of husbands are likely to influence the quality of the marital bond.

In conclusion, the findings in this study seem to suggest that sex, education, occupation, income, and childhood and adulthood socialization are major determinants of spousal interaction and that black middle-class couples are both similar and different from lower- and working-class couples.

REFERENCES

Bernard, J. *Marriage and Family among Negroes*. Englewood Cliffs, N.J.: Prentice-Hall, 1966.

Bullock, H. A. *The Texas Negro Family: The Status of Its Socioeconomic Organization*. Prairie View: Prairie View College Press, 1941.

Cromwell, V. L., and R. E. Cromwell. "Perceived Dominance in Decision-Making and Conflict Resolution among Anglo, Black and Chicano Couples," *Journal of Marriage and the Family*, 1978, 40, 749–759.

Frazier, E. F. *The Negro Family in the United States*. Chicago: The University of Chicago Press, 1939.

———. *The Negro in the United States*. New York: The Macmillan Co., 1957.

Hippler, A. E. *Hunter's Point*. New York: Basic Books, Inc., 1974.

Holloman, R. E., and F. E. Lewis. "The Clan: Case Study of a Black Extended Family in Chicago," In D. B. Shimkin et al. (eds) *The Extended Family in Black Societies*. The Hague: Mouton Publishers, 1978, 201–238.

King, C. E. "The Negro Maternal Family: A Product of an Economic and A Culture System," *Social Forces*, 1945, 24(October), 100–104.

Martin, E. P., and J. M. Martin. *The Black Extended Family*. Chicago: The University of Chicago Press, 1978.

Moynihan, D. P. "The Roots of the Problem," In L. Rainwater and W. L. Yancey (eds) *The Moynihan Report and the Politics of Controversy*. Cambridge: The M.I.T. Press, 1967.

Otterbein, K. F. *The Andros Islanders*. Lawrence: University of Kansas Publishers, 1966.

Powdermaker, H. *Copper Town: Changing Africa*. New York: Harper & Row Publishers, 1962.

Scanzoni, J. H. *The Black Family in Modern Society*. Boston: Allyn & Bacon, 1971.

Shimkin, D. B. et al. "The Black Extended Family: A Basic Rural Institution and A Mechanism of Urban Adaptation," In D. B. Shimkin et al. (eds) *The Extended Family in Black Societies*. The Hague: Mouton Publishers, 1978.

Smith, R. T. *The Negro Family in British Guiana*. New York: Grove Press, 1956.

Staples, R. "The Myth of the Black Matriarchy," In D. Y. Wilkinson and R. L. Taylor (eds) *The Black Male in America*. Chicago: Nelson Hall Publishers, 1977.

Willie, C. *A New Look at Black Families*. Bayside: General Hall, Inc., 1976.

6

RACE DIFFERENCES IN HUSBAND-WIFE INTERPERSONAL RELATIONSHIPS DURING THE MIDDLE YEARS OF MARRIAGE

Walter R. Allen

Predictions of the imminent demise of marriage as a viable institution in our society are widespread. Both popular and scholarly sources point to soaring divorce rates, demands for drastic redefinition of marriage, and the increasing numbers of adults opting for lifelong singlehood as evidence in support of such conclusions. Nowhere, we are told, is this crisis in the institution more strongly felt than among black Americans. Increasingly, more people are coming to echo Moynihan's (1965) controversial conclusions of years past, that black family life is in a stage of rapid deterioration. While superficial analyses of these patterns might justify such a conclusion, a more careful, critical reading of the facts does not.

When one attempts to infer individual inclinations and characteristics from aggregate patterns, misreadings of the true situation often result. The conclusion that marriage is a dying institution generally, and among blacks in particular, is a good case in point. Several studies of mainstream (Bane, 1976) as well as black (see Allen, 1978 and 1979 for detailed reviews) family life suggest a totally different view of marriage. Despite high group divorce and separation rates, individual norms and behaviors are shown to favor marriage. These studies point to mitigating circumstances and advise against taking high marital dissolution rates as *prima facie* evidence that marriage as a way of life has fallen into great disfavor in our society. For example, over 90 percent of first-divorced persons eventually remarry (Division of Vital Statistics, 1971). In the case of black single women, disproportionate sex ratios that represent reduced numbers of eligible black males are also factors in the

Lydia Underwood provided valuable assistance with the literature review and analyses for this chapter. Richard English, Leanor Johnson, and Robert Staples provided valuable comments on earlier drafts of this chapter.

decision not to marry initially, or to remarry (Allen, 1980). Further, one often notes extreme variations in divorce statistics across race, class, and family life stage. To attribute such differences solely to varying individual commitments is simplistically naive and denies the importance of situational constraints as determinates of individual outcomes.

Just as aggregate statistics are poor indicators of individual normative commitments to marriage, such statistics are also a questionable basis for drawing inferences about the quality of conjugal interpersonal realtionships. Nevertheless, instances in which researchers make the indefensible causal leap from group divorce statistics to conclusions about the quality of husband-wife interpersonal interactions among blacks are numerous (e.g., Bernard, 1966 and Udry, 1970). Casual perusal of the literature reveals a wealth of generalizations concerning the nature of interpersonal exchanges between black spouses. Paradoxically, few of these generalizations are empirically based, in the strictest sense of the term (Cromwell and Cromwell, 1979). Rarely will the researchers have studied black conjugal interpersonal systems in a direct, systematic, comprehensive manner. Instead, their conclusions about black husband-wife interactions tend to be impressionistic, excessively reliant on the assumed link between individual realities and aggregate patterns, or focused on a delimited aspect of husband-wife interpersonal dynamics (e.g., power relations). Clearly then, the need exists for further research into the interpersonal relationships of black married couples.

This chapter attempts to provide greater insight into the interpersonal relationships of black spouses during the middle years (roughly ages 35 to 55 years). The middle years are an important period in the study of marital interpersonal relations for several reasons. Foremost among these is the fact that at this life stage, parent, worker, and related roles usually become more manageable. Thus, marital roles and relationships assume a primacy, vis-à-vis other roles in life, much as was the case during the early phases of the couple's intimate relationship (e.g., courtship, honeymoon). For purposes of comparison, cross-sex and cross-race data were collected. Class was held more or less constant, since this was essentially a middle-class sample. In the context of this study, three dimensions of the conjugal interpersonal system were explored: marital stability, marital satisfaction or adjustment, and the distribution of power in the relationship. Our interest here was in ascertaining how the essential character of marital interpersonal systems varied by race and sex in middle-class populations.

INTERPERSONAL RELATIONS IN MARRIAGE

Research into the quality of interpersonal relationships in marriage has tended to focus on marital stability, power relationships, and marital adjustment as indictors. Researchers are likely to assume that couples in enduring marriages have high-quality interpersonal relationships. However, research by Cuber and Haroff (1965) challenges such assumptions. They show that enduring marriages are not necessarily happy marriages. Long-term married couples (10 years or more) were found to range from "deeply fulfilled people, living vibrantly" to "embittered, entrapped people living in atmospheres of hatred and despair." Further, other researchers note a tendency for the overall quality of marital interpersonal relationships to worsen with the passage of time. There is also the strong tendency among couples over time to subordinate the psycho-emotional aspects of marriage to the instrumental-economic aspects of marriage (Hicks and Platt, 1968).

An important dimension of marriage is the distribution of conjugal power. In a widely cited study, Blood and Wolfe (1960) concluded that husband and wife relative power in the marital relationship is based on resource availability. The balance of power was generally weighted toward partners having greatest assets or resources, as perceived by both spouses. Center et al. (1971), Mack (1978), and Willie (1979) further clarified our thinking about conjugal power relations by stressing the complexity of marital power systems. The relative power of spouses was found to vary as subject areas, time frames, and individual characteristics (e.g., whether wife works, personalities/attitudes of spouses) varied. The distribution of marital power has been shown to influence other important aspects of family life, such as parent-child relations, marital stability, and marital happiness. Marriages with authoritarian power arrangements were characterized by lower satisfaction ratings than those in which power was shared more equally (Eshelman, 1978).

In the literature, marital quality has most often been assessed using two measures: reported happiness and stability (Hicks and Platt, 1971). Some of the problems associated with the use of marital stability as an indicator of marital adjustment were mentioned above. Simply put, marital adjustment has been shown to be a variable quantity over the life cycle. Similarly, the relative levels of spouse adjustment are not necessarily comparable. Stable marriages are not always conclusive evidence of mutually, well-adjusted spouses; people sometimes remain in marriages because they lack other acceptable alternatives (Cuber and Haroff, 1963). Given the extremely personal and subjective nature of happiness, it is a particularly difficult quality to assess. Yet marital happiness forms the foundation on which any truly companionate marriage must be built. Burgess and Cottrell (1939) showed personal conflict, common interests, marital satisfaction, and individual personalities to all contribute to the determination of marital happiness, while Bernard (1964) refines the definition of marital happiness to make it more person and marriage specific. Thus, marital happiness is said to be best judged in terms of the alternatives. Individuals may consider marriages successful to the extent they provide the highest satisfaction possible, not the highest imaginable.

DATA AND METHODS OF STUDY

Data for this study come from a 1974 survey of Chicago, Illinois, male adolescents and their families. A stratified-cluster sample of 120 two-parent families, with a son aged 14–18 years in the home, was drawn using the following procedures: 1970 census data were used to stratify city tracts by race, income level, and educational attainment; this information (supplemented by visual examination of neighborhood and consultations with informants knowledgeable about the composition of communities in the city) was then used to select out tracts falling into one of four major groups—black or white, working-class (lower or middle) or middle-class neighborhoods. At this point, 30 blocks were then selected from each of the four tract groups using a probability of selection proportional to size of cluster sampling plan (Kish, 1965). A randomized, quota sampling plan was used at the block level to identify specific households that qualified for inclusion in the study (see Allen, 1975 for more detail on sampling plan).

In each household, interviewers sought to complete two-hour, *separate* interviews with each of the concerned family members. Of the 360 respondents originally sought (father, mother, and son in each family), 245 or 68 percent were interviewed. For these analyses, the sample breaks down as follows: black fathers (18) and mothers (32); white fathers (35) and mothers (45).

Sample Characteristics

This study assumes the socioeconomic statuses of black and white couples in this sample to be comparable. As a partial control for the confounding influences of social class status, sampling was restricted to middle-class black and white neighborhoods. Selective comparisons of the black and white families in this sample show them to be comparable in terms of our indicators of socioeconomic status level. Whites, significantly more so than blacks, had long histories in their present neighborhoods and owned or were buying their homes (Tables 6:1 and 6:2). Given that over two-thirds of the black families were long-term residents of their present neighborhoods (six or more years) and nearly three-quarters of them owned (or were buying) their homes, the statistically significant race differences on these items are tempered somewhat. Both groups were well established in their neighborhoods, only whites somewhat more so than blacks. Comparisons of parents by education, occupation, and income yield similar results (Tables 6:3–5). On the average, whites were higher than blacks across these respective dimensions. However, only in the cases of women's educational attainments and men's occupational statuses were these differences statistically significant. Most of the observed status differences were minor, particularly when placed in historical perspective. The black middle-class has historically been comparable to, rather than on par

TABLE 6:1

Permanence in Neighborhood by Race

(Percentage Distribution)

Years Lived in Present Neighborhood	Black	White
Five or Less	36.4	17.8
Six to Fifteen	51.5	40.0
Over Fifteen	12.1	42.2
(N)	(33)	(45)

$X^2 = 90$, s = .01   Cramer's V - .34   Gamma - .52

with, white middle-class families. While the two groups have many characteristics in common, white middle-class families continue to maintain their traditional economic advantage. Thus, the race differences observed here accurately reflect the reality of middle-class status for blacks versus whites in the larger society.

Measures

Multiple measures of marital relationship were used in this study. In addition to stability or years married, information was collected on related characteristics such as: whether individuals had been married more than once;

TABLE 6:2

Home Ownership by Race

(Percentage Distribution)

Rent or Own Home	Black	White
Rent	29.0	6.8
Own	71.0	93.2
(N)	(31)	(44)

$X^2 = 5$, s = .08   Cramer's V - .29   Gamma = .69

TABLE 6:3

Educational Attainment by Race and Sex

(Percentage Distribution)

Years of Completed Schooling	Black Men	White Men	Black Women	White Women
Less than eight years	27.8	5.7	9.4	
Some high school	18.7	22.9	40.6	11.1
High school graduate	22.2	22.9	21.9	42.2
Some college	27.8	28.6	21.9	33.3
College graduate	5.6	11.4	3.1	8.9
Graduate/Professional School	-	8.6	3.1	4.4
(N)	(18)	(35)	(32)	(45)

Black Women vs. White Women: $X^2 = 15$, s = .01 Cramer's V = .45 Gamma = .49

Black Men vs. White Men: $X^2 = 7$, s = .25 Cramer's V = .35 Gamma = .36

whether there were children from prior unions; age at first marriage; and whether the first marriage was earlier or later than their expected age of marriage. Conjugal power distribution was measured by a summary index of the following questions:

In all families, somebody has to decide such things as where the family will live and so on. Many couples talk such things over first, but the final decision often has to be made by either the husband or the wife. In your family, who usually makes the *final* decision about: How much money the famly can afford to spend per week on food; which house or apartment to take; where to go on a vacation; where the children should go to school; whether or not to buy life insurance?

Items were coded from "husband always" = 1 to "wife always" = 5 with the mean of responses being equal to the index score.

Marital adjustment was measured by an index using the following questions:

How much alike would you say you and your husband (wife) are? That is, in terms of your temperament, the things you think are important in life and so on? (coded from "happier than almost any marriage you know" = 1 to "very unhappy" = 5). How often do you think to yourself that if you had it to do all over again you would either marry a

TABLE 6:4

Occupational Attainment by Race and Sex

(Percentage Distribution)

Occupational Prestige Level	Black Men	White Men	Black Women	White Women
Level:				
One (janitor, steelworker, taxi driver)	16.7	2.9	23.8	5.3
Two (auto mechanic, tailor, bus driver, welder)	27.8	14.7	28.6	13.2
Three (electrician, machinist, optician, cashier)	5.6	20.6	19.0	34.2
Four (secretary, clergy, nurse, salesman)	33.3	17.6	19.0	21.1
Five (accountant, high school teacher, draftsman, manager)	16.7	23.5	9.5	23.7
Six (engineer, lawyer, doctor, college professor)	-	20.6	-	2.6
(N)	(18)	(34)	(21)	(38)

Black Women vs. White Women: 9, s = .19   Cramer's V = .38   Gamma = .46

Black Men vs. White Men: 11, s = .09   Cramer's V = .46   Gamma = .44

different person or would not get married at all? (coded from "never think that way" = 5 to "very often, nearly every day" = 1). How companionate would you say your marriage is? (coded from "very companionate" = 1 to "not companionate at all" = 5). Would you say you and your wife (husband) argue? (coded from "never" = 1 to "all the time" = 5).

Again, the mean of responses represented the summary index score.

Findings

Interestingly, our analysis revealed hardly any racial differences among subjects in terms of the average years married (22 years for whites and 20 years for blacks). This occurred in spite of widely cited differences between blacks and whites in marital longevity. Two other statistics, however, indicate pro-

TABLE 6:5

Family Income by Race

(Percentage Distribution)

Annual Family Income	Black	White
Less than 9,000	22.2	9.3
9,000 to 12,000	29.6	16.3
12,001 to 15,000	18.5	11.6
15,001 to 18,000	14.8	23.3
18,001 to 24,000	7.4	16.3
18,001 to 24,000	7.4	23.3
(N)	(27)	(43)

$X^2 = 8$, $s = .16$ Cramer's V = .34   Gamma = .45

nounced racial differences in rates of marital stability. The first shows that nearly one-quarter of the black men and women in the sample were involved in a second or successive marriage as compared to only 5 percent of the whites. Similarly, 28 percent of the black men (as compared to 3 percent of white males) and 18 percent of the black women (as compared to 2 percent of white females) reported children from previous relationships. We note also that black males entered their first marriage some average five years before white males (21 versus 26 years), while only one year separated black and white females (20 versus 21 years). It is not surprising to note, therefore, that over 60 percent of black husbands claim to have entered the first marriage at an earlier than expected age (Table 6:6). It is surprising to note, however, similar significant race differences among wives, given their comparable average age at first marriage. Conceivably, black wives' higher proportions of second marriages and children from previous unions are a factor here.

Few major differences were revealed in the distribution of conjugal decision-making power (Table 6:7). For the most part, family decision-making power seemed to be shared equally. Fewer blacks than whites reported egalitarian relationships, although these differences were not statistically significant. Husband and wife estimates of conjugal power were, on the other hand, significantly different for both races. Wives tended more so than husbands to claim egalitarian distribution of power.

Significant sex and race differences were revealed in levels of marital adjustments. Table 6:8 shows that on the average, blacks reported greater

TABLE 6:6

Expected Age of Marriage

Actual Age of Marriage	Husbands		Wives	
	Black	White	Black	White
Much Earlier Than Expected	44.4	6.3	28.1	10.0
Earlier Than Expected	16.7	12.5	21.9	25.0
At Age Expected or Later	38.9	81.3	50.0	65.0
(N)	(18)	(35)	(33)	(45)

Statistical Comparisons:

1. Black Fathers vs. White Fathers

   $X^2 = 11.7$ $V = .48$

   $s = .003$ $G = .74$

2. Black Mothers vs. White Mothers

   $X^2 = 4.0$ $V = .24$

   $s = .14$ $G = .34$

3. White Fathers vs. White Mothers

   $X^2 = 18.8$ $V = .56$

   $s = .001$ $G = .92$

4. Black Fathers vs. Black Mothers

   $X^2 = 4.0$ $V = .33$

   $s = ns$ $G = .20$

dissatisfaction ($\chi = 11, s < .02$). However, sex-race interaction affected marital adjustment such that black wives and white husbands reported greater marital satisfaction than their spouses. Respectively, 17 and 13 percent separated black wives and white husbands from spouses in the above-average marital satisfaction category. These differences indicate that irrespective of race, spouses tend not to necessarily share a consensus in the evaluation of their marriages. In somewhat of a paradox, more black than white wives expressed either extreme satisfaction or dissatisfaction with the marital relationship.

Since pronounced race-sex differences were revealed in marital satisfaction, it seemed that further, more detailed analyses of this dimension of the conjugal interpersonal relationship was called for. In particular, the impact of socioeconomic status variations on marital satisfaction was investigated. While this sample was largely comparable by class, such an analytic approach was justified by the within-group variation in socioeconomic status and the possibility that class effects on marital satisfaction varied by race and sex of the spouse. Husband's occupational status, wife's occupational status, and

TABLE 6:7

Distribution of Conjugal Power

Spouse Controlling Decision Making	Husbands		Wives	
	Black	White	Black	White
Husband	17.7	17.7	9.9	12.0
Shared Equally	64.6	70.5	76.8	80.8
Wife	17.7	11.8	13.3	7.2
(N)	(18)	(35)	(33)	(45)

Statistical Comparisons:

1. Black Fathers vs. White Fathers
   X^2 = 7.7   V = .39
   s = ns   G = -.10

2. Black Mothers vs. White Mothers
   X^2 = 4.5   V = .25
   s = ns   G = -.14

3. Black Fathers vs. Black Mothers
   X^2 = 60.3   V = .77
   s = $<$.001   G = .71

4. White Fathers vs. White Mothers
   X^2 = 43.4   V = .51
   s = $<$ .001   G = .37

family income were found to influence strongly the marital happiness levels of each race-sex spouse (Table 6:9). As prestige of both spouses' occupation and family income increased, so did their expressed levels of satisfaction with the marital relationship. Apparently, gradations in socioeconomic status affect marital adjustments within, as well as across, class groups. Interestingly, these effects were largely consistent and seemed to be independent of spouse's race or sex.

In order to clarify further the effects of socioeconomic status factors on marital adjustment during the middle years, a regression analysis was run (Table 6:10). The result of this analysis was to suggest that educational attainment level, more so than any other factor, determined an individual's level of adjustment to marriage. Moreover, the importance attributed to wife's occupation and family income by the analysis above was shown to be misplaced. With controls these variables were shown to contribute little to the determination of marital adjustment. Husband's occupational status, however, was shown to influence strongly the husband's level of marital adjustment. For wives, the number of children in the family gained in strength as a

TABLE 6:8

Level of Marital Adjustment

Adjustment Levels	Husbands		Wives	
	Black	White	Black	White
Below Average	12.5	5.7	16.2	7.0
Average	62.4	45.7	41.9	60.4
Above Average	25.1	45.7	41.9	32.6
(N)	(18)	(35)	(33)	(45)

Statistical Comparisons:

1. Black Fathers vs. White Fathers
X^2 = 10.7   V = .46
s = $<$.02   G = .31

2. Black Mothers vs. White Mothers
X^2 = 11.7   V = .40
s = $<$ -.01   G = .02

3. White Fathers vs. White Mothers
X^2 = 23.4   V = .40
s = $<$.001   G = -.10

4. Black Fathers vs. Black Mothers
X^2 = 13.6   V = .46
s = $<$.01   G = -.04

predictor of reported marital adjustment. Given some of the findings from analyses above, it was interesting to note the relatively minor contribution of race to the prediction of marital adjustment (when race was included in the regression equation). The discrepancy in explained variance across sex (R^2 = .69 versus R^2 = .32) indicates the need for looking beyond the above factors when attempting to identify source(s) of marital satisfaction among wives in both races.

DISCUSSION

This chapter addresses the issue of race differences in husband-wife interpersonal relations during the middle years of the family life cycle. In order to achieve greater sensitivity, the marital relationship was defined as encompassing marital stability, distribution of power, and adjustment. The sample

TABLE 6:9

Marital Adjustment by Socioeconomic Status

Cramer's V

	Marital Adjustment			
Variables	Wife		Husband	
	Blacks	Whites	Blacks	Whites
Husband's Education	.32*	.06	.03	.03
Wife's Education	.17	.04	.18	.04
Husband's Occupation	.70*	.34*	.65*	.37*
Wife's Occupation	.50*	.40*	.30*	.50*
Husband's Age at First Marriage	.02	.40*	.20	.21
Wife's Age at First Marriage	.05	.02	.01	,09
Family Income	.30*	.30*	.74*	.30*
Number of Children in Family	.18	.01	.07	.20

*Significant at .05 level or beyond.

consisted of husbands and wives from a sample of Chicago, Illinois, middle-class, black and white families. While there is a paucity of empirical research into the interpersonal dynamics of black marriages, voluminous conclusions have been set forth. More often than not, these conclusions are based on speculative analyses or inappropriate generalizations from aggregate statistics. This study sheds light on the nature of black conjugal interpersonal relations, using primary data from a population of black marriages that we have been told do not exist—long-term marriages among blacks whose status approximates that of middle-class.

Black couples here, more so than whites, exhibited many of the traits conventionally associated with marital instability. The incidence of second or successive marriages, children from prior unions, premature entry into marriage, and reported marital dissatisfaction all were higher for blacks. Nevertheless, there were no significant differences in the average longevity of marriage for blacks and whites in this sample (average 20 versus 22 years).

TABLE 6:10

Regression of Marital Adjustment on Socioeconomic Status

Variables	Males				Females			
	b	SE	B	F	b	SE	B	F
Husband's Education	.76	.19	.51*	16.3*	-.12	.19	-.12	.42
Wife's Education	.09	.24	.04	.16	.55	.24	.34	5.5**
Husband's Occupation	.22	.09	.21*	6.3**	.26	.09	.00	.00
Wife's Occupation	-.07	.09	-.06	.67	-.11	.09	-.14	1.5
Husband's Marriage Age	.24	.13	.22	3.6	.05	.13	.07	.16
Wife's Marriage Age	-.05	.15	-.03	.11	.15	.15	.15	1.1
Respondent's Race	.01	.10	.01	.01	.06	.1	.08	.4
Family Income	.01	.12	.00	.00	.12	.12	.13	.9
Number of Children	.18	.12	.11	2.4	.25	.12	.23	4.5**

$$R^2 = .685 \qquad R^2 = .320$$

*Path coefficient twice standard error

**Coefficients sugnificant at .05 level

Despite their comparability by class, substantial race differences were revealed in the husband-wife interpersonal systems studied here. The significant fact is that such differences aside, both black and white marriages as revealed here must be considered successful unions, for, in both cases, the marital relationship was found to be a reasonably stable, satisfying, and cooperative arrangement for the spouses. This seeming paradox forces us to confront the reality of differences in the accompanying circumstances of black and white marriage.

Black and white marriages are acted out in different contexts, and one presumes, under different constraints and expectations as well. This is not to suggest that they will not share some characteristics, rather it simply acknowledges that the essential character of marriage differs across major societal cleavages. We see in this study a microcosm of such variations; clear differences by race, socioeconomic status (within class group), and sex in the evaluation of marital relationships are revealed. Apparently, as Skolnick (1973) notes, separate marriages (or views of marriage) may exist within the same institution: a husband's as compared to a wife's; a black person's as compared to a white person's; or a lower-class person's as compared to a middle-class person's. In each instance, the social context of marriage must be fully considered, for this context defines the situational constraints to be confronted, the kinds of value orientations engendered, and the adopted styles of interpersonal interaction. In concert, these factors serve to shape the face of marital relationships.

More questions than answers have resulted from this chapter. It argues for detailed study of marital interpersonal relationships. Marital relations are multidimensional in content, crucially important during the middle years (when parent/worker roles are modified, thus allowing a reemphasis of the spouse role), and variable across major social categories. At the same time, serious doubts as to the validity of widespread negative views on black marriages have been raised. It now remains for researchers working in the area to undertake the task of exploring the true nature of black conjugal interpersonal relations with a renewed vigor.

REFERENCES

Allen, W. R. "The Antecedents of Adolescent Mobility Aspirations," diss., University of Chicago, 1975.
———. "Black Family Research in the United States: A Review, Assessment and Extension," *Journal of Comparative Family Studies,* 1978(Autumn), 167–188.
———. "Class, Culture and Family Organization: The Effects of Class and Race on Family Structure in Urban America," *Journal of Comparative Family Studies,* 1979, 10(3), 301–313.
———. "The Social and Economic Statuses of Black Women in America," *Phylon,* 1980, 42(Spring), 26–40.
Bane, M. J. *Here to Stay: American Families in the Twentieth Century.* New York: Basic Books, Inc., 1976.
Bernard, J. "The Adjustment of Married Mates," In H. Christensen (ed) *Handbook of Marriage and the Family.* Chicago: Rand McNally, 1964.
Blood, R., and D. Wolfe. *Husbands and Wives: The Dynamics of Married Living.* Glencoe, Ill.: The Free Press of Glencoe, 1960.
Burgess, E., and L. Cotrell. *Predicting Success or Failure in Marriage.* Englewood Cliffs, N.J.: Prentice-Hall, 1939.
Cromwell, V., and R. Cromwell. "Perceived Dominance in Decision-Making and Conflict Resolution among Anglo, Black and Chicano Couples," *Journal of Marriage and the Family,* 1979, 40, 749–760.
Cuber, J., and P. Haroff. *The Significant Americans: A Study of Sexual Behavior among the Affluent.* New York: Appleton-Century, 1965.
Division of Vital Statistics "Marriages: Trends and Characteristics, United States," *USDHEW, PHS,* Series 21, No. 21(Sept), 1971.

Hicks, M., and M. Platt. "Marital Happiness and Stability: A Review of the Research in the Sixties," *Journal of Marriage and the Family*, 1970, 553–574.

Kish, L. *Survey Sampling*. New York: Wiley, 1965.

Moynihan, D. P. *The Negro Family: The Case for National Action*. Washington, D.C.: U.S. Department of Labor, 1965.

Skolnick, A. *The intimate Environment: Exploring Marriage and the Family*. Boston: Little, Brown and Co., 1973.

Udry, J. R. "Marital Instability by Race, Sex and Occupation Using 1960 Census Data," *American Journal of Sociology*, 1967, 72, 203–209.

Willie, C., and S. Greenblatt. "Four 'Classic' Studies of Power Relationships in Black Families: A Review and Look at the Future," *Journal of Marriage and the Family*, 1979, 40, 691–694.

7

BLACK WIVES: PERSPECTIVES ABOUT THEIR HUSBANDS AND THEMSELVES

Donald P. Addison

Although the proportion of black American families with a woman as sole head has just about doubled from 1940 (18 percent) to 1975 (35 percent), there are still approximately 61 percent of black American family households with both husband and wife present.[1] Too much of the literature on black families is devoted to broken and low-income families. It is the intent of this chapter to examine intact black American family households from diverse occupational, economic, and educational levels. We are interested in how the black wife looks at her husband and in turn (utilizing essentially the same Likert Scale questions), her perception of how her husband thinks of her.

For quite some time, one of the major concerns relating to the family, which came as a direct result of the Moynihan Report, was the extent to which the black family was a matriarchate. Very little attention has been paid to how the wife perceives her husband and her evaluation of how she feels he thinks about her. Scott (1976) indicates, "scholars have been overly concerned with the impact of a female-headed household and not concerned enough with the impact of interpersonal relations" (p. 2).

Despite the frequent experiences of black husbands and their wives in encountering racial discrimination in economic and social life, they still survive and maintain a relatively high level of integrity. Their ability is a product of such strategies as informal adoptions (Hill, 1977), extended family assistance (Martin and Martin, 1978; McAdoo, 1980; and Staples, 1976), religious values, and adaptations to institutional policies and regulations, all of which indicate their flexibility in adjusting to the oppressions they have experienced. It is also a product of the mutually shared values and attitudes developed by the mates in the interaction process.

Surprisingly, little has been indicated about the basic dyadic relationships fundamental to whatever strategies are utilized in keeping marital partners together. Aside from a few studies about decision making (Dietrich, 1971; Heiss, 1975; King, 1967; Scanzoni, 1971; and Willie, 1976), a minimal number of studies of an empirical nature have reported other dyadic relationships that provide the basic "glue" that keeps marital partners together.[2]

It seems to us not only are goals important (Rutledge, 1980), but that patterns of interaction for meeting these goals are significant. For the husband or wife to experience external oppressive conditions and then make and sustain marital adjustments is not easy. It seems that an examination, however limited, of the interactional patterns that contribute to and help explain the basis of the observed solidarity in many of these families is of sociological importance and value.

We have noted that the abundant literature relating to the black family has been based on low-income or broken families. Unfortunately, the data based on these types of familes are drawn from, in many instances, atypical types of communities, namely, public housing units. Even more unfortunately, we believe, some studies are based on high-rise public housing units which, in the nature of the case, are unnatural structures that mitigate against "normal" familial interaction (cf. Rainwater, 1970). It should be needless to point out that most low-income families do not live in public housing units. To extrapolate from these limited contexts and cite them as being typical of the lower-class family is to present a distorted view of black family patterns.

Given these aforementioned perspectives, this study is an attempt to provide a more balanced view of black families, from a variety of areas and income levels. It was carried out in the summer of 1974, as a pilot exploratory investigation and, consequently, we were more interested in hypothesis generating than in hypothesis testing. The portion of the study reported here is a broad overall analysis of a subsample of a larger study of black families in a mid-South urban center.

BLACK FAMILY: WIFE AND HUSBAND
INTERACTION LITERATURE

There are a limited number of studies relating to the black conjugal dyad that seems to relate to this study. None, however, encompasses most of the relationships we are presenting here (See Footnote 2). The literature being reviewed in this section appears to be the most closely related.

Billingsley (1968), in using a social systems approach, asserts black families are different from white families in that white husbands perform primarily the instrumental (provider) role, while white wives perform more expressive functions. In contrast, black husbands and wives combine both these functions, primarily because of the peculiar history of black families in America and, in particular, the caste-like stratification system that relegates blacks to inferior status. Staples (1976, p. 125) and Hill (1971, p. 4) both agree with this characterization.

Scanzoni (1977), in utilizing an exchange theory approach of blacks above the underclass and linking this to the economic opportunity structure that he had developed in his earlier monograph (1970), found the relationships of black husbands and wives to have a great similarity with those of whites. Scanzoni (1977) further indicates that "the clear drift or trend within black family structure is toward convergence with family patterns existing in the dominant society" (p. 264).

Blood and Wolfe (1960 and 1970) found black wives less satisfied in terms of companionship than white wives. Black wives tell their problems to their husbands much more frequently than black husbands share their problems with their wives. Blood and Wolfe indicate further (1960):

Negro wives, as usual, can be cited as a group with severe problems. Their extremely low satisfaction with the understanding they get is unusually striking in view of the fact that Negro husbands do not differ significantly from white husbands in their pattern of responding to bad-day troubles except in their predilection for giving advice. Hence, the wife's dissatisfaction may be due primarily to the severity of the problems she faces (p. 215).

Rutledge (1980), in a unique and insightful chapter relating to marital goals and more specifically relating marital strengths to goals, as well as attempting to determine the greatest influence on marital interaction goals, concludes:

the marital relations of the black woman of this study are more characteristic of "strengths" than weaknesses. . . . the second conclusion is that extra-familial activities or activities outside the marriage/family unit are sustaining for the marital relation (p. 158).

Finally, Myers (1980), basing her study on a symbolic interactionist perspective and the relationships black women perceive in their marital situations, indicates that

Black married and unmarried women may see one function of social and symbolic relationships in marriage as an outlet of emotional support (support system) and concern of someone to confide in. Spouses (mates) who seem to fulfill that need cannot be found in the larger society due to its structure (p. 171).

The literature, especially the nondescriptive literature, is still at the embryonic stage. Because of the limited number of empirical studies relating to the black conjugal dyad, theoretical or substantial propositional works are still in their infancy. Less time needs to be spent on black/white differences or on "lower-class" families. Rather, it seems to me, more empirical research needs to be done in various regions (including suburbia, the South, North, etc.) not only on the black conjugal dyad, but on the black family in general.

METHODOLOGY

The instrument used to collect the data was a combination questionnaire and interview schedule. The format and questions were a communal endeavor involving students in two family courses at a predominately black college. None of the students had taken a family or marriage course previously. The questions were based on 12 taped exploratory interviews (conducted by the author) and the concerns of students.

The students were trained as interviewers daily for two weeks (three hours per day) before they went into the field. The respondents were wives and were interviewed in their homes without their husbands being present. The exclusion of husbands was determined after the first week of interviews when we found wives were more frequently available and more willing to participate in the interview process.

The questions were framed in the form of a Likert-type scale for evaluative purposes using the categories (1) Never, (2) Once in awhile, (3) A lot, and (4) All of the time. Most of the questions asking the wife how she perceives her husband (23 items) were asked also in terms of how she thinks her husband perceives her (24 items). Space was also allotted for elaboration of the answers if the respondent so desired.

Sample

The universe from which the sample was drawn included the total black population of Crescent City, Iowa. Ten students who were long-time residents of Crescent City (had lived in the city at least 10 years) first separately and then together selected areas and/or streets in the city that they felt could be designated as high-, medium-, or low-income areas. Each interviewer was subsequently assigned a street or area, being required to get an equal number of interviews from each income level.

Some selected characteristics of the subsample of 271 first-time married couples from which the wives were drawn appear in Tables 7:1–4.

DATA ANALYSIS AND FINDINGS

The results are presented in a straightforward manner, explaining the data in percentages and percentage differences. We have also disaggregated the two general Likert-type scales of "Wife's perception of husband" and "Wife's perception of husband's perception of her" into the following dimensions:

TABLE 7:1

Distribution of Couples According to Years Married by Percent And
Number and Mean Number of Years Married

Length of Time Married	Percent [a]
1 to 5 Years	27.7 (75)
6 to 10 years	22.5 (61)
11 to 20 years	25.5 (69)
21 to 30 years	17.3 (47)
31 to 50 years	7.0 (19)
Mean number of years married	13.808

[a] Figures in parenthesis equal actual number

TABLE 7:2

Combined Annual Income of Husbands and Wives by Percent
and Number

Annual Family Income in Dollars	Percent [a]
Below 4,999	7.4 (20)
5,000 to 7,499	13.7 (37)
7,500 to 9,999	11.8 (32)
10,000 to 12,499	10.7 (29)
12,500 to 14,999	11.1 (30)
15,000 to 17,499	13.7 (37)
17,500 to 24,999	17.3 (47)
25,000 and above	14.4 (39)

[a] Figures in parenthesis equal actual number

TABLE 7:3

Distribution of Wives and Husbands According to Educational Attainment by

Percent, Number and Mean

Educational Attainment	Wife	Husband
9th grade and below	10.3 (28) [a]	15.1 (41)
up to 3 years high school	7.7 (21)	8.5 (23)
high school graduate	32.5 (88)	25.8 (70)
some college	13.7 (37)	14.8 (40)
bachelors degree	20.3 (55)	18.8 (51)
masters degree	3.5 (13)	10.4 (28)
doctoral degree	1.1 (3)	3.0 (8)
professional degree	1.5 (4)	3.7 (10)

Mean number of years education (wife) 13.752

Mean number of years education (husband) 13.430

[a] Figure in parenthesis equals actual number

Communication, Behaviors, Emotions, and Attitudes. Included in the Communication category are the following items: Hard to talk to and Refuses to listen. The subcategory of Communication (Contents of Communication) includes Praises me, Criticizes me, and Lies. The Behaviors category contains Drinks too much, Lazy, Cuts out, Wastes money, Gambles, Works hard, Stays out late, and Beats me; the wife was asked about one more item, "Husband thinks I help him." In the Emotions category we included Jealous, Quick-tempered, Affectionate, Moody, and Weak. In the final category, Attitudes, are included Cheap, Rude, Disrespectful, and Considerate.

WIVES' PERCEPTIONS OF HUSBANDS: A GENERAL PERSPECTIVE

Communication

Basic to any relationship, whether marital or nonmarital, is the extent and type of communication that occurs. Not only is being able to talk to one's spouse important, but it is just as important to have one's spouse "listen." No successful marriage can occur without some form of understanding. Sim-

TABLE 7:4

Distribution of Wives and Husbands According to Age Including Percent And

Number

Age	Wife	Husband
16 through 24	13.3 (36)[a]	7.0 (19)
25 through 34	41.0 (111)	38.7 (105)
35 through 44	26.2 (71)	29.2 (79)
45 through 54	10.0 (27)	11.8 (32)
55 through 64	8.5 (23)	12.2 (33)
65 years and older	1.1 (3)	1.1 (3)

a
Figures in parenthesis equal actual number

ilarly, the type of communication is of paramount importance. To communicate in negative tones or in an uncomplimentary manner serves only to frustrate and negate the potentially positive aspects of any marital dyad. The wives in our study indicate (Table 7:5) their husbands by and large are not hard to talk to, with over 90 percent indicating they are "Never" (46 percent) and only "Once in awhile" (43 percent) hard to talk to. As for listening, over 91 percent indicate their husbands either "Never" (46.6 percent) or "Once in awhile" (45.5 percent) refuse to listen to them. This finding is somewhat contrary to that by Blood and Wolfe (1960, p. 195) who indicate black wives seldom tell their husbands their troubles. Although our question does not refer to telling troubles, per se, communication does not appear to be a problem for the participants in this study. It may, however, by the type of communication that occurs which poses the problem. Even here a total of 93 percent of the wives indicate the husband "Never" lies (47 percent) or at least only lies "Once in awhile" (46 percent), which would seem to indicate truthfulness or trust is not a major problem in these black families. Looking at the item "Husband criticizes me," 88 percent give what is essentially a positive response indicating either "Never" (30 percent) or "Once in awhile" (58 percent). We also looked at the item "Husband praises me," and it is here we notice a divergence from the positive perspectives we have encountered so far. A total of 63 percent indicate their husbands "Never" (11 percent) praise them or praise them "Once in awhile" (52 percent); consequently, we find only 35 percent who praise them either "All the time" (4.5 percent) or "A lot" (31 percent).

Wives' Perceptions of Husbands by Percent and Number [a]

	Never	Once In Awhile	A Lot	All The Time	No Answer
Husband Jealous	29.8 (79)	56.6 (150)	9.1 (24)	4.5 (12)	4.5 (6)
Husband Quick-Tempered	28.3 (75)	52.5 (139)	14.0 (37)	5.3 (14)	2.2 (6)
Husband Considerate	5.6 (15)	28.8 (77)	49.1 (131)	16.5 (44)	1.5 (4)
Husband Drinks Too Much	60.6 (160)	31.4 (83)	4.9 (13)	3.0 (8)	2.6 (7)
Husband Is Lazy	59.3 (159)	34.3 (92)	4.5 (12)	1.9 (5)	1.1 (3)
Husband Hard To Talk To	46.6 (124)	43.6 (116)	5.6 (15)	4.1 (4)	1.8 (5)
Husband Beats Her	90.7 (235)	8.9 (23)	0.4 (1)	0	4.4 (12)
Husband Refuses To Listen	46.6 (123)	45.5 (120)	5.7 (15)	2.3 (6)	2.6 (7)
Husband Cuts Out	76.2 (189)	19.4 (48)	2.8 (7)	1.6 (4)	8.5 (23)
Husband Critizes Her	30.8 (82)	58.3 (155)	7.9 (21)	3.0 (8)	1.8 (5)
Husband Lies	47.3 (121)	46.5 (119)	4.7 (12)	1.6 (4)	5.5 (15)
Husband Wastes Money	44.0 (117)	42.9 (114)	10.2 (27)	3.0 (8)	1.8 (5)
Husband Is Affectionate	9.1 (24)	26.5 (70)	48.1 (127)	16.3 (43)	2.6 (7)
Husband is Moody	19.2 (51)	65.7 (174)	11.3 (30)	3.9 (10)	2.2 (6)

[a]
Figures in parenthesis equal actual number

TABLE 7:5   continued

Wives' Perceptions of Husbands by Percent and Number

	Never	Once In Awhile	A Lot	All The Time	No Answer
Husband Praises Her	11.7 (31)	52.5 (139)	31.3 (83)	4.5 (12)	2.2 (6)
Husband Stays Out Late	50.4 (131)	41.9 (109)	6.2 (16)	1.5 (4)	4.1 (11)
Husband Is Cheap	73.2 (191)	21.8 (57)	3.1 (8)	1.9 (5)	3.7 (10)
Husband Is Rude	66.8 (175)	29.0 (76)	2.3 (6)	1.9 (5)	3.3 (9)
Husband Gambles	73.4 (193)	24.3 (64)	1.9 (5)	0.4 (1)	3.0 (8)
Husband Is Weak	78.8 (205)	18.5 (48)	1.9 (5)	0.8 (2)	4.1 (11)
Husband Is Disrespectful	74.5 (196)	17.5 (46)	3.8 (10)	4.2 (11)	3.0 (8)
Husband Works Hard	8.0 (21)	12.6 (33)	26.7 (70)	52.7 (138)	3.3 (9)

Behaviors

Although a married couple may be engaging in positive communication processes, it does not necessarily follow that subsequent behavioral patterns will also be positive. There is an element of truth in the saying, "Don't do as I do, do as I say." Therefore, it is necessary to look at behavior patterns with an attempt to determine those patterns of behaviors prevalent in these black families.

When we look at behaviors (Table 7:5) beginning with "Husband drinks too much," 7 percent of the wives indicate their husband drinks "All the time" (3 percent) or "A lot" (4 percent) with over 90 percent indicating otherwise. All too often one of the caricatures of black males is about how lazy or shiftless they are. In our sample, over 90 percent of the wives indicate husbands are lazy "Never" (59 percent) or "Once in awhile" (34 percent) with only 6 percent indicating they are lazy "A lot" (4.5 percent) or "All the time" (1.9 percent). As for "Cutting out" (being unfaithful), approximately 95 percent of the sample indicates their husbands "Never" cut out (76.2 percent) or cut out "Once in awhile" (19.4 percent). When answering the question "My husband beats me," over 90 percent indicate "Never" with 8.9 percent indicating they are beaten "Once in awhile" and 0.4 percent indicating "A lot." None indicate they are beaten all of the time. When it comes to wasting money, approximately 87 percent indicate their husbands "Never" (44 percent) waste money or waste money "Once in awhile" (42 percent). As for gambling, given the image of the bourgeois male poker player as well as the stereotypes of dice rollers and numbers players, we are again shown evidence that questions these caricatures. Over 97 percent indicate their husbands either "Never" (73.4 percent) gamble or gamble only "Once in awhile" (24.3 percent). Given the portrait of the struggling wife with the nonworking husband, it is interesting to note over 75 percent indicate their husbands work hard with 52.7 percent indicating "All the time" and 26.7 percent indicating "A lot."

Emotions

One can and often assumes that black married couples must be under constant emotional strain since they are undoubtedly under constant pressure from external economic and social institutions. Aggression, both direct and indirect, are subjects of frequent discussion when concern is expressed about the black community. It has already been indicated that in this sample, the vast majority of wives (over 90 percent) are never beaten by their husbands. Literature dealing with emotional relationships existing within black couples are mostly descriptive accounts or quite frequently figments of the imagination of some novelist, comedian, or cartoonist. The experiences of Bootsie are legendary and have been assumed to be true. Of course, it is therefore incumbent upon us to present some empirical data and at least begin to separate fact from fiction.

Looking at Table 7:5 we see that surprisingly only 19.3 percent of the wives indicate their husbands are quick-tempered either "All the time" (5.3 percent) or "A lot" (14 percent). In a somewhat related item, "Husband is moody," a relatively low percentage (15.2) indicate their husband is moody either "All the time" (3.9 percent) or "A lot" (11.3 percent). Thus, for these black wives, husbands being "moody" or "quick-tempered" is atypical. Jealousy is another emotion being considered. The wives indicate over 85 percent of their husbands are either jealous "Never" (29.8 percent) or only "Once in awhile" (56.6 percent). It is not hard to find literature indicating openly or implicitly that the black male is a weak, unprincipled individual with minimum concern for his wife or family. As far as the wives in this study are concerned, 2.7 percent of them consider their husbands weak either "All the time" (0.8 percent) or "A lot" (1.9 percent), which obviously means an overwhelming majority believe their husbands are not weak. The final item we considered under the Emotions category is Affection. We find here many of the wives (64.4 percent) feel their husbands are affectionate with 16.3 percent indicating "All the time" and 48.1 percent indicating "A lot."

Attitudes

The final category we are considering is that of Attitudes, which means for us, a general predisposition of behavior. It is being used in the more popular sense and reflects how a spouse, with the terms identified, perceives the other spouse. Most of the wives (Table 7:5) find their husbands are "Never" cheap (73.2 percent) with only 5 percent finding them cheap "A lot" (3.1 percent) or "All the time" (1.9 percent). The items indicating whether a husband is considered rude or disrespectful pose an interesting analysis. Most wives (66.8 percent) place their husbands in the "Never" rude category, and 74.5 percent place them in the "Never" disrespectful category, while in somewhat of a contrast, 1.9 percent indicate their husbands are rude "All the time" and 4.2 percent indicate their husbands are disrespectful "All the time." However, in neither category are husbands considered rude or disrespectful a substantial amount of the time. The final item in this category is "Husband is considerate." Most wives (65.6 percent) indicate their husbands are considerate either "All the time" (16.5 percent) or "A lot" (49.1 percent) with only 5.6 percent indicating their husbands are "Never" considerate.

Having presented the results of the scale on how the wife perceives her husband, the next step is to present the results of the scale indicating the wife's perceptions of the husband's perceptions of her. We will proceed in essentially the same manner using the same categories and methods of analysis.

WIVES' PERCEPTIONS OF THEIR HUSBANDS' PERCEPTIONS OF THEM

Communication

Wives apparently feel (Table 7:6) they are not hard to talk to with only as few as 7.3 percent indicating their husbands find them hard to talk to "All the time" (1.9 percent) or "A lot" (5.4 percent). There is obviously a difference between being able to talk to your spouse and having your spouse listen. In reply to the item, "Husband thinks wife refuses to listen," a great majority (93.4 percent) indicate they "Never" (54.8 percent) or only "Once in awhile" (38.6 percent) perceive their husbands as thinking they refuse to listen. We can suggest, therefore, that communication in terms of having a wife listen does not seem to be a basic problem for the husbands in this sample.

Aside from listening and talking, there are other levels of communication, namely, the types and contents of the communication. Only 5.4 percent of the wives indicate their husbands think they lie "A lot" (2.7 percent) or "All the time" (2.7 percent). The data further indicate some (64.4 percent) of the wives think their husbands believe they "Never" lie. When it comes to the item "Husband thinks wife criticizes him," 90 percent of the wives indicate either "Never" (36.4 percent) or "Once in awhile" (53.6 percent) with only 1.1 percent being shrewish. As far as the item "Husband thinks wife praises him" is

Husbands' Perceptions of Wives by Percent and Number[a]

	Never	Once In Awhile	A Lot	All The Time	No Answer
Wife Jealous	31.2 (81)	49.2 (129)	14.6 (38)	5.0 (13)	4.1 (11)
Wife Quick-Tempered	24.7 (65)	49.8 (131)	19.8 (52)	5.7 (15)	3.0 (8)
Wife Considerate	6.5 (17)	30.7 (80)	46.4 (121)	16.5 (43)	3.7 (10)
Wife Drinks Too Much	86.0 (221)	11.7 (30)	1.9 (5)	0.4 (1)	5.2 (14)
Wife Lazy	58.6 (153)	36.4 (95)	3.8 (10)	1.1 (3)	3.7 (10)
Wife Hard To Talk To	46.0 (120)	46.7 (122)	5.4 (14)	1.9 (5)	3.7 (10)
Wife Beats Him	91.9 (224)	6.9 (17)	1.6 (4)	0.4 (1)	9.2 (25)
Wife Refuses To Listen	54.8 (142)	38.6 (100)	4.6 (12)	1.9 (5)	4.4 (12)
Wife Cuts Out	85.4 (222)	13.5 (35)	0.8 (2)	0.4 (1)	4.1 (11)
Wife Criticizes Him	36.4 (95)	53.6 (140)	8.8 (23)	1.1 (3)	3.7 (10)
Wife Lies	64.4 (168)	30.3 (79)	2.7 (7)	2.7 (7)	3.7 (10)
Wife Wastes Money	38.3 (100)	46.0 (120)	12.3 (32)	3.4 (9)	3.7 (10)
Wife Is Affectionate	8.8 (23)	26.8 (70)	46.7 (122)	17.6 (46)	3.7 (10)
Wife Is Moody	22.5 (58)	60.5 (156)	15.5 (40)	1.6 (4)	4.8 (13)
Wife Praises Him	12.7 (32)	57.0 (143)	26.7 (67)	3.6 (9)	7.4 (20)
Wife Stays Out Late	85.5 (218)	13.7 (35)	0.8 (2)	0	5.9 (16)

TABLE 7:6   continued

Husbands' Perceptions of Wives by Percent and Number

	Never	Once In Awhile	A Lot	All The Time	No Answer
Wife Is Cheap	86.3 (221)	11.3 (29)	1.6 (4)	0.8 (2)	5.5 (15)
Wife Is Rude	78.3 (202)	20.2 (52)	1.2 (3)	0.4 (1)	4.8 (13)
Wife Gambles	93.5 (243)	5.4 (14)	0.8 (2)	0.4 (1)	4.1 (11)
Wife Is Weak	72.5 (187)	23.6 (61)	3.5 (9)	0.4 (1)	4.8 (13)
Wife Is Disrespect-ful	81.9 (213)	15.8 (41)	1.9 (5)	0.4 (1)	4.8 (11)
Wife Works Hard	10.5 (27)	26.0 (67)	33.3 (86)	30.2 (13)	4.8 (13)
Wife Helps Him	6.2 (16)	17.0 (44)	41.7 (108)	35.1 (12)	4.4 (12)

a
Figures in parenthesis equal actual number

concerned, 12.7 indicate "Never," while 30.3 percent indicate their husbands think they praise them either "All the time" (3.6 percent) or "A lot" (26.7 percent). This reflects the idea that most wives think their husbands see them as offering much more praise than criticism.

Behaviors

Most of the literature relating to black wives (other than the matriarchy myths) relates to them as being nurturant mothers or supportive wives who also perform instrumental roles in order to enable their families to survive. Little is discussed in terms of other behaviors that must occur in any marital relationship. This section contains perspectives on behaviors as wives perceive their husbands' perceptions of them.

Very few wives (Table 7:6) have husbands who think they drink too much, with only 2.3 percent indicating their husbands think they drink either "A lot" (1.9 percent) or "All the time" (0.4 percent). Eighty-six percent indicate their husbands "Never" think of them as drinking too much. As we have indicated, the literature on black wives and their behaviors is limited; however, being lazy is not one of the caricatures one ever sees. In this sample, only 4.9 percent indicate their husbands perceive them as being lazy "A lot" (3.8 percent) or "All the time" (1.1 percent). In a related item, "Wife works hard," 63.5 percent indicate their husbands think they work hard either "A lot" (33.3 percent) or "All the time" (30.2 percent) with the wives indicating only 10.5 percent of the husbands perceive them as "Never" working hard. Closely related to the lazy and hard-work items is the item "Husband thinks wife helps him." A significant majority (76.8 percent) feel their husbands think they help them either "A lot" (41.7 percent) or "All the time" (35.1 percent), with 6.2 percent indicating their husbands feel they "Never" help.

Do black wives hit or beat their husbands? Once again the literature is sparse and more descriptive than empirical. The wives in this sample indicate that 91.9 percent of them "Never" beat their husbands, while 6.9 percent beat them "Once in awhile." A very small percentage (1.6) indicate they beat their husbands "A lot," and 0.4 percent indicate "All the time." Do black husbands look at their wives as being faithful? In answer to this question, the item "Husband thinks wife cuts out" shows 85.4 percent of the husbands think their wives "Never" cut out, while 1.2 percent think their wives cut out either "A lot" (0.8 percent) or "All the time" (0.4 percent). When it comes to being frugal, how does the black husband perceive his wife? The item "Wife wastes money" shows only 38.3 percent feel their wife "Never" wastes money, while 46 percent are looked at as wasting money "Once in awhile." The other 15.7 percent either waste money "A lot" (12.3 percent) or "All the time" (3.4 percent). When it comes to gambling, black women (not necessarily wives) have been pictured as numbers players spending small amounts on their favorite numbers daily. They have not been noted for gambling either descriptively or empirically. In our sample, wives indicate their husbands think they "Never" gamble by an overwhelming 93.5 percent. The data further indicate that when it comes to husbands feeling their wives stay out late, none have husbands that feel they stay out late "All the time," while only 0.8 percent indicate their husbands think they stay out late "A lot." The majority of the husbands (81.5 percent) think their wives "Never" stay out late.

Attitude

What is the perception wives think their husbands have of them in regard to such traits as being cheap, rude, disrespectful, or considerate? Most (86.3 percent) indicate their husbands look at them as "Never" being cheap. Only 2.4 percent feel their husbands look at them as being cheap either "A lot" (1.6 percent) or "All the time" (0.8 percent). As for being rude, the majority of wives feel they are looked at as "Never" (78.3 percent) being rude with only 1.6 percent indicating they are considered rude "A lot" (1.2 percent) or "All the time" (0.4 percent). Being rude or disrespectful are closely related, and 81.9

percent of the wives feel their husbands "Never" look at them as being disrespectful, while a meager 2.3 percent indicate their husbands look at them as being disrespectful either "A lot" (1.9 percent) or "All the time" (0.4 percent). Being considerate, the final item, is obviously an important trait which undoubtedly can help promote positive marital interaction. Most wives (46.4 percent) feel they are looked at as being considerate "A lot," 16.5 percent feel they are perceived as considerate "All the time," and only 6.5 percent indicate their husbands perceive them as "Never" being considerate.

Emotions

How patient are black wives? The item indicating the extent to which wives are perceived to be patient or not is "Wife is quick-tempered." Most wives (49.8 percent) feel they are quick-tempered "Once in awhile." It is interesting to note that 24.5 percent feel they are perceived as being quick-tempered "A lot" (19.8 percent) or "All the time" (5.7 percent). Related to the problem of temper is one of moodiness, and 60.5 percent of the wives feel their husbands perceive them as being moody only "Once in awhile," while 22.5 percent indicate their husbands "Never" perceive them as being moody. Are black women the jealous type? This category is a perplexing one. Although 31.2 percent feel their husbands think they are "Never" jealous, over 20 percent indicate their husbands feel they are jealous either "A lot" (14.6 percent) or "All the time" (5.0 percent). The matriarchy myth is based, to a large degree, on the idea of the black wife or mother as being strong. In answer to the item "Wife is weak," 72.5 percent of the wives indicate their husbands perceive them as being weak "Never," while 23.6 percent feel their husbands think they are weak only "Once in awhile." The last item we are considering in the Emotion category is Affection. The largest percentage is 46.7 percent, found in the "A lot" category with the next largest percentage indicating wives think husbands perceive them as being affectionate 26.8 percent in the "Once in awhile" category.

DIFFERENCES IN PERCEPTION

Having presented the results of the wives' perceptions of their husbands and the wives' perceptions of the husbands' perceptions of them, we now will look briefly at the perceived differences between these two. This should shed some light on the wives' impressions of their relationships with their husbands. We have merged the categories "A lot" and "All the time" into a category called "Frequently" and have retained the categories "Never" and "Once in awhile." Tables 7:7 and 7:8 contain the frequencies presented previously in Tables 7:5 and 7:6, with the merged categories. The figures contained in parentheses

TABLE 7:7

Differences in Wives' Perceptions of Husbands and Husbands' Perceptions of Wives in Percentages [a]

	Never			Once In Awhile			Frequently		
	W - H		H - W	W - H		H - W	W - H		H - W
Jealous	29.8	(1.4)	31.2	56.6	(7.4)	49.2	13.6	(6.0)	19.6
Quick-Tempered	28.3	(3.6)	24.7	52.5	(2.7)	49.8	19.2	(6.3)	25.5
Considerate	5.6	(0.9)	6.5	28.8	(1.9)	30.7	65.5	(2.7)	62.9
Drinks Too Much	60.6	(25.4)	86.0	31.4	(20.3)	11.7	8.0	(5.7)	2.3
Lazy	59.3	(0.7)	58.6	34.3	(2.1)	36.4	6.3	(1.3)	5.0
Hard To Talk To	46.6	(.06)	46.0	43.6	(3.1)	46.7	9.8	(2.5)	7.3
Beats	90.7	(0.4)	91.1	8.9	(2.0)	6.9	0.4	(1.6)	2.0
Refuses To Listen	46.6	(8.2)	54.8	45.5	(6.9)	38.6	8.0	(1.4)	6.6
Cuts Out	76.2	(9.8)	85.4	19.4	(5.9)	13.5	4.4	(3.2)	1.2
Criticizes	30.8	(5.6)	36.4	58.3	(2.7)	53.6	10.9	(0.9)	10.0
Lies	47.3	(17.9)	64.4	46.5	(16.2)	30.3	6.3	(0.9)	5.4

a. Percentages do not add to 100 due to rounding error.

Differences in Wives' Perceptions of Husbands and How Wives Think Husbands Perceive Them in Percentages [a]

	Never			Once In Awhile			Frequently	
	W - H		H(?)	W - H		H(?)	W - H		H(?)
Wastes Money	44.0	(5.7)	38.3	42.9	(3.1)	46.0	13.2	(2.5)	15.7
Affectionate	9.1	(0.3)	8.8	26.5	(0.3)	26.8	64.4	(0.0)	64.4
Moody	19.2	(3.3)	22.5	65.7	(5.2)	60.5	15.1	(2.0)	17.1
Praises	11.7	(1.0)	12.7	52.5	(4.5)	57.0	35.8	(5.5)	30.3
Stays Out Late	50.4	(35.1)	85.5	41.9	(28.2)	13.7	7.7	(6.9)	0.3
Cheap	73.2	(10.1)	83.3	21.8	(10.5)	11.3	5.0	(2.7)	2.3
Rude	66.3	(11.5)	78.3	29.0	(8.8)	20.2	4.2	(2.6)	1.6
Gambles	73.4	(19.9)	72.5	18.5	(19.9)	23.6	2.7	(1.1)	3.9
Weak	78.8	(6.3)	72.5	18.5	(5.1)	23.6	2.7	(1.2)	3.9
Disrespectful	74.5	(7.4)	81.9	17.5	(2.3)	15.3	8.0	(5.7)	2.3
Works Hard	8.0	(2.5)	10.5	12.6	(13.4)	26.0	79.4	(15.8)	63.6

a Percentages do not add to 100 due to rounding error.

indicate the percentage differences within the cell. Using 9.6 percent and above as an indication of significant differences, the following discussion is presented reflecting differences in the two types of perceptions.

Behaviors

It is in the behaviors category that most of the significant differences occur. Wives look at themselves as drinking considerably less (Table 7:7) than their husbands, with a 25.4 percent difference in the "Never" drink category and a 19.7 percent difference in the "Once in awhile" category. "Cutting out" (Table 7:7) reflects a small but significant difference of 9.8 percent in the "Never" category. However, it should be kept in mind that both husbands and perceived wives have high percentages in the "Never" cuts out category (76.2 percent and 85.4 percent, respectively). Closely related is the item "Stays out late" (Table 7:8). This item has the largest percentage differences of all categories with 85.5 percent of the wives indicating their husbands perceive them as "Never" staying out late, while 50.4 percent of the wives indicate their husbands "Never" stay out late, leaving a difference of 35.1 percent. In the "Once in awhile" category, the difference is 28.2 percent with the husbands' perceived behavior having a higher percentage. When it comes to gambling (Table 7:8), there is a large difference with most (93.5 percent) of the wives indicating they are perceived as "Never" gambling, while 73.4 percent indicate their husbands "Never" gamble—a 19.9 percent difference between the two. There continues to be a 19.9 percent difference with the husbands again having the larger percentage in the "Once in awhile" category. Although both perceptions in the "Works hard" item contain a majority in the "Frequently" category, there is a percentage difference of 15.8 percent with husbands working hard being the higher percentage.

Communication

Only one item in the communication category reflects a significant difference (17.9 percent). Wives indicate they perceive that 47.3 percent of the husbands "Never" lie, while the perception husbands have of their wives in terms of lies indicates 64.4 percent are perceived as "Never" lying (Table 7:7).

Attitude

There are two sections in the Attitude category that reflect significant differences. Two items under "Husband thinks I am cheap" reveal husbands are considered cheaper. Eighty-six percent of the wives indicate their husbands think they are "Never" cheap as opposed to 73.2 percent of the wives who indicate their husbands are never cheap (Table 7:8). This is a difference of 13.1 percent. A 10.5 percent difference occurs in the "Once in awhile" category with the wives indicating 21.8 percent of the husbands are cheap "Once in awhile." In the Rude category, the "Never" response category reflects a difference of 11.5 percent with wives (66.8 percent) indicating their husbands are "Never" rude. On the other hand, the wives indicate that 78.3 percent of the husbands see them as "Never" rude.

CONCLUSIONS

The data presented here at least have brought into question some negative stereotypes and caricatures. Unfortunately, there is a limited amount of published empirical data to which we could refer. More research on the black family, particularly relating to interaction within the family as well as to the relationships of black families to the socio-economic-political institutions, is a pressing need. Until such research is forthcoming, misconceptions and distortions relating to the black family can be expected to continue.

In general, the negative caricatures of black males, at least as far as the wives in this study were concerned, do not hold. They were overwhelmingly described as not lazy, physically abusive, or being gamblers, and as faithful and emotionally strong. Of course, black males are subject to the same human qualities as any other group of males. For example, their wives indicated the men were jealous once in awhile and that they could be quick-tempered and critical. However, the point is that many positive characteristics described these men in contrast to the picture often painted in past literature.

The results showing what wives think their husbands think of them must be taken with caution since the desire to give socially acceptable responses may have influenced the wives' reactions. Their responses tended to be positive. Nevertheless, the results presented here are simply a beginning. Further investigation needs to be done to check and attempt to validate these findings.

Our findings with regard to differences between the wives' perceptions of their husbands and the wives' perceptions of their husbands' impressions of them suggest that wives expect to be given the same regard and to be seen in the same favorable light as they generally seem to view their husbands. In most cases, there was no significant difference (according to our formula) between perceptions and expectations of perceptions. Whether or not husbands would respond this way is a topic for future research.

The results presented have been limited to broad interpretations. Subsequent analysis will involve statistical analysis of a more sophisticated type involving such variables as income, occupation, education, length of marriage, job satisfaction, etc. With a more indepth analysis, despite the sample limitations (wives as only respondents and non-probability), we intend to proceed inductively, possibly developing some hypotheses and a theoretical structure.

NOTES

1. A comprehensive report citing changes in the black family as well as other factors relating to blacks in general is contained in *The Social and Economic Status of the Black Population in the United States: An Historical View, 1790–1978*, U.S. Department of Commerce, Bureau of the Census (1979), Current Population Reports, Special Studies Series, p-23, No. 80. See especially Chapter V.

2. There have been other studies that are tangentially related which are concerned with various aspects of dyadical relationships. However, their focus has been with such aspects as role relationships or marital happiness. (Aldous, 1969; Axelson, 1970; Hancy, Michielutle, Vincent, Cochrane, 1975; Himes, 1960; Jackson, 1972; King, 1954; Ladner, 1971; Lopata, 1971; Parker and Kleiner, 1969; Osmond, 1977; Renne, 1970; Scanzoni, 1975; Steinmen and Fox, 1970; and Rainwater, 1966.

REFERENCES

Alexson, L. J. "The Working Wife, Difference in Perception among Negro and White Males," *Journal of Marriage and the Family*, 1970, 32(3), 457–464.

Aldous, J. "Wives' Employment Status and Lower Class Men as Husband Fathers: Support for the Moynihan Thesis," *Journal of Marriage and the Family*, 1969, 31(3), 469–476.

Blood, R. O., Jr., and D. Wolfe. "Negro-White Differences in Blue-Collar Marriages in a Northern Metropolis," *Social Forces*, 1970, 48, 59–64.

Dietrick, K. "A Reexamination of the Myth of Black Matriarchy," *Journal of Marriage and the Family*, 1975, (37)2, 367–374.

Haney, C. A., et al. "Some Consequences of Illegitimacy in a Sample of Black Women," *Journal of Marriage and the Family*, 1975, 37(2), 359–366.

Heiss, J. *The Case of the Black Family: A Sociological Inquiry*. New York: Columbia University Press, 1975.

Hill, R. *The Strength of Black Families*. New York: National Urban League, 1971.

———. "Informal Adoption among Black Families," Washington, D.C.: National Urban League Research Department, 1977.

Himes, J. S. "Interrelation of Occupational and Spousal Roles in Middle Class Negro Neighborhood," *Marriage and Family Living*, 1960, 22, 362–363.

King, C. E. "The Sex Factor in Marital Adjustment," *Marriage and Family Living*, 1954, 16, 203–208.

King, K. "A Comparison of the Negro and White Family Power Structure in Low Income Families," *Child and Family*, 1967, 6, 65–74.

Ladner, J. *Tomorrow's Tomorrow: The Black Woman*. Garden City, New York: Doubleday & Co., Inc., 1971.

Lopata, H. Z. *Occupation Housewife*. New York: Oxford University Press, 1971.

Martin, E. P., and J. Martin. *The Black Extended Family*. Chicago: University of Chicago Press, 1978.

McAdoo, H. P. "Black Mothers and the Extended Family Support Network," In La Frances Rodgers-Rose (ed) *The Black Woman*. Beverly, Calif.: Sage Publications, 1980.

Myers, L. W. "On Marital Relations: Perceptions of Black women," In La Frances
     Rodgers-Rose (ed) *The Black Woman*. Beverly, Calif.: Sage Publications, 1980.
Osmond, M. W. "Marital Organization in Low Income Families: A Cross-Race
     Comparison," *International Journal of Sociology of the Family*, 1977, 7,
     143–156.
Parker, S., and R. Kleiner. "Social and Psychological Dimensions of the Family Role
     Performance of the Negro Male," *Journal of Marriage and the Family*, 1969,
     31, 500–506.
Rainwater, L. *Behind Ghetto Walls: Black Family Life in a Federal Slum*. Chicago:
     Aldine Publishing, 1970.
Renne, K. "Correlates of Dissatisfaction in Marriage," *Journal of Marriage and the
     Family*, 1970, 32, 54–87.
Rutledge, E. M. "Marital Interaction Goals of Black Women: Strengths and Effects,"
     In La Frances Rodgers-Rose (ed) *The Black Woman*. Beverly, Calif.: Sage
     Publications, 1980.
Scanzoni, J. "Sex Roles, Economic Factors, and Marital Solidarity in Black and
     White Marriages," *Journal of Marriage and the Family*, 1975, 37, 130–144.
_____ . *The Black Family in Modern Society*. Chicago: University of Chicago Press,
     1977.
Scott, P. B. "A Critical Overview of Sex Roles Research on Black Families," *Woman
     Studies Abstracts*, 1975, 5, 1–10.
Staples, R. *Introduction to Black Sociology*. New York: McGraw-Hill, 1976.
Steinmann, A., and D. J. Fox. "Attitudes toward Woman's Family Role among Black
     and White Undergraduates," *The Family Coordinator*, 1970, 19, 4.

8

CAREER, MARRIAGE, AND MOTHERHOOD: "COPPING OUT" OR COPING?

Cheryl B. Leggon

Most of the sociological literature on the conflicts between working on the one hand and marriage and motherhood on the other focuses on white women. This bias implies one of two things: either that career and motherhood pose no problems for black women; or, if they do, that black women have already solved them. Further support for both implications is provided by the literature documenting differences between the socialization of white women and that of black women, especially in terms of work orientation: black women seem to have less conflict than white women about working. This difference is attributed to the fact that since more black women have mothers who worked, they have a precedent or role model, which in turn, causes them to feel more confident than their white counterparts about their ability to fulfill obligations to both family and job. Whereas black women tend to experience much less conflict and guilt than white women over having a job, both black and white professional women tend to experience problems engendered by the conflicting demands of marriage, motherhood, and career.

Through focusing on black women in the elite professions of business, law, and medicine, this chapter will examine the differences in socialization patterns between middle-class black and white women and the impact of these differences upon resolution(s) of the conflict between career, marriage, and motherhood. Specifically, this chapter addresses the following questions: To what extent are the middle-class black woman's views on career, marriage, and motherhood similar to those of her white counterpart? In what ways do they differ? What accounts for the difference(s)? What coping mechanisms have black professional women devised to deal with the conflicting demands of career, marriage, and motherhood?

SOCIALIZATION PATTERNS

Socialization patterns have been shown to vary by gender (Kessler and McKenna, 1978; Komarovsky, 1946, 1950; Oakley, 1972; Wallin, 1950; and Weitzman, 1978), by socioeconomic class (Brofenbrenner, 1965 and Gans, 1962), by ethnicity (Strodbeck, 1968), and by race (Billingsley, 1968; Frazier, 1939; Hill, 1971; and Stack, 1974). In addition, some intraracial differences along class lines have been documented (Ladner, 1971; Martin and Martin, 1979; Willie, 1974; and Wilson, 1978).

Differences in patterns of socialization along gender lines are much more pronounced for whites than for blacks. White middle-class males are social-ized to be aggressive, independent, and individualistic—characteristics asso-ciated with occupational success. White middle-class females are socialized to be nurturant, supportive, and dependent—characteristics associated with successful interpersonal relationships (Weitzman, 1978). Therefore, white males and females differ fundamentally in their orientation toward work: for white males, work is the basic component of their identity from which their principal ego-satisfactions are derived. For white females, work is a less central component of their identity, because they are trained to derive their principal ego-satisfactions from being nurturant and supportive in the domes-tic arena (Ginzberg, 1966).

Regardless of sex, black parents socialize their children to be aggressive, sexually assertive, emotionally expressive, and independent (Lewis, 1975). Consequently, there is "less role differentiation between black than white spouses" (Lewis, 1975). The socialization of black children is characterized by a synthesis of gender traits, whereas that of white children tends to be characterized by a dichotomization of gender traits (Allen, 1978, p. 178). Although white males are socialized to expect to work all of their adult lives, white females are socialized to work until they marry. This socialization practice is based on the assumption that after marriage, they will be supported financially by their husbands; regardless of how realistic this is, the point is that many white females—and especially those in the middle class—are socialized to hold this view. This indicates that marriage is an alternative avenue for upward socioeconomic mobility for white women, at least theoreti-cally; this does not hold, not even theoretically, for black women. Because black males earn less than white males, black women are socialized to expect to work most of their adult life whether or not they marry:

For black women this has meant that they are trained from childhood to become workers, and expect to be financially self-supporting whether they are married or single; work to them, unlike to white women, is not a liberating goal, but rather an imposed lifelong necessity (Lerner, 1973, p. xxiv).

Thus, it is not surprising that the proportion of wives in the labor force continues to be much higher for blacks than for whites: in 1977, 57 percent of all black wives were in the labor force as compared to 44 percent of white wives (Hill, 1978). Compared to that of white wives, black wives' earnings constitute a higher proportion of total family income (Geschwender, 1978 and Allen, 1978). Therefore, black women tend to view the responsibilities to work and to family as being consonant; their work is one of the important contributions that they make to their family. White women, on the other hand, tend to view their occupational responsibilities as competing with their familial responsibilities.

CAREER VERSUS JOB

Although black women may experience less guilt about working on a job, they experience just as much guilt and just as many conflicts over having a *career* as do white women. The literature on black and white working women fails to distinguish between those working at a job and those with a career. This is a crucial distinction because of the important differences between careers and jobs in terms of preparation, orientation, occupational socialization, and requirements of time, effort, energy, and commitment. Briefly, I shall discuss each.

1. *Preparation and Occupational Socialization.* In general, a career requires more extensive preparation, in terms of formal training, and more intensive occupational socialization than does a job. In fact, a career often consists of a number of jobs that are related to and viewed as the means of reaching a career objective.

2. *Orientation.* People working a job tend to have a different orientation toward it than do people with a career: the former tend to view their job in a limited temporal perspective—as a 9-to-5, five-days-a-week concern; for the latter, a career knows no temporal bounds—evenings, weekends, and holidays are often times for work. Finally, a career is viewed as a more integral part of one's life and one's personal identity than is a job.

3. *Sunk Costs—Time, Effort, Energy, and Commitment.* Careers are characterized by a greater amount of "sunk costs" in terms of the number of years of formal education (and the money associated therewith), preparation, and training invested in a career. The greater the amount of sunk costs, the greater is the commitment to the career.

Ginzberg (1966) has identified four basic types of career patterns:

1. the straight career pattern, characterized by consistency, continuity, and progression within the same field;

2. the broad career pattern, characterized by remaining within one's original area of work, but shifting either field or function;

3. the changed career pattern, characterized by changes in one's fields and/or functions in which later choices have no direct relation to previous ones; and

4. the variant career pattern, characterized by floundering.

According to Ginzberg (1966), there is a positive correlation between continuous work histories and the straight and broad career patterns; moreover, single women and married women without children usually have straight and broad career patterns. Although the occupational career patterns of women are not normally continuous, this trend seems to be changing. For white women, the higher the class status, the higher the probability that work will be interrupted at marriage and the less the chance that women will return to the labor force after childbirth; this is not the case for black women, a greater percentage of whom work after they are married and after they have children.

Insofar as the distinction between job and career is concerned, jobs are characterized by the changed or variant career pattern, whereas careers are characterized by the broad or straight career pattern. Professions constitute a special category or type of careers insofar as they are characterized by the straight career pattern. This is particularly true of the "elite" professions of medicine and law: because they require a great deal of formal training and preparation, their practitioners tend to be more committed to them and less likely to change fields. Given the greater commitment required by a profession as compared to a job, how do women cope with the incompatible demands of career and family? One method used by the educated, upper-middle-class white women in Ginzberg's (1966) study is to lower their achievement goals. During his follow-up interview five years after his study, Ginzberg found that those women who had expected their careers to take precedence over marriage and family worked full-time, whereas those who did not think they could have both a career and a family devoted the least time to work. Thus, the self-fulfilling prophecy was operating: those who expected to be able to handle both a career and a family, and those who did not expect to be able to handle both, had their expectations realized.

Before examining the extent to which this applies to black professional women, and in order to better comprehend the differences between black and white professional women, a brief historical overview of their participation in the labor force is useful.

BLACK AND WHITE PROFESSIONAL WOMEN

Black and white women entered the labor force in different ways and at different times because advanced education was denied longer to black women than to white women. For example, although from its inception in 1833 Oberlin College accepted both blacks and women, only nine black women had graduated from the college by 1871.

During the nineteenth century, few women worked; when they did, it was because they were childless or because their husbands were inadequate providers. However, the significant exceptions to this were black wives in the South and immigrant wives in the North (Degler, 1964). In 1890, one-quarter of black wives and two-thirds of black widows were gainfully employed. Most of these women worked as field hands or domestic servants, the same kinds of jobs black women had always done under slavery (Blau, 1979). Although white women began working in the factories in the early nineteenth century, black women were denied access to factory employment, except for the Southern tobacco and textile industries, until World War I. The entry of blacks and women into new fields of employment generally occurred during wartime because they were usually employed only in those jobs for which white males were unavailable. For white women, mass entry into the business world came with the development of the typewriter. Although white women entered government service during the Civil War, black women were not admitted to such jobs until World War II. Even then, black women were restricted to very few jobs. Moreover, light-skinned blacks were preferred over dark-skinned blacks for those jobs. It was not until August 8, 1968, with Executive Order No. 11478, that discrimination in employment by the Federal government and by the District of Columbia government were prohibited (Eastwood, 1979).

Although black women work more years of their lives than do white women, their unemployment rate is greater, and their earnings are lower. From 1975 to 1977, joblessness among black women *increased* by 13 percent, whereas joblessness among white women *decreased* by 11 percent; during the first half of 1978, the unemployment rate for adult black women was 2.1 times the rate for adult white women. From 1940 to 1960, the relative status of black females in terms of income improved markedly within each region of the United States. Redistribution of the black population from the South to the North and West further narrowed the gap between black and white females. This increase in the status of black females relative to white females was not due to a steep increase in their median income, but to the fact that the median income of white females did not increase proportionately to that of other sex-race categories (Glenn, 1963). In 1969, black women earned three-fourths of what white women earned, but only 28 percent of what white men earned.

In 1975, many black women were working full-time to achieve the earnings of white women who were working part-time (Hill, 1978). Even black professional women have been losing ground: in 1971, black professional women working year-round, full-time earned approximately 66 percent of the earnings of white male professionals working year-round and full-time; four years later, they earned 56 percent of their white male counterparts' earnings.

Proportionately, more black women than white women participate in the labor force, although the differential has been declining recently, according to Blau (1979). Between 1954 and 1977, the labor force participation rate among black women rose from 46.1 percent to 50.9 percent. For that same 23-year period, the labor force participation rates for white women increased from 33.3 percent to 48.1 percent (Hill, 1978). By 1977, 51 percent of non-white women were in the labor force. A primary factor in the racial differential in women's labor force participation rates is the greater financial necessity of market work for black women. Although 68 percent of all women in the labor force work out of economic necessity (Scholzman, 1979), this necessity is more acute for black women because of two factors: a higher proportion of black women are divorced, widowed, or separated, and among those married and living with their husbands, the lower average earnings of black men (as compared to white men) increase the importance of a wife's contribution to family income (Blau, 1979). Another factor of prime importance in accounting for the greater labor force participation rate of black women as compared to white women is that the expectation of lifelong employment applies as much to middle-class black women as to working-class black women. Middle-class economic status is most difficult for blacks to obtain and even more precarious to maintain.[1] Moreover, as a group, black middle-class families have been unable to consolidate and pass along their gains to their offspring (Farley, 1979).[2] Unlike its white counterpart, the black middle class lacks a business tradition, which places its members in a weaker position to support their professionals. This, in turn, means that the practice of most black lawyers and physicians with predominantly black clientele is marginal in terms of their clients' ability to pay, and in terms of content (e.g., for black attorneys, criminal law constitutes the bulk of the solo practitioner's caseload).

Black women constitute the sex-race category that is the most underrepresented in the sociological literature on the professions (Leggon, 1979). Most of the sociological literature on the professions is based on samples composed solely of white males; the seminal studies of black professionals (Woodson, 1934 and Edwards, 1959) are based on samples consisting entirely of males. When mentioned, women are usually relegated to footnotes, which clearly indicates that they are considered to be peripheral members of the professional community. Research on women in the professions tends to focus on white women (Bailyn, 1964; Epstein, 1970; and Ginzberg, 1966). In addition to being underrepresented in the literature, the plight of black female professionals is often misrepresented.

Research findings of comparisons between black and white professional women imply that black women are doing "very well": they earn 99% of what their white counterparts earn, and they occupy more positions open to blacks than white women occupy open to whites. Quite obviously, the problem with this type of comparison is that the most accurate assessment of the socioeconomic status of black women is obtained by comparing them to white males rather than to white females. Comparing black women to white women tends to distort their status by making it appear to be much better than it actually is. Comparing black women to white men yields a truer picture of their socioeconomic status. Black women earn 66 percent of the earnings of white males. Furthermore, that black women occupy more occupational positions open to blacks than white women occupy open to whites is no satisfactory indication that black women are more occupationally successful than white women (insofar as occupational distribution is an indicator of occupational success) because the range of occupations open to blacks is narrower than that for whites. Similarly, although black females are more widely distributed among professions open to women than are black males in professions open to men, there are fewer positions open to women. Within the professional category, the majority of women are concentrated in the two traditionally "female" professions of school teacher and nurse. Black male professionals, on the other hand, are more widely distributed than black female professionals. In fact, of all the sex-race categories, black women are the most restricted occupationally, and their employment distribution is "skewed toward the lower rungs of the occupational ladder" (Blau, 1979). Even within the so-called elite professions of medicine, law, and business, women are highly concentrated in the least prestigious and least remunerative areas of specialization. In medicine, these areas include pediatrics and general or family practice. In law, "family law" including divorce and adoption and "civil rights" law are the areas of concentration; and in business, the areas are personnel and public relations. These areas of specialization tend to be less remunerative and less prestigious because women are concentrated therein as practitioners, and the clientele of these specialties consists primarily of members of groups accorded low social status in the United States.

Black professional women tend to be treated in two ways in the sociological literature:

1. "Invisible Women." Their unique combination of ascribed statuses—black and female—tends to be treated as if it were equal only to the sum of its parts. In other words, black professional women tend to be subsumed under either the category of black professionals, or under the category of female professionals (Leggon, 1979).

2. Two negatives make a positive. This view, first elaborated by Epstein (1973), maintains that the double minority statuses of black and female give black women "advantages" over both white women and black men.

One such advantage is that employers prefer to hire black women because they get "two minorities for the price of one."[3] Even if this were true, it would have a very limited effect because, as Epstein notes parenthetically, access to professional careers is denied to all but the smallest fraction of black women (Allen, 1978). Another so-called advantage is that black women experience less guilt than their white counterparts over working. This advantage applies only to black women working jobs. Because of the greater demands on time, effort, and energy that distinguish a career from a job, professional women— black as well as white—experience problems engendered by the conflicting demands of career, marriage, and motherhood.

CAREER, MARRIAGE, AND MOTHERHOOD

To ascertain the extent to which black women experienced conflict between the demands of profession, marriage, and motherhood, I interviewed a sample of 25 black females in the Chicago Metropolitan Area in the following occupational categories: 6 in medicine, 12 in law, and 7 in business administration (i.e., women with masters degrees in business administration). Names were obtained from the membership rolls of professional associations: the Cook County Bar Association, the nation's oldest and largest local black bar association; and the League of Black Women, an organization founded in 1972 with membership consisting of women from all areas of life and with a representative cross-section of professionals. In order to eliminate bias accruing from a sample composed entirely of women who join professional associations, each woman contacted was asked to name other black women in business, medicine, and law. This snowball technique proved useful in locating most of the universe of black women in these designated professions. During the interview period for this study, from 1974 to 1975, Chicago had the largest number of black attorneys of any American city, approximately 330, of whom approximately 35 were female; and approximately 212 black doctors. It was difficult to estimate the number of black female physicians because most of the referral lists of physicians to which I had access consisted of last names and first initials; perhaps this is because many people are wary of female doctors except in a "traditionally female" specialty such as pediatrics. It was even more difficult to estimate the number of black women with masters degrees in business administration because the offices of the deans of the major graduate schools of business in the Chicago Metropolitan Area did not keep records by race and/or sex.

Because my study examined very complex and sensitive areas, I decided that the best method of data collection would be a two-part interview schedule consisting of questions to elicit basic socioeconomic data and open-ended questions comprising an indepth interview, designed to discover the respondents' perceptions of themselves and their situations. Because of the subject matter and in order to reduce interviewer bias, I personally interviewed all of the subjects. Their responses were recorded verbatim in shorthand or on tape. Because I am a black female, I hoped that the subjects would be more candid in their responses than they might be with a white female or with a male, black or white.[4]

Although the validity of the responses to the interview questions may be challenged on the basis that the study contains no corroborating mechanism(s) or cross-checks with "reality," it must be kept in mind that it is the respondents' perceptions of role conflicts that are of paramount importance. Nevertheless, in order to provide some measure of continuity in research, the wording of my interview schedule was patterned as closely as possible to that of National Opinion Research Center Study No. 431 and to Alice Rossi's supplemental schedule on sex roles in the follow-up study thereto. Each interview focused on attitudes toward the roles of professional and female as traditionally defined, the compatibility or incompatibility of the demands associated with each, and the coping mechanisms persuant thereto.

Before proceeding with the findings, a brief overview of selected salient characteristics of the sample is useful. Over three-fourths of the respondents grew up in the central city of a metropolitan area with a population of more than two million. Consonant with sociological theory that eldest, only, and youngest children tend to be the most successful occupationally, the majority of respondents were either the oldest or youngest child, or the oldest girl. For both law and medicine, the majority of the respondents were in specialties traditionally sex-typed as "women's specialties." To review briefly: for law, these specialties are domestic relations or family law (divorce, adoption), and public law, including administrative agency work; for medicine, pediatrics and family practice; and for business, personnel and public relations. The evidence is insufficient to indicate any discernible trend toward concentration of women in business, since many respondents had temporary assignments and duties; this is especially true of management trainees.

FINDINGS

Determination of the extent to which black professional women feel that the demands associated with the roles of "professional" and "female" are incompatible requires finding out what the role of "female" as traditionally defined, prescribed, and proscribed means to them. Therefore, to discover the meaning of the role of "female," I asked for the respondents' reaction, ranging from "Agree strongly" to "Disagree strongly," to the following statement: "Even if she has a career, a woman always has the option of being a housewife." Table 8:1 shows that more than half of the respondents agreed that women have the housewife option, even if they have a career. However, when broken down by age, more younger (i.e., women who entered a profession after 1965) than older women *disagree*. Although one young attorney was "infuriated" that this (housewife) was the alternative, an older attorney argued that the housewife option

tends to make a woman very, very comfortable in what she does. This is an alternative consideration, not avenues [sic] of retreat, but a different way of getting what you want.... it is built-in support.

A similar point was made by a physician who said that her husband's income and his attitude allowed her to "goof off financially," by which she meant enabled her not to be exclusively money-oriented and, consequently, enabled her to have more freedom than if she were her own sole support. One young woman in business maintained that being a housewife was "hardly an option." An interesting variation of the attitude toward the traditional female role was offered by another young businesswoman who did not think that "any woman has the option of being a housewife [because] a woman cannot choose to be married, that decision is made by the man."

Another indicator of the extent to which respondents were committed to the role of female as traditionally prescribed (and proscribed) was the viewpoint they espoused:

1.   the "traditional" viewpoint, which stresses the difference between the roles of men and women, in which women's lives center on home and family and their job participation is in those fields sex-typed as female; or

2.   the "feminist" viewpoint, which stresses greater equality and similarity in the roles of men and women than now exist, with greater participation of women in leadership positions in politics, the professions, and business.

As shown in Table 8:2, approximately 77 percent of the women in business, law, and medicine espoused the "feminist" viewpoint.

Commitment to the role of professional is a function of the following factors: the amount of "sunk costs" involved in preparing for the profession; satisfaction with the type of work performed; satisfaction with salary and estimated chances for professional advancement; and whether the respondent would choose the same profession if she had it to do all over again. The greater the sunk costs involved, i.e., the more time, effort, money, and energy one

TABLE 8:1

Agreement with Housewife Option by Age and Occupation

| | Pre-1965* | | | | Post-1965 | | | |
| | Law & Medicine | | Business | | Law & Medicine | | Business | |
	N	%	N	%	N	%	N	%
Strongly Agree	4	44	0	0	2	22	0	0
Somewhat Agree	3	33	1	50	2	22	0	0
Somewhat Disagree	0	0	1	50	3	33	0	0
Strongly Disagree	2	22	0	0	2	22	3	60
Neutral	0	0	0	0	0	0	2	40
Total	9	99**	2	100	9	99**	5	100

*Women entering their profession before 1965 constitute the "older" women.

**Does not total to 100 because of rounding error.

invests in a profession, the greater the probability that one will continue to pursue that career. Therefore, the earlier the career decision is made and acted upon, the greater the commitment to one's chosen profession. For half of the physicians and lawyers, the career decision was made before or during high school; however, more than half of the women in business decided during or after their junior year in college. Therefore, it is not surprising that in contrast to the conscious, deliberate choice of physicians and attorneys, the women in business just "kind of drifted" into their profession. As one younger respondent put it, "It was my junior or senior year in college and I didn't think I could cut graduate school to get a Ph.D., but I thought I could make two years, so I decided to get an MBA." An older respondent, who married in her senior year of college, returned to school to work on a Ph.D., but

decided it wasn't worth it because of the pressures I had to tackle....I needed a summer job and got one doing economic research....I continued working there after graduation....when my husband got a job here, I was able to be transferred....I liked the job and later decided to get an MBA.

TABLE 8:2

Feminist VS. Traditional Viewpoint by Age and Occupation

| | Pre-1965 | | | | Post-1965 | | | |
| | Law & Medicine | | Business | | Law & Medicine | | Business | |
	N	%	N	%	N	%	N	%
Strongly Agree	5	55	1	50	7	77	2	40
Moderately Agree	2	22	0	0	0	0	2	40
Partly Agree Partly Disagree	1	11	0	0	2	22	1	20
Moderately Disagree	0	0	0	0	0	0	0	0
Strongly Disagree	0	0	0	0	0	0	0	0
Don't Know	1	11	1	50	0	0	0	0
Total	9	99*	2	100	9	99*	5	100

*Does not total 100 due to rounding error.

What emerges from these anecdotes, then, is that women got their MBAs by default or because they chose to follow the "line of least or lesser resistance."

An overwhelming majority (99 percent) of the respondents were at least somewhat satisfied with the type of work they did, their job as a whole, and their salary (Table 8:3). Moreover, 86 percent of physicians and attorneys felt that their own chances for professional advancement were good, as compared to only 71 percent of the women in business. A significantly greater percentage of women in law and medicine than in business would choose the same profession again: 94 percent and 77 percent, respectively, as Table 8:4 shows.

Measuring commitment to the role of professional as a function of sunk costs, job satisfaction, and choosing the same profession again indicates that as groups, physicians and lawyers tend to be more committed to their respective professional roles than do women in business.

Strain(s) engendered by incompatible role demands are directly proportional to the commitment to each role with which the conflicting demands are

TABLE 8:3

Job Satisfaction by Occupation

	Type of Work				Salary				Employer				Job As A Whole			
	Law & Med.		Business		Law & Med.		Business		Law & Med.		Business		Law & Med.		Business	
	N	%	N	%	N	%	N	%	N	%	N	%	N	%	N	%
Extremely Satisfied	10	62	5	71	5	31	3	43	4	33	1	14	6	37	4	57
Somewhat Satisfied	6	37	2	28	7	43	3	43	3	25	4	57	10	62	1	14
Neutral	0	0	0	0	2	12	0	0	3	25	0	0	0	0	0	0
Somewhat Dissatisfied	0	0	0	0	2	12	0	0	2	17	2	28	0	0	1	14
Very Dis- satisfied	0	0	0	0	0	0	1	14	0	0	0	0	0	0	1	14
Total[b]	16	99	7	99	16	98	7	100	12	100	7	99	16	99	7	99
N.A.	2		0		2		0		6		0		2		0	

a
Percentages do not add to 100 due to rounding error.

b
No answer.

125

TABLE 8:4

Would Choose Same Profession Again, By Occupation

	Yes N	Yes %	No N	No %	Total N	Total %	N.A. [a]
Law and Medicine	16	94	1	6	17	100	1
Business	4	66.6	2	33.3	6	100	1

a
No answer.

associated. Specifically, the stronger the commitment to the role of professional and to the traditional role of female, the greater the strain(s) engendered by the incompatibility of the demands associated with each role. This strain can be eliminated or reduced by either eliminating one of the roles completely (e.g., giving up one's career) or by reducing one's commitment to one of the roles (e.g., "no matter what, my job comes first!"). Implicit in the preceding discussion is the assumption that the role demands associated with the role of professional are diametrically opposed to those associated with the role of female as traditionally defined. Indeed, I contend this to be the case. This contention is supported by much of the sociological literature on socialization patterns which indicates that those qualities deemed necessary to succeed professionally are the opposite of those defining a successful "female." Success for males is synonymous with occupational success; for females, it is synonymous with nonoccupational pursuits—marriage and motherhood.

Because a woman assumes the roles of professional, wife, and mother does not *ipso facto* mean she has reconciled successfully the incompatibility of the demands attached to each role. A specific indicator of this incompatibility is the strength of the effect(s) on the respondents of the societal expectations that a woman should marry and that whether she works or not, the home is the woman's responsibility. Both of these expectations are particularly binding on the older women as a group, regardless of profession, as illustrated by the remarks of one physician:

I was never going to get married, but I changed my mind in college because I lacked real companionship and figured that I had to get married because in those days it was not done to "shack up with someone"; [besides I] knew that marriage was expected of women in my generation.... I wasn't going to have children either, but my husband wanted them, so...

Another older married respondent agreed: "a man can divorce himself from home a little more than can a lady." These expectations cause ambivalence at the least and guilt at the most in the younger respondents, as one young attorney, married to an attorney, described:

Many women know that what they are doing is intellectually as important as what their husbands do, but they still feel guilty about not doing everything and keeping up the house. In the final analysis, it falls on the woman's head if the house is messy.

An older married attorney holds just the opposite viewpoint:

You must figure out what it is you are going to do. You can have a family and rear children and make yourself a complete pivot (so that all are totally dependent on you). If you feel you have to do all this (cook, clean, etc.), you are just holding yourself down. . . . Most people feel that the combination of job, marriage and family is much too much, but they don't want to give up doing anything.

In other words, to justify their role of professional to the larger society, as well as to themselves, and in order to alleviate the guilt attendant to assuming such a "deviant" role as that of professional, some women feel that they must be "Superwife," Supermom," and "Superwoman."

When married respondents were asked whether or not they anticipated problems before their marriage in combining marriage and career, the vast majority replied that they did not (Table 8:5). One reason so few older women anticipated problems in combining career and marriage is that they decided *a*

TABLE 8:5

Married Respondents Anticipating Problems Combining Career and Marriage by

Profession and Time of Entering

Profession

	Pre-1965						Post-1965					
	Law		Medicine		Business		Law		Medicine		Business	
	N	%	N	%	N	%	N	%	N	%	N	%
No	2	66	3	100	1	100	2	100	1	50	2	100
Yes	1	33	0	0	0	0	0	0	1	50	0	0
Total*	3	99	3	100	1	100	2	100	2	100	2	100

*Percentages do not total 100 due to rounding error.

priori to place their family ahead of their career. This position is expressed by one of the older business women:

My first responsibilities are as a wife and mother .... (and my husband has responsibilities in terms of his career). Coming along during the days I did, the husband's career sets the pattern of your life and it's terribly important for him to succeed .... I tended not to seek out opportunities for changes in jobs and I tended to be more content with my situation than I actually may have been because it was terribly important for me to be in a [working] situation where I knew the people and my husband was terribly successful. I could not have pressure from the job and pressures from the home.

These sentiments are shared by an older physician married to a physician: "my career was the secondary career .... [we] never discussed it [which career would take precedence]." The opposite solution—choice of career over marriage—was adopted by one young, single physician: "if my husband gave me the choice of him or my career, I would take the career." This respondent's father had always told her to prepare herself for a profession, so that if she married and it did not work out, "she would not have to take anything off of anybody."

Some choose to deal with the conflicting demands of profession and marriage by remaining single. One such person, a single, older attorney born and raised in the South, stated that "marriage was considered another job, especially in the rural South where the woman looked after the husband. If you are working, studying, going to school, it's too much." Remaining single does not mean the same thing for older respondents as for the younger respondents; the latter are availing themselves of the option of "shacking up" or living together without benefit of clergy. Case in point, one young attorney, married and divorced at an early age, who vowed never to remarry, although she had been living with her steady male companion for the past four years. Another resolution, particularly favored by physicians, was to marry someone in the same profession. After having dated one man who wanted her to stop medical school, a young physician decided that she would "marry someone in medicine, so that he could understand what I am going through during my work hours." She acted on her decision, and subsequently married a physician.

Whether he is in the same profession or not, most respondents agree that their spouse's approval and support of their professional role greatly ease the tension generated by the incompatible demands of profession and marriage. This is attested to by one woman in business whose husband deliberately attempted to sabotage her career by "taking the car so I couldn't use it .... He doesn't like the idea of women working although he tries to act like he does .... Instead of helping, he works against me." His subversive behavior was prompted not only by his dislike of working women in general, but by his inability to deal with the fact that his wife earned more money than he.

Educational differentials between husband and wife, when the latter is better educated than the former, can also cause problems for the married professional woman. One attorney married to a nonprofessional considerably less educated than she described her marriage as "pretty unhappy" because he resented the fact that she was better educated and made more money than he. All other things being equal, husbands with working mothers are more favorably disposed toward their wives working. It is difficult to determine the extent to which this proposition holds for the respondents in this study because their husbands' favorable attitude toward their career could also have stemmed from the fact that they were professionals, often in the same profession. In sum, as a method of reducing the tension caused by the conflicting role demands associated with marriage and profession, moral support from a woman's husband is more likely to obtain when both spouses are professionals— preferably in the same profession.

In all cases, when married respondents anticipated problems in combining marriage and career, they materialized (Table 8:6). One of the most frequently cited problems was the amount of time spent away from the children, as one young doctor married to a doctor described:

[we] probably overcompensate with the children when we are with them by letting them stay up late because we are not here in the day . . . but the quality not the quantity of time spent with the children is more important.

Supportive parents and relatives who may even share childcare responsibilities, as well as paid babysitters, aid in reducing the tension generated from the combination of professional and maternal demands. Generally, black professional women tend not to experience as much guilt and anxiety as their white counterparts over delegating some childrearing chores to others—family or

TABLE 8:6

Cases In Which Those Married Respondents Anticipating Trouble Combining Career

And Marriage Had it Materialize by Profession and Time

Of Entering Profession

| | Pre-1965 | | | | | | Post-1965 | | | | | |
| | Law | | Medicine | | Business | | Law | | Medicine | | Business | |
	N	%	N	%	N	%	N	%.	N	%	N	%
No	0	0	0	0	0	0	2	100	0	0	2	100
Yes	3	100	3	100	1	100	0	0	2	100	0	0
Total	3	100	3	100	1	100	2	100	2	100	2	100

paid help. This is because they are socialized to expect to work whether or not they marry and have children and because more often than not their own mother worked. Therefore, for black professional women, the incompatibility of professional and maternal demands is easier to cope with than the incompatibility between professional and marital demands. One option available for the younger group is not having children. As one young attorney, married to an attorney, put it:

I went to school for a long time and my husband did too, and we have been preparing to be in a situation where we will have the money and freedom to do what we want to do and enjoy [it]. I have no desire to cramp my style with a child . . . . I wouldn't want to impose my child on anyone.

For most of the married women, the expectation that motherhood, marriage, and career would be equally important was borne out, as was the expectation that motherhood would take precedence over career. All of those anticipating career taking precedence over marriage had their expectation met, as Table 8:7 shows. The expectation that career and marriage or career, marriage, and motherhood would be equally important was held before marriage by most of the married respondents and is held by most of the nonmarried respondents. As one single respondent pointed out, the problems anticipated depend "on whom you are going to marry."

That quote succinctly summarizes my findings: most of the problems that my respondents discussed resulted from the conflicting demands of career with marriage rather than with motherhood. For these black professional women, the conflicts between the demands of profession and marriage were more important in terms of both frequency and intensity than the conflicts caused by the demands of profession and motherhood. Although some of my respondents cited not having enough time to spend with their children and worries over parental responsibilities as problems, these were problems that both they and their husband experienced. Moreover, they tended to resolve them, at least partially, through the support of relatives and paid babysitters. Such support was more acceptable to black respondents than to their white counterparts. Far less easily resolvable for them were the problems resulting from the clash between their obligations as professionals and as wives. This was especially true in cases in which the wife was better educated than the husband or made more money than he, or both. Solutions ranged from deciding *a priori* that marriage would take precedence over career, to marrying someone in the same profession, to deciding that career would take precedence over marriage, and therefore deciding not to marry at all. In sum, both black and white professional women experience problems caused by the conflict between career and marriage, but in different ways and for different reasons.

TABLE 8:7

Anticipated Preferences Before Marriage by Occupation and Marital Status

| | Single | | | | | | Married | | | | | |
| | Law | | Medicine | | Business | | Law | | Medicine | | Business | |
	N	%	N	%	N	%	N	%	N	%	N	%
Career over Marriage	0	0	1	100	0	0	1	20	0	0	0	0
Marriage over Career	1	20	0	0	3	75	2	40	0	0	1	20
Career = Marriage	2	40	0	0	0	0	1	20	3	60	1	20
Motherhood over Career	0	0	0	0	0	0	0	0	0	0	2	40
Career over Motherhood	1	20	0	0	1	25	2	40	0	0	0	0
Motherhood = Career = Marriage	1	20	0	0	0	0	0	0	2	40	0	0
Total	5	100	1	100	4	100	6	120[a]	5	100	4	80
No Answer											1	

[a]
Percentages total to more than 100 because one respondent gave two answers to the same question.

131

SUMMARY AND CONCLUSIONS

Through focusing on black women in the elite professions of business, law, and medicine, this paper examined the problems caused by the conflicting demands of career, marriage, and motherhood, the extent to which these problems are different from those of their white counterparts, the causes of these differences, and the coping mechanisms black professional women have devised to deal with these problems.

Black women define working as another contribution they make to their family, and therefore feel much less guilt than do white women over working on a job. However, *both* black and white professional women experience problems caused by the conflicting demands of career, marriage, and motherhood because a career is much more demanding than a job in terms of the greater commitment (including time, energy, and effort) it requires.

Strains engendered by incompatible role demands are directly proportional to the commitment to each role with which the conflicting demands are associated. Specifically, the stronger the commitment to the role of professional and to the "traditional" role of female, the greater the strain(s) engendered by the incompatibility of the demands associated with each role. Commitment to the role of professional is a function of the amount of sunk costs involved in preparation for a professional career; satisfaction with the job as a whole; and whether the respondent would choose the same profession if she had it to do all over again. The greater the sunk costs and the greater the work satisfaction, the greater the commitment to the role of professional. As groups, physicians and lawyers tend to be more committed to their respective professional roles than do women in business. Although the vast majority of married respondents, regardless of age, did not anticipate problems before marriage in combining marriage with career, their reasons for this expectation vary with age and occupation. Many of the older women increased the compatibility or decreased the incompatibility of the role demands of professional and wife by deciding *a priori* that their marriage would take precedence over their career. Many respondents maintained that marriage can be combined easier with business and law than with medicine. Most physicians, married and single, concurred and posited marriage to another physician as the best way for them to combine their career with marriage because this enables their mate to understand, sympathize, and empathize with the demands that their profession makes on them. Whether or not they share the same profession, most respondents agree that the greater the personal and occupational security of one's mate, the more able and willing he is to accept and encourage a professional wife.

For black professional women (as for their white counterparts) the self-fulfilling prophecy holds; regardless of the content of the expectation—career taking precedence over motherhood and marriage; motherhood taking precedence over career; career, motherhood, and marriage being equally important—

the expectation was met. In sum, the most important problems for black professional women are caused by the conflict between the demands of career and marriage, whereas for their white counterparts, it is the conflict between the demands of career and motherhood. Therefore, in light of this distinction, future research should identify and delineate additional mechanisms used to cope with these conflicting demands.

NOTES

1. For both sides of this issue, see Wilson (1978) and Hill (1978).

2. Some sociologists, such as William J. Wilson (1978) argue that black middle-class families *have* been able to consolidate their gains and pass them on to their offspring; thus, middle-class black children have greater access to society's power, privilege, and resources than do lower- or under-class black children.

3. Even though census data refute the claim that black women compete with black men for the same jobs, this claim cannot be dismissed easily, for, as George Herbert Mead said, "if a thing is not recognized as true, then it does not function as true in the community" (Merton, 1968, pp. 20ff.).

4. In addition to their effect(s) on the candidness of the subjects' responses, race and sex affect whether or not an individual will even agree to be interviewed. When telephoning a potential respondent to set up an interview, I was asked if I were black, and when I replied "yes," she said, "O.K., then I'll be interviewed, but I don't have the time for a white woman."

REFERENCES

Allen, W. R. "Black Family Research in the United States: A Review, Assessment and Extension," *Journal of Comparative Family Studies*, 1978, 9(2), 167–189.

Bailyn, L. "Notes on the Role of Choice in the Psychology of Professional Women," *Daedalus*, 1964, 93, 700–708.

Billingsley, A. *Black Families in White America*. Englewood Cliffs, N.J.: Prentice-Hall, 1968.

Blau, F. "Women in the Labor Force: An Overview," In J. Freeman (ed) *Women: A Feminist Perspective*. Palo Alto, Calif.: Mayfield Publishing Co., 1979.

Bronfenbrenner, U. "Socialization and Social Class Through Time and Space," In H. Proshansky (ed) *Basic Studies in Social Psychology*. New York: Van Nostrand, 1965.

Degler, C. N. "Revolution without Ideology: The Changing Place of Women in America," *Daedalus*, 1964, 93, 653–670.

Eastwood, M. "Feminism and the Law," In J. Freeman (ed) *Women: A Feminist Perspective*. Palo Alto, Calif.: Mayfield Publishing Co., 1979.

Edwards, G. F. *The Negro Professional*. Glencoe, Ill.: The Free Press of Glencoe, 1959.

Epstein, C. F. *Woman's Place*. Berkeley, Calif.: University of California Press, 1970.

———— "Positive Effects of the Multiple Negative: Explaining the Success of Black Professional Women," *American Journal of Sociology*, 1973, 78, 913–918.

Farley, R. "Racial Progress in the Last Two Decades: What Can We Determine about Who Benefitted and Why?," Paper presented at the ASA Meetings, Boston, Mass., September, 1979.

Frazier, E. F. *The Negro Family in the United States*. Chicago: University of Chicago Press, 1939.

Gans, H. *The Urban Villagers*. New York: Free Press, 1962.

Geschwender, J. A. *Racial Stratification in America*. Dubuque, Iowa: Wm. C. Brown Company Publishers, 1978.

Ginzberg, E. *Lifestyles of Educated Women*. New York: Columbia University Press, 1966.

Glenn, N. D. "Some Changes in the Relative Status of American Non-Whites: 1940–1960," *Phylon*, 1963, 24, 443–448.

Hill, R. *The Strengths of Black Families*. New York: Emerson Hall, 1971.

———. "The Illusion of Black Progress," Washington, D.C.: National Urban League Research Department, 1978.

Kessler, S. J., and W. McKenna. *Gender: An Ethnomethodological Approach*. New York: John Wiley & Sons, 1978.

Komarovsky, M. "Cultural Contradictions and Sex Roles," *American Journal of Sociology*, 1946, 52, 184–189.

Ladner, J. *Tomorrow's Tomorrow: The Black Woman*. Garden City, N.Y.: Doubleday, 1971.

Leggon, C. B. "Racism and Sexism: The Case of the Elite Black Female Professional," unpublished manuscript, 1979.

Lerner, G. *Black Women in White America: A Documentary History*. New York: Random House, 1973.

Lewis, D. "The Black Family: Socialization and Sex Roles," *Phylon*, 1975, 36(Fall), 221–237.

Martin, E. P., and J. M. Martin. *The Black Extended Family*. Chicago: University of Chicago Press, 1978.

Merton, R. K. *Social Theory and Social Structure*. New York: The Free Press, 1968.

Oakley, A. *Sex, Gender and Society*. New York: Harper Colophon, 1972.

Scholzman, K. L. "Women and Unemployment: Assessing the Biggest Myths," In J. Freeman (ed) *Women: A Feminist Perspective*. Palo Alto, Calif.: Mayfield Publishing Co., 1979.

Stack, C. *All Our Kin: Strategies for Survival in a Black Community*. New York: Harper & Row Publishers, 1974.

Strodbeck, F. "Family Interaction, Values, and Achievement," In D. McClelland, et al. (eds) *Talent and Society*. Princeton, N.J.: Van Nostrand, 1968.

Wallin, P. "Cultural Contradictions and Sex Roles: A Repeat Study," *American Sociological Review*, 1950, 15(2), 288–295.

Weitzman, L. J. "Sex-Role Socialization," In J. Freeman (ed) *Women: A Feminist Perspective*. Palo Alto, Calif.: Mayfield Publishing Co., 1979.

Willie, C. V. "The Black Family and Social Class," *American Journal of Orthopsychiatry*, 1974, 44, 50–60.

Wilson, W. J. *The Declining Significance of Race*. Chicago: University of Chicago Press, 1978.

Woodson, C. G. *The Negro Professional Man and the Community*. New York: Negro Universities Press, 1934.

9

PARENTING STYLES: MOTHER-CHILD INTERACTIONS AND SELF-ESTEEM IN YOUNG BLACK CHILDREN

John Lewis McAdoo

This chapter is a preliminary report of a larger study dealing with mother-child interaction and its effects on the self-esteem of black preschool children. Very few studies were found that observed black parents interacting with their children (Baumrind, 1971 and Radin, 1971) and that measured the effects of that interaction on the self-esteem of the children (McAdoo, H., 1976a). Since almost 50 percent of all black families are headed by a single parent (McAdoo, H., 1976b), it is important that both descriptive and normative data on the types of interaction between a black mother and her child are available.

Harrison (1976) has noted that a married mother has two dominant roles, wife and mother. When she becomes employed she adds a third role, worker. Whenever there is inter-role conflict between the three roles, a white mother usually relinquishes her role as worker, while a black mother, because of economic necessities, is forced to retain her worker role. The black mother, in situations of extreme inter-role conflict, removes the role of wife. This could explain the large percentage of single-parent homes in the Black community.

Noting the rapid increase in the number of single-parent families, Bronfenbrenner (1975) has suggested that a more ecological approach to family research is needed. The family should be viewed as a system and future studies should attempt to isolate the important variables related to the interaction patterns within that system. Thus, this study was designed to examine the role of mother and its effect on the development of social competency of the black child.

Lynn (1965), Lamb (1966), and other researchers have extensively explored the predictability of psychoanalytic theory, learning theory, and Parsonian theory in relation to the role of the mother in the socialization of her child. As Lamb (1966) concluded, none of the above theories is entirely consistent with the evidence; however, all three, in certain aspects, seem to be correct. He was not sure that popular methodologies should be used to validate unambiguously any theory. It is suggested that the ecological system approach may be more appropriate to explain and predict the mother's behavior in relation to her child.

An ecological model allows movement away from traditional deficit models of analysis and begins looking at the total environment and its effect upon the three important dimensions—the setting of the child, the social networks and institutions, and the ideological system. This research is related to the setting and examines relevant people and the effect of their interaction with the child on the development of social competence in the child. More specifically, we are concerned with the dimensions of maternal behavior and attitudes that affect the development of self-esteem in the child.

The present study was an attempt to explore the characteristics of black mother-child interaction, using a more ecological approach to observing mother-child interaction patterns. It allows us a framework to collect and analyze data by observing parent-child interactions in the natural environment of the home. The question was asked: What are the predominant patterns of interaction that take place between an upper or lower middle-class black mother and her child? In addition, the relationship between these established patterns of interaction and the child's self-esteem was investigated.

Several researchers (Baumrind, 1971 and Radin, 1972, 1975) have suggested that maternal warmth (nurturance) facilitates the child's identification with the mother, particularly the female child. Identification with the mother should lead to an incorporation of the mother's ideas, attitudes, beliefs, and feelings about the child. The mother communicates to the child a positive acceptance of the child as a person. Maternal nurturance is one dimension in the development of social competence in preschool children.

Another dimension important to the development of social competence is maternal nonnurturance. It is suggested that nonnurturance would not facilitate positive communication and identification between the mother and her child. For the purpose of this study, the nonnurturance dimension was divided into two categories: neutral and restrictive. Neutral nonnurturance was defined as those mothers' behaviors that were not warm and loving and supportive of the child. Restrictive nonnurturance behavior on the mother's part is a negative reaction by the mother to the child's attitude and behavior.

Nonnurturance may also lead the mother to handle the symptoms of the problem and not the needs of the child, or to controlling behavior on the part of the mother, and the cutting off of the usual patterns of identification and communication of the child. Nonnurturance in the mothers could lead the children to develop negative images of themselves and their worth as human beings, as well as having negative feelings about those around them.

While nurturance and nonnurturance are not the only dimensions of the mother-child relationship, a study of these variables will facilitate the process of identifying other variables that are also important in the mother-child interactional patterns that promote social competence in preschool children.

A socially competent child was defined as one who exhibits a positive feeling of self-worth and who has some degree of control over his or her environment (White and Watts, 1973). It is suggested that the development of self-esteem is the key variable in developing socially competent children. Therefore, it is important that the interrelationship between nurturance, nonnurturance, and self-esteem is explored.

Radin (1972) and others were concerned with the parent-child interaction and its effects on cognitive growth. Baumrind (1973) was concerned with the types of parenting and its effects on cognitive and moral development of the child. Biller (1977) focused on parenting styles and their effects on sex-role development. However, none of the above authors related their work to the development of identity and self-esteem in preschool children.

Baumrind (1971) observed the relationship between three types of parenting styles—authoritarian, authoritative, and permissive—and competence in preschool children. She found that authoritative parents promoted purposive and dominant behavior in boys and girls. Authoritative control was associated with the development of social responsibility in boys and with achievement (but not friendly, cooperative behavior) in girls. Authoritarian child-rearing practices were associated with either markedly high or markedly low over-all competence in preschool children. Children from permissive homes exhibited similar levels of cooperation as the children of authoritarian parents.

Radin (1972) has also studied patterns of interaction between white middle and working-class mothers and their children. She identified three verbal interactional patterns in her groups of mothers: nurturant, restrictive, and nonnurturant. She studied the relationship between these patterns of interaction and the child's cognitive growth one year later. Radin (1972) found that children of verbally nurturant mothers did well in school, while children of restrictive mothers did poorly on cognitive tasks in kindergarten.

Indeed, neither of the studies attempted to measure both verbal and nonverbal interactions between mothers and their preschool children. Radin (1972) has suggested that tone of voice, physical interaction, and meeting of implicit and explicit needs on a verbal level were important dimensions. However, no systematic attempt was made to observe these categories on a nonverbal level. The research team felt that this was an important dimension of interaction to explore and developed a nonverbal observational instrument to measure this behavior (McAdoo et al. 1976).

Interestingly, this suggested a relationship between parental interaction patterns, ethnic identity, and self-esteem. Clark (1939, 1952) and others (Asher and Allen, 1969 and Goodman, 1952) have suggested that black children have low self-esteem and negative ethnic identity. Self-concept and ethnic identity was assumed to have a linear relationship and as a result of one instrument, the dolls test, black preschool children were said to hate themselves and their ethnic group.

Recent studies using better methodologies have demonstrated that black children have a more positive view of themselves (McAdoo, H., 1973) and their ethnic identity (Fox and Barnes, 1977; Hraba and Grant, 1970; McAdoo, J., 1970; and Ward and Braun, 1972). Liscomb (1975), Goodman (1952), and others (Cole, 1967 and Horowitz, 1939) have stressed the importance of observing parental attitudes as an intervening variable to self-esteem and ethnic identity development. However, none of the authors appeared to have studied the interaction patterns that lead to the development of positive self-esteem and ethnic identity in preschool children.

Since Radin's work (1972) is one of the few empirical studies that attempts to observe the mother-child interaction patterns in a natural setting without other family members being present, the present study utilized her verbal observation categories with the black sample. In addition, a different measure of nonverbal interactional patterns was developed. Finally, self-esteem was assumed to be a more important variable than cognitive growth, since the way children feel about themselves and their world may influence their cognitive development; thus, self-esteem was assessed in the study.

The experimental hypotheses were: (1) black mothers would be verbally nurturant with their children; (2) there would be a negative relationship between verbal nurturance and nonnurturance; (3) there would be a positive relationship between verbal nurturance and nonverbal interaction; (4) black children would be positive in their self-esteem; (5) there would be a positive relationship between maternal nurturance and the child's self-esteem; and (6) there would be a positive relationship between the amount of nonverbal interaction and the child's self-esteem.

METHOD

Sample

The sample consisted of 40 black mothers and their preschool children, 20 boys and 20 girls, age four to six years, living in a suburban town located within the Baltimore-Washington metropolitan area. This town offered an excellent opportunity to study upper and lower middle-class blacks who lived in the same neighborhood and attended the same schools. The families were randomly selected from a pool of black families and were located by advertisement in nursery schools, local church bulletins, and door-to-door canvasing.

Interviews

There were a total of four interviews, two with the mother and child present and two with the child alone. Four black female interviewers were trained to do the interviewing. The interviewers were trained over a four-week period using role playing and video tapes. The first interview was with the entire family to explain the project, to gain their permission for participation, to obtain some socioeconomic background data, and to help the child feel relaxed around the interviewer. In the second interview, only the mother and the child were present during the hour and a half session. The child was given a puzzle to complete at the end of the session.

The mother's verbal responses to the second interview were recorded on tape in order to allow the interviewer the opportunity to code the nonverbal interactions between the mother and her child. The crucial point of the child's presence during the interview was to set up a situation in which the mother would have to respond to the child's behavior or needs. It also kept the child in the room to allow us to code the verbal and nonverbal behavior in a manner that would not disrupt the interview.

The child was seen alone in our office on two different occasions. The interviewer administered the Modified Thomas Self Concept Scale (McAdoo, 1974) on both visits. At the end of the second interview, the child was given a box of crayons and a balloon, and the parents were given a twenty-dollar gift certificate for their participation.

Instruments

There were four instruments used: (1) the procedure devised by Radin (1972) to collect verbal interaction data; (2) the McAdoo and Teresa (1976) nonverbal interaction scale; (3) the Cognitive Home Environment Scale (CHES) (Radin, 1972) to examine parental attitudes; and (4) the Modified Thomas Self Concept measure.

Radin's verbal interaction scale. All verbal interactions during the second interview were recorded. After the interview, two trained coders reviewed the entire tape and divided it into four 15-minute segments. The two consecutive 15-minute periods with the most verbal interactions were coded by the verbal coders. The average intercoder reliability was 0.92. The verbal interactions were scored according to seven factors: (1) reinforcing; (2) responding to implicit needs; (3) relating to explicit needs; (4) initiating motivating behaviors; (5) expressing warmth; (6) influencing and limit-setting categories; and (7) restricting behaviors (Radin, 1972).

Nurturant behavior, for example, involved any response after the child's behavior, such as saying "good," or expressing appreciation; asking the child what he wanted, setting a limit, but providing an explanation for the limit. Restrictive behavior, for example, would be to order the child to do something, but give no explanation, scolding, name-calling, sarcasm, yelling, etc.

Nonverbal interactions. The nonverbal interactions between mother and child were recorded on a timed grid placed after each question on the questionnaire. The interviewer recorded nonverbal interactions at 15-second intervals, a maximum of two minutes per question during the first, middle, and last 10 questions on the questionnaire. There were five categories of nonverbal behavior: tone of voice, physical touch, meeting implicit needs, meeting explicit needs, and no interaction. Within these five categories were measures of degrees, i.e., positive tone of voice, negative tone of voice, and neutral.

Following the interview, the scores on the number of nonverbal interactions were obtained by counting the number of 15-second intervals in which nonverbal interaction occurred between mother and child. A proportional score was obtained by dividing the frequency of interaction by the maximum number of 15-second intervals possible in which nonverbal interaction could have occurred.

Cognitive Home Environment Scale. Parental attitudes toward child-rearing was measured by the mother's responses to questions regarding her perceived strictness to tolerate misbehavior on the part of the child, similarities between her own and her parents' childrearing practices, expectation of child care provisions in event of death or disability, and the extent to which that person would rear the child differently. These questions were scored for frequency and percentages on the total group's response to the questions.

Modified Thomas Self Concept measure. The modification of the Thomas Self Concept Test (McAdoo, H., 1974) measures the child's self-concept through the use of questions based upon the child's own Polaroid photograph. The children were asked to give their views of and how they are moved by three "significant others" in their lives (mother, teacher, peer). The questions form a core of 14 bipolar adjectives, items representing the value on which the children reported their perceptions. The Thomas' items are presented in an "either-or" format, using the child's own name, i.e., "Is David happy or is David sad?", while referring to the child's own picture. The more desirable choice was scored +1. The +1 items across all categories were added together to get a total score of the child's view of himself or herself.

The Thomas test was modified to make the scale more appropriate. Thomas' original test did not include the father as a "significant other." It also had a negative sex-typing for girls on two questions. In the original Thomas scoring, the dimensions of "strong–weak" and "big–little" were scored differently for girls, with "strong" and "big" given a negative score. The author did not feel this was a valid reversal and, therefore, both sexes were scored similarly (McAdoo, H., 1974). In addition, the Thomas asked how the child liked to be with men and did not ask a comparable question about women. Therefore, these three changes were made. The Thomas' scores were restandardized using the three modifications, based on a sample of 100 black preschool children in the metropolitan Washington, D.C., area (McAdoo, H., 1974). These new standardized scores were felt to be preferable to the original Thomas standardization sample of children in Head Start Centers in the 1960s in Grand Rapids, Michigan.

TABLE 9:1

Mean and Standard Deviation of Black Mothers' Verbal And

Nonverbal Interactions with Their Preschool Children

Variable	Number	Mean	Standard Deviation
Verbal Interaction			
Reinforcing Frequency	40	5.95	21.66
Explicit	40	18.60	23.22
Implicit	40	21.78	22.35
Motivating Behaviors	40	10.10	21.16
Warmth	40	7.23	21.48
Influencing & Limit Setting	40	9.08	21.29
Restrictive	40	8.65	21.59
Total Nurturance	38	35.08	20.59
Total Restrictive	38	10.21	11.44
Total Interaction Frequencies	38	49.18	25.95
Total Child Initiated	38	17.50	15.15
Nonverbal Interaction			
Total Number Intervals Used	39	83.21	29.49
Total Ratio # Interactions per Interval	40	.29	.22
Total Ratio # Noninteractions per Interval	40	.76	.18
Total Ratio Positive Interactions per Interval	40	.09	.20
Total Ratio Negative Interactions per Interval	40	.05	.16

RESULTS

Verbal Interactions

Generally, the mothers in the sample gave more nurturant responses (M = 35.08) than restrictive (M = 10.21) responses toward their children. This suggests that the children were receiving positive and warm responses for their actions. Mothers were attempting to meet their children's implicit and explicit needs in ways that would be supportive rather than detrimental to their developing personalities (Table 9:1). However, this was not a permissive setting interaction pattern. Limits were defined clearly; however, explanations were given beforehand so the child could understand the reasons for the parental limit-setting.

When the mother's behavior was examined across the factors, the most frequent type of response was in relating to the implicit needs of the children (M = 21.78). In other words, the mother initiated the child in conversation, stopped to listen when the child talked, etc. Inherently, meeting implicit needs refers to satisfying the child's physical or emotional needs even though the child may not have expressed the need. The second most frequent type of behavior was meeting the explicit needs of the child. Explicit behavior refers to the need-meeting behavior of the parent that is an overt response to the child's overt seeking of parental response. It is an acknowledgment on the part of the mother of the need and a physical or verbal response to the child. The child initiated many of the interactions (M = 17.50).

Nonverbal Interactions

The nonverbal interactions were coded starting 15 seconds after each question was read. Coding continued once every 15 seconds from that point until the mother had finished answering the question or for a maximum of two minutes per question. The average number of 15-second intervals used were 83.21. Since some mothers did not interact for the total two minutes for each of the 30 minutes, a ratio scoring was used in order to be able to make the data comparable across all mothers. The ratio reflected the number of nonverbal interactions occurring divided by the number of intervals used in coding. Thus, we could compare responses of mothers who gave long answers with those who gave short ones. The ratio of the total number of interactions per interval was an average of .29 for all of the mothers. The ratio of noninteractions was higher, at .76. This indicates that the nonverbal interactions occurred only roughly one-fourth of the time. However, when nonverbal interaction did occur, it tended to be positive (.09) rather than negative (.05).

Because social class is reportedly related to mother-child interactions, we divided the sample into two groups categorized by education and occupation: lower middle-class and upper middle-class. No significant difference between the two categories was found on any of the variables (Table 9:2). This would

TABLE 9:2

t-Test of Socioeconomic Status Differences on Verbal and Nonverbal Interactions by Black Mothers

Variable	Factor	Number	Mean	Standard Deviation	t	df	p
Verbal Interaction							
Total Nurturance	Upper Class	16	33.50	.17.37	-.43	35	n.s.
	Middle Class	21	36.52	23.51			
Total Restrictive	Upper Class	16	10.13	12.95	-.11	35	n.s.
	Middle Class	21	10.57	10.69			
Total Interaction Frequencies	Upper Class	16	47.19	23.44	-.48	35	n.s.
	Middle Class	21	51.43	28.52			
Total Child Initiated	Upper Class	16	17.81	17.25	.01	35	n.s
	Middle Class	21	17.76	14.00			
Nonverbal Interaction							
Total Number Intervals Used	Upper Class	17	86.35	24.44	.57	36	n.s.
	Middle Class	21	80.71	34.05			
Total Ratio # Inter-actions per Interval	Upper Class	18	.31	.28	.33	37	n.s.
	Middle Class	21	.29	.16			

indicate that the mothers responded in the same way regardless of status difference within the middle-class.

Self-Concept

Contrary to the self-hatred hypothesis in which the black child is seen as having a low self-esteem, these preschool children felt good about themselves and had strong self-concepts (M = 50.07, SD = 11.49). The children felt that they were highly valued by their parents, teachers, and peers. However, no relationship was found between how the children viewed themselves or how they perceived others viewing them and the type or frequency of verbal and nonverbal interaction.

While no significant differences were found on the Thomas Self Concept (TSC) measure, when we compared socioeconomic status differences, the upper middle-income children felt slightly more positive toward themselves on the total TSC as a group than the lower-income children did. The upper middle-class fathers and mothers were perceived as more positively valuing the child's attributes than the lower middle-class parents did. The upper middle-class children also perceived significant others outside the family, their peers, and their teachers as valuing them more highly than did the lower middle-class children (Table 9:3).

In response to questions related to the degree of strictness among the sample, no significant socioeconomic differences were found. Forty-eight percent of the sample felt they were not strict at all, while 28 percent felt that they were moderately strict, and 24 percent felt they were very strict.

The majority of the mothers in the sample (57 percent) felt that the child should obey right away. Almost 40 percent of the mothers felt that the child should obey, but he or she did not have to obey right away. One mother said that it did not matter. Most of the mothers felt that they were very tolerant toward acting-out behavior in their children. Forty-eight percent of the mothers would tolerate a great deal of misbehavior in their children and 46 percent of the sample stated that they could accept some misbehavior in their children. Only 6 percent of the total sample felt that they would not allow misbehavior in their children.

Almost all of these mothers felt that they were raising their children differently than they were raised. Ninety-six percent of the sample felt that they were not as strict as their parents. When asked who would you expect to care for your child in the event that you were not able to, 55 percent of the mothers expected their parents to care for the child. Forty-four percent expected that their brothers and sisters would care for the child, and only one respondent felt that a friend would raise her child. None of the sample indicated that their children would be reared at public expense in event of their disability.

The mothers were almost evenly divided on the question of whether their parents or siblings would raise the child differently. Forty-three percent of the

TABLE 9:3

t-Test of Socioeconomic Status Differences of the Children's Total Thomas Self Concept Scores

And the Thomas Sub-Scores

Factor		Number	Mean	Standard Deviation	t	df	p
Thomas' Self Concept Standard Score	Upper Class	18	53.72	8.78	1.26	33.78*	n.s.
	Middle Class	21	49.00	14.30			
Self	Upper Class	18	51.11	7.05	0.73	32.75*	n.s.
	Middle Class	21	51.81	12.22			
Mother	Upper Class	18	54.39	9.04	1.21	33.78*	n.s.
	Middle Class	21	49.71	14.72			
Father	Upper Class	18	54.06	5.88	0.98	28.72*	n.s.
	Middle Class	21	50.95	13.03			
Teacher	Upper Class	18	53.05	8.69	0.80	36.02*	n.s.
	Middle Class	21	50.30	12.07			
Peer	Upper Class	18	51.39	12.84	1.35	36.87*	n.s.
	Middle Class	21	45.14	15.98			

*Separate variance estimates.

145

mothers felt that their kin would raise their children differently, and 38 percent said that their kin would raise the children in the same manner. About 19 percent were not sure if their kin would raise the children any differently.

In summary, the black mothers in this sample present themselves as being moderately strict and perceived themselves as much less strict with their children than their parents were with them. On one hand, they expected their instructions to be obeyed by their children, on the other they were generally more tolerant of misbehavior on the part of their children. They fully expected their kin to care for their children in the case of death or disability, and the overriding decision of which kin seemed to be more related to questions of financial ability and health than to similarity in patterns of discipline. Several mothers commented that their parents are much less strict with their children than they were with them. Others commented that they felt their parents might spoil their children. The brothers and sisters were presented as being on the same general socioeconomic level with them and would be more in tune with the expectations of children of that level.

SUMMARY

Our purpose was to explore the types, frequency, and amounts of verbal and nonverbal interaction that takes place between a working mother and her child and to note the relationship between that interaction and the self-esteem of the child. The black mothers were found to be verbally nurturant with their children. They were warm and loving and attempted to meet the child's needs as expressed by the child or as the mother's perception of need. There were no significant differences between the upper and lower middle-class mothers in their verbal and nonverbal interaction patterns.

The black mothers in this sample appear to handle the roles of wife, mother, and worker fairly well when we take into consideration the quality of their relationships with their children. The interaction patterns observed wei warm, firm, and loving, and devoid of conflict. While no direct relationship was found between self-esteem or social competency and interaction patterns, the high self-esteem of the children would suggest that the mothers in this sample, regardless of socioeconomic status or their employment, are effectively carrying out their mother role.

The middle-income mothers of preschool children in the sample interacted with their parents and siblings by telephone on a regular basis and appeared to be involved positively in the kin network exchange (McAdoo, H., 1976). Many of them sent their children to stay with relatives during holidays and vacations when they had to work. They expected their kin to help them and did not feel that the type of discipline and control used by relatives was significantly different from their own. The patterns of mutual obligation-expectation found in extended family patterns with older children were also found in this study (McAdoo, H., 1976).

Thirty-five of the 40 middle-income mothers were working to supplement the family income. Our data suggest that there is little evidence of role strains related to their three roles. This suggests that they were able to compartmentalize the different roles effectively. Because of the geographical closeness of their kin, they have been able to use the kin network system to lessen inter-role tensions. They seem to be able to discuss work strains with their kin and friends and send children for weekend visits to alleviate parenting tensions.

While no direct relationship was found between parental interaction and self-esteem, it was obvious that the preschool children felt good about themselves as a group. Upper middle-income children felt slightly more positive about themselves than lower middle-income children. All of the children felt that significant others—mother, father, teacher, and peers—valued them highly. Perhaps a different measure is needed to correlate the warm, loving, fairly firm interaction patterns between mothers and children, the way the children feel about themselves, and the way they view significant others perceiving them.

One implication of the study is that mothers who are not under severe economic or social pressure are able to handle their various inter-role functions adequately. These preschool mothers used the kin network system to control inter-role strain. It might be informative to compare differential methods for combating inter-role strain to determine their effectiveness. One study might compare the use of kin network versus use of fictive kin versus use of social agencies in reducing inter-role conflict.

We need to study the extreme points of role strain on the mother to determine at what point inter-role strain becomes too much for the mother and her kinship system to handle effectively. This could help us to determine if Harrison (1976) is right in suggesting that the wife role becomes the first casualty. It is just as reasonable for us to suspect that it is the role of worker, particularly in those families in which the conflict is over the wife working, that is most vulnerable. This type of research would be most valuable in planning programs related to resolving inter-role stress in working mothers.

As a result of our study, it is reasonable for us to believe that any mother, single or married, who has relative economic sufficiency, provided by either her own or wider family network resources, and who has made the adjustments to her roles of provider, mother, wife, and worker, will have positive interaction patterns with her children. Further, the children will develop a sense of self-worth and feel that they are highly valued by relevant others in their community.

Most of the mothers were working to supplement the family income. They seem to be able to handle the roles of wife, mother, and worker. Because of the employment responsibilities that took them away from home for long periods of the day, these mothers appeared more tolerant of misbehavior in their children. However, even they set firm limits as to behavior.

Finally, we utilized only one aspect of the ecological approach, a participant observation in the naturalistic setting of the home. It is important that we be able to observe the extended kin and community network systems and the degree to which other institutions impinge upon the family to cause internal strains. In this way we can help the single-parent mother to develop ways of avoiding some of the strains in her various roles and to determine that aspect of her community that can be used most effectively in alleviating such strains.

The results of this study should go a long way toward dispelling the negative myths about black mothers in the child development literature. This study indicates that when race and sex of the interviewer and social class are controlled and black mothers are interviewed in a naturalized setting, they have the same kinds of relationships with their children as mothers of other ethnic groups.

REFERENCES

Asher, S., and A. Allen. "Racial Preference and Social Comparison Processes," *Journal of Social Issues*, 1969, 25(1), 157–166.

Baldwin, C. "Comparison of Mother-Child Interaction at Different Ages and in Families, Different Educational Levels, Ethnic Backgrounds," Paper presented at annual meeting of Society for Research in Child Development, Philadelphia, Penn., 1973.

Baumrind, D. "Current Patterns of Parental Authority," *Developmental Psychology Monographs*, 1971, 4(1), Part 2.

Biller, H. B. *Father, Child and Sex Role*. Lexington, Mass.: Heath Lexington Books, 1971.

Blanchard, R. W., and H. B. Biller. "Father Availability and Academic Performance among Third-Grade Boys," *Developmental Psychology*, 1971, 4, 301–305.

Bronfenbrenner, U. "Social Change: The Challenge to Research and Policy," Paper presented to the Society for Research in Child Development, annual meeting, April, 1975.

———— . Paper presented to American Ortho Psychiatric Association, Washington, D.C., 1975.

Clark, K. "Racial Identity and Preference in Young Children," In E. E. Macoby, et al. (eds) *Readings in Social Psychology*. New York: Holt & Co., 1952.

———— , and M. Clark. "The Development of Consciousness of Self and the Emergence of Racial Identification in Negro Preschool Children," *Journal of Social Psychology*, 1939, 10, 591–599.

Dyk, R. B., and H. Witkin. "Family Experiences Related to the Development of Differentiation in Children," *Child Development*, 1965, 36, 21–55.

Fagot, B. I. "Sex Differences in Toddlers' Behavior and Parental Reaction," *Developmental Psychology*, 1974, 10(4), 554–558.

Fox, D. and U. Barnes. "Racial Preference and Identification of Blacks, Chinese and White Children," Paper presented at the American Educational Research Association meeting, New York, N.Y., 1971.

Goodman, M. *Race Attitudes in Young Children*. Cambridge, Mass.: Addison-Wesley, 1952.

Harrison, A., and J. H. Minor. "In Role Conflict, Coping Strategies, and Role Satisfaction among Black Working Wives," *Journal of Marriage and the Family*,
1978, 40, 799–805.

Helbrun, A. E. "An Empirical Test of the Modeling Theory of Sex Role Learning,"
Child Development, 1965, 36, 789–799.

Hess, R. D., et al. *The Cognitive Environments of Urban Preschool Children*.
Chicago: The University of Chicago Graduate School of Education, 1968.

Hollander, M., and D. Wolfe. *Nonparametric Statistical Methods*. New York: John
Wiley & Sons, 1973.

Horowitz, R. "Racial Aspects of Self-Identity in Nursery School Children," *Journal of
Psychology*, 1939, 1, 91–99.

Hraba, J., and J. Grant. "Black is Beautiful: A Reexamination of Racial Preference
and Identification," *Journal of Personality and Social Psychology*, 1970, 16(3),
398–402.

Kagan, J. "The Concept of Identification," *Psychology Review*, 1972, 6, 396–405.

Lamb, D. B. *The Role of the Father in Child Development*. New York: John Wiley &
Sons, 1976.

Lipscomb, L. "Parental Influences in the Development of Black Children's Racial
Self-Esteem," Paper presented at the American Sociological Meeting, San
Francisco, Calif., 1975.

Lynn, D. B. *The Father: His Role in Child Development*. Monterey, Calif.: Brooks-
Cole Publishing Co., 1975.

Lytton, H. "Three Approaches to the Study of Parent-Child Interactions," *Journal of
Child Psychology and Psychiatry*, 1973, 14, 1–17.

Macoby, E. E., and H. Levin. *Patterns of Childrearing*. Evanston, Ill.: Row Peterson
& Co., 1957.

McAdoo, H. "The Socialization of Black Children: Priorities for Research." In L. E.
Gary (ed) *Social Research and the Black Community: Selected Issues and
Priorities*. Washington, D.C.: Howard University Institute for Urban Affairs
and Research, 1974, pp. 66–75.

——— . "A Reexamination of the Relationship between Self-Concept and Racial
Attitudes of Young Black Children," Given at conference on Demythologizing
the Inner City Child, Atlanta, Georgia State University, 1976a.

——— . "Factors Related to Stability in Upwardly Mobile Black Families," *Journal of
Marriage and the Family*, 1978, 40(4), 80–99.

——— . "The Development of Self-Concept and Race Attitudes of Young Black
Children Over Time," Given at conference on Empirical Research in Black
Psychology, III, Ithaca, New York, Cornell University, 1976b.

McAdoo, J. "An Exploratory Study of Racial Attitude Change in Black Preschool
Children, Using Differential Treatment," *Dissertation Abstracts International*,
1970 and Ph.D. diss., University of Michigan, 1970 (University Microfilms
No. 71-4678).

——— . "The Relationship between Black Father-Child Interaction and Self-Esteem
in Preschool Children," Given Conference on Empirical Research in Black
Psychology, III, Ithaca, New York, Cornell University, 1976.

Moynihan, D. *The Negro Family: The Case for National Action*. Prepared for Office
of Policy Planning and Research, 1965.

Radin, N. "Father-Child Interaction and the Intellectual Function of 4-Year-Old-Boys," *Developmental Psychology*, 1972, 6, 353–361.

_____ . "Maternal Warmth, Achievement Motivation and Cognitive Functioning in Lower Class Preschool Children," *Child Development*, 1971, 42(5), 1561–1565.

_____ ."Observed Paternal Behavior with Preschool Children," Final report, National Institute of Child Health and Human Development Grant, 1975.

_____ , and H. Sonquist. *The Gale Preschool Program: Final Report*. Ypsilanti, Mich.: Ypsilanti Public Schools, 1968.

Sears, P. S. "Child Rearing Factors Related to Playing of Sex-Typed Roles," *American Psychologist*, 1953, 8, 431.

Thomas, W. *The Thomas Self-Concept Values Test*. Grand Rapids, Mich.: Project on Student Values, 1967.

Ward, S., and J. Braun. Self-Esteem and Racial Preference in Black Children," *American Journal of Orthopsychiatry*, 1972, 42(4), 64–74.

White, B., and J. Watts. *Experience and Environment*. Englewood Cliffs, N.J.: Prentice-Hall, 1973.

Yarrow, R. R. "Problems of Methodology: A Parent-Child Research," *Child Development*, 1963, 34, 215–226.

10

BLACK FAMILY DESIGN

Castellano B. Turner and William A. Darity

The purpose of this chapter is to discuss some issues related to the process of family formation among contemporary black American couples. First, we will place the behavior of blacks into both a historical and a contemporary context. Next, we will review briefly the salient theory and research that attempts to explain variations in patterns of black fertility in the United States. Finally, we will describe a research project that provides a partial test of some current theories concerning black fertility.

The process of family design in the United States has for some time been closely tied to family planning and birth control usage. For that matter, the present population policy of the United States government is largely built around and limited to support for voluntary planning. In spite of the panic generated by Ehrlich's (1968) description of the impending national and international crisis of the "population bomb," no clear direction has been provided for responding to the "crisis." As we indicated in a previous report, most population policy proposals that have surfaced in recent years are unacceptable to ethnic minority groups because they focus solutions on the poor and minority groups (Turner and Darity, 1975). However, as Ehrlich (1970) pointed out, it is affluent whites who have contributed most to the problems of population growth, including heavy pollution and excessive consumption of limited resources.

Part of the difficulty in developing adequate population policy stems from the fact that social scientists have met with little success in explaining reproductive behavior among either blacks or whites (Taeuber and Taeuber, 1966). In a recent report from the Institute for Social Research at the University of

The research upon which this chapter is based was supported by a grant from the National Institute of Child Health and Human Development, No. HD05325.

Michigan (*ISR Newsletter*, 1978), it is made clear that we have relatively meager insight into *why* people have children. Rainwater (1965), in his now classic *Family Design*, provided an important beginning for finding some of the answers, but the book is itself a testament to the difficulty involved in determining the origins of the desire for children. We believe that clarity has been especially elusive when considering black Americans.

BLACK AMERICANS, BIRTH CONTROL, AND POPULATION POLICY

Among the many critical dilemmas that have surfaced in the recent debate over population policy is one that faces black Americans in particular. This dilemma involves the issue of whether birth control and family planning programs are a new form of black genocide. On the one hand, there is a clear and widely understood connection between the capacity to partake of American affluence and the judicious limitation of family size (Davies, 1967; Jaffe, 1964; and Lipson and Wolman, 1972). Moreover, contraceptive technology has made possible the disconnection of sexual activity from fertility. On the other hand, during the last 15 years there has been a growing fear among blacks that sinister motives lay behind the larger white society's interest in population stabilization and its new enthusiasm for making birth control technology readily available in black communities (Kammeyer et al., 1975 and Willie, 1971). Still, there has been no consensus among blacks about the genocidal implications of birth control programs; there have been black men and women, radicals and conservatives, on both sides of the question. The history of the debate and the basis for the fears have been reviewed by Weisbord (1973). One important question remaining, however, is whether identification with one's minority group status (i.e., race consciousness) and such genocide fears have an impact on the fertility-related behavior of blacks.

SOME HISTORICAL BACKGROUND

In the past, family planning programmers have given relatively little consideration to the historical origins of blacks' sensitivity concerning family limitation (Turner, 1979). One of the defining characteristics of slavery in the United States was that slaves were considered property. As such, slaves were widely treated like breeding stock. Matings were often arranged and terminated based on the financial interests or the whim of the slave owner. Sometimes slave women were even rewarded for producing a large number of children, who were routinely sold off. Autonomous decisions about family formation and family size were a rare privilege for slaves. Sexuality and procreation were also controlled at times by means of punitive castration (Population Reference Bureau, 1975).

External control of black fertility did not end with slavery. Involuntary sterilization began to be sanctioned around the turn of the twentieth century for state prisoners, and the burden of such sterilizations fell heavily on blacks. Sterilization as a method of punishment and control in prisons and state hospitals developed fully by the 1930s, and the percentage of blacks sterilized involuntarily was greater than for whites. Repugnant as this history may seem to most, there are still some whites who continue to support such practices (Paul, 1968 and Morrison, 1965). Such longstanding external exploitation and brutal control of black individuals and black families by whites in this fundamental area of life must be considered the background for current concerns about black family size limitation, especially if dictated, even indirectly, by the population policies of the white majority.

RECENT BLACK-WHITE FERTILITY DIFFERENTIALS

Two questions about recent black fertility patterns have received attention from social scientists. First, why does overall black fertility continue to be higher than white fertility—2.44 to 1.80, respectively (U.S. Bureau of the Census, 1974)? This fertility differential is strongest at the lower socioeconomic status level. Second, why do college-educated black women have *lower* fertility rates than white women of the same educational level? These questions can be answered in part by a brief review of relevant research and theoretical formulations. This literature has focused primarily on three determinant variables: social class, especially education; geographical region; and psychological variables, especially values and attitudes.

Education

For both black and white women, fertility level is closely related to educational attainment (U.S. Bureau of the Census, 1973). Since blacks are overrepresented at the low end of the educational attainment scale, it would seem reasonable to infer that educational attainment can account for the black-white fertility differentials. Upon closer inspection of the census data, however, it becomes clear that education per se does not account for the black-white fertility differentials, since black women with an education below the twelfth grade have significantly higher fertility than white women matched for level of education (Roach et al., 1967).

When education and other socioeconomic strata indices are controlled, and black-white differentials remain, the alternative explanations have gravitated around the notion of a "culture of poverty" (Jaffe and Polgar, 1968). We believe, however, that such complex explanations are not yet required, since there has been an erroneous assumption routinely applied in the analysis of education as a determinant. This assumption is that the school-recorded educational attainment level (grades completed) has the same meaning for blacks and whites in the United States. Once stated, it becomes obvious that such an assumption contradicts the facts. Clark (1965), among others, has demonstrated that the *quality* of education provided to blacks in this country is on the whole substantially lower than that provided to whites. What is the mechanism by which education might influence fertility? Let us suppose that low educational attainment increases fertility because of decreased opportunity to gain, for example, information about human physiology and general planning skills. Black women might be assumed, therefore, to be leaving school with less information and fewer problem-solving skills than white women of the same recorded educational attainment, especially at the lowest levels of attainment. By way of support for this formulation, several researchers have remarked upon the "substantial ignorance" concerning reproductive physiology among black interviewees (Beasley et al., 1966 and Kantner and Zelnick, 1969). In reading such reports, one gets a clear sense of the authors' surprise. Our interpretation assumes that the black-white differentials in fertility may still be based on educational level, because black educational attainment is actually lower than that of whites with the same recorded attainment. One method for testing this assumption would call for using standardized school achievement scores rather than grades completed to match blacks and whites. If education defined in terms of knowledge and skills gained is the determinant variable, then the black-white differential should disappear when blacks and whites are matched on standard achievement measures.

A related line of research focuses on lack of "access" to family planning techniques as the major basis for current fertility differentials (Hill and Jaffe, 1971). Such researchers tend to see lack of adequate education as one form of limited access. However, access problems are also directly related to poverty, e.g., prohibitive distances and costs for services to the poor. Such research reports tend to be antagonistic toward the notion of "culture of poverty" as an explanation for high fertility and low birth control effectiveness (Bogue, 1969; Reissman, 1968; and Jaffe and Polgar, 1968). One major argument is that there are relatively small differences by race and socioeconomic strata on such questions as ideal and desired number of children, whereas there are significant differences on expected and actual fertility. The implication is that the differences would disappear if people could be helped to get what they really desire.

Geographic Region

In all of the attempts in the literature to explain the differential in black-white fertility rates, we know of none that claims that *race* (as such) causes the differences. Race is, however, demonstrably related to a number of the demographic and socio-psychological variables that relate to fertility levels. Being from the rural South is related to higher fertility rates for both blacks and whites, but, just as in the case of educational attainment, blacks have been proportionately over-represented in the rural South. Research has indicated that black women from Southern rural backgrounds not only show higher fertility than other groups (Farley, 1970 and Ritchey, 1973), but also report less knowledge and use of contraceptive techniques (Westoff and Ryder, 1965). This regional difference holds even when education is controlled. We are not aware of any systematic research attempts to specify the meaning of this relationship. Those who have reported this pattern discuss it primarily in terms of the more gradual shift from traditional values in isolated farm areas and in terms of continuing economic benefits that accrue from having many children on farms. Urban couples are faced with substantially lower family size norms, so that these couples rarely have large families to gain potential economic benefits (Rainwater, 1965).

Psychological Determinants

There has been considerable theorizing and some research on psychological factors involved in fertility control. Some writers maintain that there are strong and long-standing *values* in connection with family life and procreation among black Americans, and that such values might explain differential fertility. Murray (1977), in particular, suggests that important basic needs and values are expressed by blacks in the process of procreation —e.g., survival, power, and freedom. Staples (1971) believes that black women prize the creativity of giving birth and caring for young. Scanzoni (1977) places a somewhat more cynical interpretation on the same observed behavior. He sees procreation as an "alternative" means of personal expression and achievement used by blacks who are blocked from satisfying participation in the occupational opportunity structure. He used the observation of low fertility in college-educated black women as an example: i.e., when black women have access to educational and occupational opportunities they are less likely to seek such "alternatives" as producing children in order to make life meaningful. Johnson (1979) modifies this interpretation by suggesting that simple acceptance into the opportunity structure would not in itself lead to *lower* fertility among blacks. It is the lack of structural assimilation of minority group members, she reasons, that requires greater sacrifices of child-centered behavior from upwardly mobile black women.

The influence of identifying with one's minority group status itself on fertility rates is difficult to discern. (We have chosen to discuss "minority group status" as a psychological variable here because there have been a number of studies linking certain social-psychological attitudes to identification with one's minority group status). It is certainly possible that individuals could make decisions to have more children for political reasons. Goldscheider and Uhlenberg (1969) found support for the influence of minority group status in determining fertility across a number of ethnic minority groups in the United States, including blacks. Kennedy (1973) also found some support for this relationship in Northern Ireland, although religion and other factors were more important in determining fertility. Johnson (1979), however, found no support in her analyses that minority group status has an independent influence on black fertility in the United States.

There have been a number of studies on attitudes conceptually related to minority group status and aspects of fertility and family planning. Groat and Neal (1967), for example, found that alienation level was related to fertility. We have previously reported that race consciousness level was found to relate positively to desired number of children in a sample of New England blacks (Turner and Darity, 1971). Fears of black genocide have been found to be related negatively to the use of family planning methods (Darity and Turner, 1972 and Farrell and Dawkins, 1979). The major implication of these attitude studies is that the sentiments of blacks about their situation in the United States may indirectly cause an increase in fertility.

THE RESEARCH PROJECT

In this section we will use data from a large-scale interview study of black Americans to test the relationships of the three explanatory variables discussed in the previous section under education, geographical region, and psychological determinants, to two aspects of family planning: *ideal* family size and *actual* family size. As Kennedy (1973) has pointed out, there is particular value and importance in doing comparisons between segments of an ethnic minority group. When testing the differences between fertility of Catholics and Protestants in Northern Ireland, any differences found could be a function of religion rather than minority group status of the Catholic population. The solution he found was to compare the fertility of Irish Catholics in a location where they were a majority with those in a location where they were a minority. This effectively controls the influence of religion, which is known to influence fertility. Similarly, by comparing subgroups of blacks who differ from each other on variables that are hypothesized to relate to fertility, we are essentially controlling the influence of race. This approach, of course, would not readily control the influences stemming from interactions of race with other variables. For example, being a black person in an area where there are very few other blacks may well lead to experiences different from someone living with large numbers of blacks nearby. (As will be seen, this particular influence has been controlled in the study to be described).

The literature we reviewed suggests the following three hypotheses, which are testable in our data:

1.   Blacks with low educational attainment will report higher ideal and
     actual family sizes than blacks with high educational attainment.

2.   Blacks living in the South will report higher ideal and actual family
     sizes than blacks living in the North. The reader should note that the
     literature has most often identified specifically "southern *rural*
     background" as most clearly relating to higher fertility. The analysis
     presented here is, in effect, a conservative test of the difference that
     geographical region makes in fertility behavior. If we find signifi-
     cant differences between blacks in the two urban areas (one in the
     North and one in the South), one could reasonably conclude that a
     comparison of northern urban with southern rural blacks would
     show at least as much difference. The characteristics of the South
     and of rural areas that might influence fertility would be similar and
     would have a cumulative effect.

3.   Blacks who respond to attitude items in a direction suggesting
     higher race consciousness and/or genocide fears will report higher
     ideal and actual family sizes than blacks not responding in such a
     direction. The items in our attitude item pool tapping such senti-
     ments all identify blacks as the relevant population. We are assum-
     ing that this, in itself, makes these items relevant to "race
     consciousness". Likewise, the items all have direct or indirect rele-
     vance to the issue of "genocide fears."

Method

Sample. In this study we sampled 1,000 black households with the goal of
interviewing female-male partners. The final sample of usable interviews was
1,890. The two cities where the respondents lived were Philadelphia, Pennsyl-
vania, and Charlotte, North Carolina. These cities were chosen for three
reasons: (1) they are geographically diverse, i.e., north and south; (2) they both
have large and socioeconomically diverse populations (since both cities have
approximately 30 percent blacks, the issue of variation in the density of the
ethnic minority population, discussed earlier, was effectively controlled); and
(3) they share with many other American cities certain characteristics and
problems.
   The sampling procedure began with the identification of communities
which, according to census data, were composed of at least 50 percent blacks.
Using United States census reports, each community was placed into one of
two categories, based on the average income of its residents: low socioeconomic status or middle to high status. Street lists were then used to produce a
stratified random sample of 60 percent from the low status communities and
40 percent from the middle to high socioeconomic status communities. Next,

households were chosen from the street lists by means of a computerized random sampling procedure.

Interview procedure. In each selected household, a female between 15 and 44 years of age was contacted. Arrangements were made to interview her and her most significant male partner (usually her husband, but if she was single, divorced, or widowed, then her boyfriend). When male partners were available, a male-female interviewing team entered the home together and conducted simultaneous interviews in different parts of the residence. This procedure was followed to ensure noncontamination of responses by partners.

In addition to demographic information, the interview schedule included questions on many different aspects of family planning—knowledge, attitudes, and practices. Among the attitude items were several intended to reflect race consciousness and genocide fears.

Results

The dependent variables in this analysis were: (1) ideal number of children, based on the question "How many children would you say makes the best family size?" and (2) actual number of children, based on the question "How many children do you have?" Follow-up questions were used to clarify the meaning, e.g., not adopted, etc.

Table 10:1 presents the results of analyses relating education to ideal and actual numbers of children. The comparisons of the two levels of education were done for males and females separately as well as for the combined sample. (This method of presentation will be followed throughout the remaining tables.) The pattern of the table follows consistently what one would expect based on previous reports in the literature. Throughout Table 10:1, it is the group with the lower educational attainment that shows the largest percentages in the "3 or more" category. This is true for the ideal, but clearly the differences between the educational level groups are not great, and the only comparison that shows a statistically significant difference is for females and males combined. The picture is very different when the comparison focuses on the actual number of children. Obviously, educational level is highly related to fertility in this sample. The first hypothesis, we conclude, has received strong support. Based on these data, it seems that blacks with less education are more likely to have "3 or more" children than are more educated blacks.

Table 10:2 reveals a similar pattern. The relationship between geographical region and ideal number of children is, however, even weaker and inconsistent, and there are no significant differences for either sex of the combined group. The relationship between region and actual number of children is significant both for males and females separately and for the sexes combined.

TABLE 10:1

Percent Reporting Ideal and Actual Number of Children in Family As "3 or

more" As Related to Education, Controlling For Sex

| Variable | Sex | Education | | Chi-Square |
		Less than High School Graduation	High School or More	
Ideal Number of Children	Male	65.9	59.4	3.58
	Female	60.9	57.0	1.38
	Combined	63.3	58.1	5.00*
Actual Number of Children	Male	33.9	22.1	14.65**
	Female	39.3	22.6	32.09**
	Combined	36.6	22.4	54.39**

*p < .05

**p < .001

Again, this finding provides strong support for the hypothesis and is consistent with past research. It appears from these data that blacks who reside in the South are much more likely to have "3 or more" children than blacks living in the North.

Table 10:3 presents the results of the analyses relating each of six attitude items to ideal number of children. As was noted earlier, we regard each of the items as reflecting both "race consciousness" and "genocide fear." All of the items identify concerns about black Americans, and each bears on some aspect of family planning or population control. An inspection of the table suggests some moderate support for the third hypothesis. Three of the six items show statistical significance for at least one of the sex groups. It should also be noted that, with the exception of the female group on item 3, the pattern of the relationship is consistent throughout, i.e., those with larger family size ideals are more inclined to agree with these statements. This finding fits our expectations based on existing literature. In this sample, those blacks who have particular concerns about racial survival and are fearful that survival is threatened by birth control programs believe that having more children is a good idea. They may be saying that having more children is the appropriate method to counter the threat. These items may, on the other

TABLE 10:2

Percent Reporting Ideal and Actual Number of Children in Family As "3 or

more" As Related to Region, Controlling For Sex

Variable	Sex	Region		Chi-
		North	South	Square
Ideal Number of Children	Male	62.8	60.2	.24
	Female	57.9	62.0	.86
	Combined	60.2	61.2	.07
Actual Number of Children	Male	25.8	38.3	8.30*
	Female	27.7	38.6	7.96*
	Combined	26.8	38.5	17.05**

*$p < .01$

**$p < .001$

hand, reflect a generally alienated stance toward the larger society, and that also would likely relate to a tendency to follow subgroup norms (rather than those of the larger society) in producing children.

The one item showing significance for the female group mentions "birth control clinics." Since women are the ones most often involved in such clinics, it is not surprising that the item appears to be more salient for them. An inspection of the two items on which the males show significant differences by size of ideal family reveals that both items suggest a directive for blacks to have more children. The black males are, at least, consistent in their attitudes.

When we move from attitudes to behavior, however, the pattern shifts considerably. Table 10:4 presents the analyses relating actual number of children to the six items. It is immediately st..ing that the number of significant differences has dropped to one, i.e., for the females on item 1, which was the only one for which they showed significance on the ideal number of children. This suggests that the pattern for women is consistent between ideals and behavior. Not only are women who have concerns about whites running birth control programs in black communities more inclined to see ideal family size as larger, they are also more likely to have produced more children.

TABLE 10:3

Percent Agreement with "Race Consciousness" and "Genocide" Items As Related

to Ideal Number of Children, Controlling Respondent Sex

| Item | Sex | Ideal Number of Children | | Chi-Square |
		2 or less	3 or more	
1. Birth Control Clinics in Black neighborhoods should be operated by Blacks	Male	59.3	63.7	1.50
	Female	50.5	57.5	4.50*
	Combined	54.3	60.4	6.76**
2. Black families should not limit their sizes	Male	35.7	43.8	2.54*
	Female	27.6	31.7	1.78
	Combined	31.1	37.5	7.82**
3. As the need for cheap labor goes down there will be an effort to reduce the number of Blacks	Male	46.2	49.6	.84
	Female	58.7	52.3	3.71
	Combined	53.1	51.0	.69
4. As Blacks become more militant there will be an effort to decrease the Black population	Male	59.7	63.2	.92
	Female	64.3	64.3	.00
	Combined	62.1	63.8	.44
5. The survival of Black people depends on increasing the number of Black births	Male	50.0	59.3	6.83**
	Female	50.6	52.3	.21
	Combined	50.3	55.7	5.04*
6. Birth control programs are a plot to eliminate Blacks	Male	37.8	44.5	3.54
	Female	37.3	37.9	.02
	Combined	37.4	41.1	2.33

*p $<$ .05

**p $<$ .01

TABLE 10:4

Percent Agreement with "Race Consciousness" and "Genocide" Items as Related

to Actual Number of Children, Controlling Respondent Sex

| Item | Sex | Actual Number of Children | | Chi-Square |
		2 or less	3 or more	
1. Birth Control Clinics in Black neighborhoods should be operated by Blacks	Male	62.4	60.9	.11
	Female		60.9	6.43**
	Combined	56.8	60.9	6.76**
2. Black families should not limit their sizes	Male	39.6	43.8	1.14
	Female	28.5	33.6	2.28
	Combined	33.7	38.1	3.10
3. As the need for cheap labor goes down there will be an effort to feduce the number of Blacks	Male	50.2	43.6	2.77
	Female	55.8	53.0	.53
	Combined	53.1	48.8	2.65
4. As Blacks become more militant there will be an effort to decrease the Black population	Male	63.1	58.5	1.41
	Female	63.2	66.9	1.08
	Combined	63.1	63.1	.00
5. The survival of Black people depends on increasing the number of Black births	Male	55.0	57.9	.45
	Female	49.7	56.0	3.10
	Combined	52.2	56.9	3.15
6. Birth control programs are a plot to eliminate Blacks	Male	43.9	37.2	2.94
	Female	37.4	38.4	.06
	Combined	40.4	37.8	.93

*p < .05

**p < .01

Closer inspection of the table also reveals considerable inconsistency in the pattern of differences. Actual number of children seems to be unrelated to the attitudes of "race consciousness" and "genocide fear," especially among the males in the study. We conclude that the hypothesis relating actual number of children to attitudes finds very little support in these data.

CONCLUSIONS AND IMPLICATIONS

The findings of the research reported here provide support for some of the current theories about black American fertility. Educational attainment did make considerable difference in determining actual fertility levels. The relationship of education to ideal family size was minimal. Many of the studies reviewed in this chapter have indicated that poor black women do not want more children than do other groups, but they have continued to give birth to more children (Bogue, 1969 and Jaffe, 1964). In our data also, education was much more powerful in its relationship to actual numbers of children than to ideals. The implication of such a finding is that increasing educational opportunities of poor blacks and other poor people in the country would probably lead to an overall drop in fertility for these groups and for the country as a whole. Unfortunately, quite a different stance is often taken regarding the fertility of the under-educated. They are blamed for having children even though society has withheld the tools that could help in limiting family size. Moreover, for those who have little and have been kept out of the mainstream of American affluence, children may indeed be among the few sources of personal satisfaction and a sense of accomplishment available.

The findings concerning the importance of geographical region are also consistent with past research. As noted earlier, comparisons of blacks in two urban areas is a conservative test of the impact of region. The sample was controlled for urbanity and race. The fact that blacks in a northern and a southern city showed little difference in their ideal family size but striking difference in their actual fertility suggests that fertility trends are likely to change in the future. As in the case of differences by education or other socioeconomic status indicators, regional differences in actual fertility are likely to gradually disappear because norms are essentially the same. It is only the wherewithal to reach goals that has not been available equally to all.

We must conclude that our data provide little indication that "race consciousness" and "genocide fears" relate substantially to actual fertility. Since such attitudes relate more positively to the ideal family size, policy makers may have considerable need for concern. If the well-being of black Americans continues to be threatened by racism and unequal opportunity, some blacks may see a push for higher black birth rates as the only strategy for survival.

REFERENCES

Beasley, J. D., et al. "Attitudes and Knowledge Relevant to Family Planning among New Orleans Negro Women," *American Journal of Public Health*, 1966, 56(November) 1847–57.

Bogue, D. J. "Family Planning in the Negro Ghettos of Chicago," Paper presented at the Milbank Conference on Negro Population, New York, 1969.

Clark, K. B. *Dark Ghetto: Dilemmas of Power*. New York: Harper & Row Publishers, 1965.

Davies, V. "Fertility Versus Welfare: The Negro American Dilemma," *Phylon*, 1967, 27(3), 226–232.

Ehrlich, P. *The Population Bomb*. New York: Ballantine Books, 1968.

————. "The Population Crisis: Where We Stand," *Bulletin of the Field Museum of Natural History*, 1970, 41, 2–9.

Farley, R. "Fertility among Urban Blacks," *The Milbank Memorial Fund Quarterly*, 1970, 43(2), 183–206.

Goldscheider, C., and P. R. Uhlenberg. "Minority Group Status and Fertility," *American Journal of Sociology*, 1969, 74(4), 361–372.

Groat, H. T., and A. G. Neal. "Social Psychological Correlates of Urban Fertility," *American Sociological Review*, 1967, 32, 945–959.

Hill, A. C., and F. S. Jaffe. "Negro Fertility and Family Size Preferences— Implications for Programming of Health and Social Services," In R. Staples (ed) *The Black Family*. Belmont, Calif.: Wadsworth Publishing Co., 1971.

ISR Newsletter, "The Value of Children: Why Couples Choose Parenthood," August, 1978, pp.3+ (Institute for Social Research, University of Michigan, Ann Arbor).

Jaffe, F. S. "Family Planning and Poverty," *Journal of Marriage and the Family*, 1964, 26(4), 467–470.

————, and S. Polgar. "Family Planning and Public Policy," *Journal of Marriage and the Family*, 1968, 30(2), 228–235.

Johnson, N. "Minority-Group Status and Fertility of Black Americans, 1970: A New Look," *American Journal of Sociology*, 1979, 84(6), 1386–1400.

Kammeyer, K.C.W., et al. "Family Planning and the Distribution of Black Americans," In N. R. Yetman and C. H. Steele (eds) *Majority and Minority*. Boston: Allyn & Bacon, 1975.

Kantner, J., and M. Zelnick. "United States: Exploratory Studies of Negro Family Formation—Common Conceptions about Birth Control," *Studies In Family Planning*, November, 1969.

Kennedy, R. E. "Minority Group Status and Fertility: The Irish," *American Sociological Review*, 1973, 38, 85–96.

Lipson, G., and D. Wolman. "Polling Americans on Birth Control and Population," *Family Planning Perspectives*, 1972, 4, 39–42.

Morrison, J. L. "Illegitimacy, Sterilization and Racism: A North Carolina Case History," *Social Service Review*, 1965, 39(1), 1–10.

Murray, R. F. "The Ethical and Moral Values of Black Americans and Population Policy," In R. M. Veatch (ed) *Population Policy and Ethics: The American Experience*. New York: Halsted Press, 1977.

Paul, J. "The Return of Punitive Sterilization Proposals: Current Attacks on Illegitimacy and the AFDC Program," *Law and Society Review*, 1968, 3(1), 77–106.

Population Reference Bureau. "Family Size and the Black American," *Population Bulletin*, 1975, 30, 4.

Rainwater, L. *Family Design: Marital Sexuality, Family Size, and Contraception.* Chicago: Aldine, 1965.

Reissman, C. K. "Birth Control, Culture and the Poor," *American Journal of Orthopsychiatry*, 1968, 38(4), 693–699.

Ritchey, P. N. "The Fertility of Negroes without Southern Rural Experience: A Reexamination of the 1960 GAF Findings with 1967 SEO Data," *Population Studies*, 1973, 27, 134.

Roach, J. L., et al. "The Effects of Race and Socioeconomic Status on Family Planning, "*Journal of Health and Social Behavior*, 1967, 8(1), 40–45.

Scanzoni, J. H. *The Black Family in Modern Society.* Chicago: University of Chicago Press, 1977.

Staples, R. "Toward a Sociology of the Black Family: A Theoretical and Methodological Assessment," *Journal of Marriage and the Family*, 1971, 33, 119–138.

Taeuber, K. E., and A. F. Taeuber. "The Negro Population in the United States," In J. P. Davis (ed) *The American Negro Reference Book*. Englewood Cliffs, N.J.: Prentice-Hall, 1966.

Turner, C. B. "Black Americans, Family Planning, and Population Policy," Invited address to the Margaret Sanger Centennial Conference, Smith College, Northampton, Mass., 1979.

————, and W. A. Darity. "Fears of Genocide among Black Americans as Related to Age, Sex and Region," *American Journal of Public Health*, 1973, 63(12), 1024–1034.

U.S. Bureau of the Census. "Women by Number of Children Ever Born," *Subject Reports*, Final Report PC(2)-3A, Washington, D.C.: U.S. Government Printing Office, 1973.

————. *The Social and Economic Status of the Black Population in the United States, 1974.* Washington, D.C.: U.S. Government Printing Office, 1975.

Weisbord, R. G. *Genocide?: Birth Control and the Black American.* New York: Two Continents Publishing Group, Ltd., 1975.

Westoff, C. F., and N. B. Ryder. "Contraceptive Practice among Urban Blacks in the United States, 1965," *The Milbank Memorial Fund Quarterly*, 1970, 43(3), 215–233.

Willie, C. V. "A Position Paper," Presented to the President's Commission on Population Growth and the American Future, Washington, D.C.: Population Reference Bureau Selection No. 37, 1971, 1–4.

PART TWO:

MARRIAGE AND FAMILY THERAPY

11

MARRIAGE AND FAMILY THERAPY WITH BLACK CLIENTS: METHOD AND STRUCTURE

Lorraine Brannon

Whenever two people are involved in an intense interpersonal relationship like marriage, problems will inevitably arise. It is healthy for a couple to attempt to resolve their own problems. It is, however, detrimental to deny the existence of problems or to continue a process of resolution that is obviously unsuccessful. At this point it is healthy to seek professional help.

In my experience as a marriage and family therapist with black couples, I have found that there are usually one of two major obstacles that serve as deterrants to their seeking professional help. One is the perceived stigma associated with seeking assistance for emotional concerns. If one has a physical problem, no second thoughts are given to immediately seeking help from an appropriate professional. Somehow this logic breaks down when one has emotional problems. To have emotional problems and to see a psychologist or other mental health professional, for many people, translates into "I am crazy." Unfortunately, the word *crazy* is associated with spectacular media portrayals of an individual who rants and raves, and no one wants to think of himself or herself as behaving in that way. It is helpful and more acceptable to many clients if "emotional problems and concerns" are defined as "problems associated with daily living" (Szasz, 1969) and as problems stemming from one's attitude and how one responds to other people, i.e., you are upset, you are dissatisfied with your life, you experience anxiety and do not know the reasons why, you just want to scream, you just want to get away from it all, or you find that you are unable to cope with situations the way you once did.

A second major obstacle to seeking professional help is resistance. It has been my experience that the black male is usually resistant and occasionally vehemently opposed to participating in marital therapy. Vontress (1970) found that in therapy with black couples, black males provide a greater challenge to therapists than black females. Asking for help is often perceived as a "blow" to an already fragile ego. Black males often correlate solving one's own problems with one's masculinity. Consequently, to seek help is synonymous with admitting defeat and admitting defeat is synonymous with being less than a man!

These obstacles, unfortunately, deter many couples who could benefit from marital therapy from seeking it. Instead they choose to deny the existence of a problem and hope that somehow—miraculously—things will work themselves out. The divorce statistics would seem to indicate that miraculous solutions are at a premium.

TAKING THE FIRST STEPS

When people are able to admit honestly that they have problems that require outside intervention, they have taken the first positive step. The next step is to select a therapist. I purposely use the word *select* because they are not obligated to accept the first therapist to whom they are referred. In working with black clients, situations arise that serve to remind me of the effects of racism on our self-esteem. We have been conditioned to believe that we have to take what we can get and we are often, therefore, not very selective. When seeking therapeutic assistance, it is often well worth the time and money to "shop around" for a therapist exactly as one would for anything else. Clients should get the answers to any questions that are important to them. There are no questions that are "off limits," including ones about the therapists' training, experience, and fees. Clients should select a therapist whom they have confidence in and with whom they feel comfortable; one they feel they can talk to, confide in, and share information with; and one who will truly understand the individual and his or her problems. Above all, a therapist should not intimidate the client. When seeking a therapist, many people feel comfortable when referred by someone they know or by someone they believe to be a credible source. The majority of my clients are referred by current or former clients, physicians, attorneys, or other psychologists who recommend marital therapy or family therapy after assessing a child in the family. The Washington, D.C., Association of Black Psychologists and the D.C. Psychological Association maintain referral registers and many clients are referred as a result of telephoning these professional associations.

Most of my clients are black, are from the middle income group, and live either in the District of Columbia or one of the nearby Maryland or Virginia suburbs. In practically every instance, both husband and wife are employed. The type of employment varies, but the majority hold professional positions (doctors, lawyers, college professors, public school teachers) or administrative-level government positions. They range in age from 27 to 42 years with an average age of 34, have been married an average of six years, and have an average of one child who is an average of five years of age.

WHAT TO EXPECT

Each therapist may have a slightly different structure for marital therapy. Some therapists utilize a co-therapist in marital and family therapy situations as opposed to a single-therapist approach. I have used both methods but prefer the single-therapist approach. My preference is to tape the session and listen to the recording later when I am not involved actively in the situation. I also use the tape to provide immediate feedback to my clients. Initially, some clients are a bit uneasy and will react to the tape either in voice tone and/or quality or by constantly watching it. I will not tape, however, if there is any strong objection. The format I prefer is a fairly common approach, described by Fitzgerald (1973), which utilizes the first few sessions for the purpose of gathering information. The initial session is a joint one in which both parties verbalize their perceptions of the area(s) of difficulty. This session provides a wealth of nonverbal and verbal information regarding the way the couple interacts, their patterns of communication, and their perceptions of roles within the marriage, as well as their perceptions of themselves and each other as male and female.

The next several sessions are for the purpose of gathering individual information. An extensive history, encompassing mate selection; interpersonal relationships with parents, siblings, and significant others; and sex history, is taken. It is during these sessions that secrets between the couple are usually shared with the therapist. These individual sessions provide a great deal of insight into the spouse's willingness to share information with his or her partner, areas causing personal discomfort, and serious differences in background that may be underlying facilitators of the current difficulties being experienced by the couple.

Once the information-gathering sessions are complete, the couple, along with the therapist, identify two or three goals of therapy. When establishing goals, it is extremely important that they be (1) mutually agreed upon and (2) as specific as possible. The purpose of establishing goals is to provide a yardstick by which progress or lack of it can be measured by all parties involved. If the identified goals are too large and all encompassing, the purpose will be defeated. In 1975, Adams and Orgel conducted a mental health study in the Washington, D.C., Metropolitan Area. Included in the results of the study was a sample format for a written contract. The contract I use is a modification of that format. The contract is a written agreement between the therapist and client(s) and includes the goals of therapy; the date, time, length, and number of sessions; the fee; any rules the client(s) are to follow, for example, the procedure for cancellations; and provisions for renegotiation of the contract and/or the goals. A written contract is very helpful to clients because it removes the aura of mysticism from the therapeutic setting and process. The consistent message that I give in marital therapy is that the couple is expected to work. The therapist serves to identify, clarify, structure, guide, interpret, and work with the couple; but by no means will the therapist do the work *for* the couple. In addition, I stress to the couple that the majority of their work will take place outside the usual 50-minute, once-a-week session. For that reason, I give homework assignments to my clients. Inevitably, in marital therapy, these assignments include things that the couple have to communicate about and often mutually agree upon. For example, the initial homework assignment is to agree mutually on two or three goals of therapy. Many couples contend that they do not have time to reflect on and discuss therapeutic content between sessions. Because the majority of the work must be done outside the therapy session, it becomes obvious that if the couples have no time to talk, they will not be able to work toward resolving their dilemma. Consequently, another common assignment given is to etch out of their busy schedules, a segment of private time devoted exclusively to a discussion of the content and process of the previous therapy session. Trust level is an area that generally suffers when a relationship begins to deteriorate. With respect to this area, the couple are asked to re-establish trust levels and to decide mutually the method to be used in doing so. Before they can begin to work toward re-establishing trust levels, they have to agree mutually on whether there is honestly the will (desire) and motivation to do this. In other words, "talk is cheap." They can talk about re-establishing trust all they want to, but their behavior will definitely reveal their honest desire.

If the couples identify a problem during the therapy session and they are unable to resolve it, I will generally assign the problem as homework. The specific assignment is to continue to discuss the problem and the issues and to arrive at a viable solution. A helpful adjunct to arriving at a solution is for the couple to identify areas of common responsibility as opposed to blaming each other.

There are only a few rules and regulations to which the couple must adhere during the sessions. One, they are to talk to each other and look at each other when doing so. For example, the husband is not allowed to direct a question to his wife through me or vice versa. Two, they are not to attack each other or me physically, and three, they are not to destroy the furniture in the room. A final rule is that they are in marital therapy and will only be seen together. I will not see one spouse without the other unless previously agreed upon. For example, if the wife arrives before her husband, I will not talk with her individually while we are waiting for her husband to arrive or vice versa. Quite often one or both spouses will attempt to manipulate the situation or gain a "one upmanship" position with such tactics. Consequently, the therapy session does not begin until both spouses have arrived.

The content and process of the therapy sessions vary. There are occasions when a great deal of structure is needed, and I will provide it. On other occasions, however, a less structured approach is utilized. The couples are allowed to interact in whatever manner they choose. Quite often they choose to argue (yell and scream) with each other. My role in these situations is that of a participant-observer. Fitzgerald (1973) discusses process focus versus content focus. It is not what one says (content) but rather how one says it (process). I allow the couple to complete their argument without interruption. When I do respond, I comment on the type of interaction (process) I observed as opposed to commenting on what (content) they argued about. They are usually unaware of how they sound as evidenced by their responses to such questions as "Do you have any idea how you sound to me?" It is quite surprising and often shocking to the couple to receive the immediate feedback that I provide, in most instances, when I rewind the tape and allow them to listen to themselves. Their reactions to how they sound to each other and to themselves becomes a topic for discussion as does my perception and interpretation of the process.

One of the goals of therapy is to teach both marriage partners to interact with each other in a different manner. My presence as an objective participant requires the spouses to deal with each other in a different way. I emphasize the positive side of the couple's interaction and/or re-define the situation as different from the way the couple defines it (Haley, 1974). The couples have usually reached the point at which they are able to see only the negative side of their spouse's action. I try to point out the positive side and get them to begin to focus on this area. For example, the wife might define her husband's invitation to dinner as a bribe for some deceptive action she expects to follow. I might re-define it as his attempt to bring them closer together. Trust levels again become important in instances such as this one. The wife has to sincerely begin to learn to trust her husband, accept his actions at face value, and discontinue her anticipation of the worse.

Following the Gestalt model (Fagan and Shepherd, 1970), I do not allow the couple to speak in the past tense. I help them focus on the "here and now." For example, if they had a disagreement yesterday, rather than recount it, I require them to re-argue the subject in the present tense. I also encourage them to focus on feelings. Fritz Perls describes this as the "lose your mind and come to your senses" situation (Fagan and Shepherd, 1970). In other words, rather than intellectualizing about the situation, the wife focuses on feelings by responding, "I am afraid to trust you because I am afraid of being hurt." Getting the spouses to become aware of their feelings as well as each other's feelings, and then to express them is difficult, but it is not impossible. It requires constant coaching on my part. Because awareness involves more than feelings, Gestalt techniques also help persons focus on their bodies, acts, and behaviors. It is often easier to talk about these behaviors in the third person, "it" and "they" language. For that reason "it" is changed to "I". Thus, a dialogue, as might be described by Perls, between client and therapist might be as follows:

THERAPIST: What is your hand doing?

    CLIENT: It is trembling.

      T: Please change the word "it" to "I."

      C: I am trembling.

The latter is a more responsible statement. The language that the couples use is very important, and I take responsibility for changing inaccurate language that promotes irresponsibility. For that reason, I also do not allow my clients to use words like *if, but, I can't,* and *I feel guilty* because use of these words implies an external source of control and responsibility. They are asked to substitute the word *and* for *if* and *but, I don't want to* for *I can't,* and *I resent* for *I feel guilty*. For example, "my wife makes me feel so guilty with her accusations" is translated into "I resent my wife's accusations" and "I want to trust my husband but I can't" is translated into "I want to trust my husband and I don't want to." Changing the words highlights the emotional conflict and puts the control and responsibility exactly where it really is—with the individual. Each individual must learn to accept responsibility for his or her own choices and actions and to express this. This is not an easy task to master because most people have been using inaccurate language for quite some time. Initially, it is a "tug of war" until the couple begin to monitor and change their own language. I rarely answer questions during therapy sessions. I ask the client to change the question into a statement because this task makes visible the material from which the question grew. Asking questions can be interpreted in therapy as sustaining dependency (Fagan and Shepherd, 1970). Changing a question into a genuine statement, again, forces one to take responsibility, in this instance, for one's expressions and feelings. The emotional conflict can only be dealt with when it is brought out into the open.

There are two possible outcomes of marital therapy. One is the discovery that your marriage is salvageable. The other is the discovery or confirmation that it is not. The expectation in the latter instance is that as a result of marital therapy, the couple will feel more confident in their decision to separate or divorce.

DIFFERENCES BETWEEN BLACK AND WHITE CLIENTS IN THERAPY

Psychodynamically, there are probably no differences between black and white clients. The concepts of id, ego, superego, conscious, unconscious, defense mechanism, and others are present regardless of race. Both black and white people experience intrapsychic difficulties; however, black people have to cope with the additional strain of racism and discrimination which definitely impacts on the development of the black "psyche."

A belief shared by many clinicians and researchers but with which I disagree is that insight-oriented psychotherapy is not suitable for minority group and poor clients. Somehow, it is assumed that if a person is poor or belongs to a minority group he or she is unable to think, discern, and see intuitively into a situation or problem. My experience indicates that this phenomenon may be more a function of social class than race. That is, the poor, which as a consequence of racism includes many black people, may lack knowledge of the nature and utility of psychotherapy that their middle-class black and white counterparts may have acquired through more sophisticated exposure. Once the client understands the therapeutic process, insight development is possible and does occur. There do, however, appear to be several differences between black and white clients who seek therapeutic intervention. One difference is that many black clients are not as familiar with psychotherapy as middle-class white clients are. They may have faulty, inaccurate perceptions about what therapy entails, about who seeks therapy, and for what reasons. As a result, the therapist will have to educate the client about what to expect. A second difference, according to Jones (1979), is the unfavorable attitude that black clients have about seeking mental health care. He notes that black people probably have to be suffering more severely than white people before they decide to seek therapy. Consequently, by the time the average black person seeks therapy, he or she will present with more severe problems. In addition, therapeutic intervention is utilized more often in a crisis situation as a last resort and consequently is usually a low priority once the crisis subsides.

A third difference is that white clients remain in therapy for longer periods of time—a minimum of six months (Fitzgerald, 1973), which would roughly be 24 once-a-week sessions. It has been my experience with black couples that because they are usually motivated by a crisis, they prefer short-term or brief psychotherapy. The black couples I have seen have remained in therapy for an average of 10 sessions as compared to an average of 20 sessions for white clients. Generally, the reason expressed by the black clients for terminating therapy is a financial one. Either the couples feel they have exhausted the funds allotted for psychotherapy or they feel the money can be better utilized elsewhere. This latter reason reflects the subtle attitude, even of couples involved in therapy, that psychotherapy is a low priority after the crisis has been dealt with successfully.

Fourth, a belief shared by many practitioners is that black clients disclose less about themselves than white clients and that black males disclose less than black females (Jourard and Lasakow, 1958). Once a relationship is established, black clients are more ready to communicate about externals than about internal conflicts and anxieties (Krich, 1974). It appears that black clients are more reactionary and again more motivated to seek therapy as a result of an external crisis as opposed to desiring personal growth and development as is the situation with many white clients.

Flowers (1972) observed a definite difference in the time values of black clients. The lower-income black clients with whom she worked were frequently "tardy for no reason" as compared with the middle-income white clients. After considerable exploration, she concluded that the tardiness was neither resistance to therapy nor manipulation as her traditional training dictated, but rather a difference in values which she learned to accept and accommodate. Awareness of this difference in values is extremely important because a therapist who is unfamiliar with the black clients' value system will certainly interpret some of their behaviors inaccurately.

This difference in cultural values is also highlighted when working with families. McAdoo (1977) points out that the majority of the literature about families focuses on only one segment of black families. These findings are then generalized, and the false impression is created that all black families are characterized by disintegration, instability, and pathology. On the contrary, black families are usually characterized by close family ties that often include an extended family. The concept of an extended family and interdependence among the members as opposed to a small nuclear family is another difference between black and white clients. All families, regardless of race, experience stress related to economic and geographical change. Black families have the added burden of having to raise their children to effectively manipulate and negotiate a society that does not reinforce positive evaluations of their ethnic group. During periods of crisis, the extended family and a supportive church family is often depended on to provide support and resources beyond those available in the nuclear family. Therapists must be acutely aware of the strong interdependence of family members that exists in black families, to a far greater extent than in white families (McAdoo, 1977).

Still another difference between black and white clients stems from the emotional stress experienced by many black people who are striving for upward mobility. Most black people who are now part of the upwardly mobile group have roots in a less affluent background. McAdoo (1977) points out that the upwardly mobile black person is often compelled to make an emotional separation from the draining, ongoing, everyday needs of his or her family of orientation although continuing to maintain physical interaction and contact with them. She proceeds to suggest that some of the antagonism and alienation that exists between working and middle-class black people may be attributed to this separation. This social class division may be stronger among blacks than it is among whites (McAdoo, 1977). The type of stress and isolation associated with this emotional separation increases the need for supportive therapy provided by someone outside the family who is aware of this type of cultural factor.

A critical difference between black and white clients is that racism has impacted on the psychological development of black people and continues to impact on us daily. A therapist who denies this and chooses to ignore the sociocultural influences on the behavior of the black client runs the risk of labeling many behaviors that are different from white middle-class norms as pathological. Some behaviors that may indicate or suggest pathology in a white person may indicate adaptability in a black person. Black people, as a whole, have on occasion been referred to as paranoid. Paranoia, by definition, means that you believe someone is "out to get you" or "wants to do harm to you" when in actuality (reality) it is not true. For a black person, to live and survive in this racist society and not be paranoid is pathological! The paranoia that is exhibited in this type of situation is a "healthy paranoia" that has facilitated our survival. However, it is not my intention to suggest that black people do not become psychotic. My intention is to highlight an important consideration that impacts on the behavior of black clients. A black client may be somewhat defensive, guarded, and slow to develop trust in others (especially whites), but we have good reasons grounded in reality for this behavior. Consequently, a therapist working with black clients must take into account the social realities of the black experience and understand the stress factors pressing on black people everyday of our lives.

MAIN SOURCES OF CONFLICT WITH BLACK COUPLES

One dangerous mistake, when working with black clients, is attributing all of their problems to race. Black people are subject to the same intrapersonal psychological dynamics as non-black people. Race, class, and powerlessness, however, interact with intrapsychic variables to produce behavior that is a product of all the factors.

Marriage is an extremely complex relationship, and consequently, the sources of conflict are also complex. There is rarely only one focal problem, but rather a combination of problems, difficulties, and issues. In marital therapy, the model for marriage that the two individuals have is extremely important. Each of us is a unique individual who has been affected by different experiences. The model that most of us have for marriage is that of our parents or that of the setting in which we were raised. Verbal and nonverbal cues from the familial setting stick in our minds and affect our interpersonal interactions quite often without our awareness of the process. Role perceptions are one source of conflict. Perceptions of the female/wife/mother role are based, in large part, on the role played by mother or mother figure in the family. Perceptions of the male/husband/father role, likewise, are based on the role played by father or father figure in the family. This concept holds true regardless of the race of the couple involved.

In addition to role perceptions within the marriage, perceptions of self are often another source of conflict. The conflictual perception of self in black couples can be viewed as one effect of racism. Therefore, in marital therapy with black couples, it is of crucial importance that the therapist be aware of, understand, and be sensitive to the effects of racism on the self-concept in black people. There is a plethora of literature indicating that the therapist's race is a significant factor related to level of understanding in the therapeutic process and that clients and therapists have difficulties responding positively to someone of the opposite race (Banks, 1972; Banks, Berenson and Carkhuff, 1967; Brannon, 1976; Bryson and Cody, 1973; Carkhuff and Pierce, 1967; Hollingshead and Redlich, 1958; and Vontress, 1970). Within the area of mental health, the inequitable service delivery to minority clients, as well as the less-positive treatment outcomes, has been well documented (Comer, 1973; Fiman, 1975; and Hollingshead and Redlich, 1958). One hypothesis to account for this phenomenon is the large number of culturally alien therapists (Fiman, 1975) who have had very little, if any, form of training that is geared toward the specific requirements of minority populations. The literature also clearly documents the effects of racism on the black psyche. Black males, more so than females, have been subjected to tactics designed to strip them of their identities, self-confidence, and self-respect (Cameron, 1967). Black males grow up receiving conflicting messages regarding appropriate male behavior. Grier and Cobbs (1968) point out that black males are punished for exhibiting behavior that is defined as masculine for the rest of society, i.e., expressions of assertion, aggression, demanding certain privileges, pursuing, etc. For purposes of survival, black females taught their sons to suppress masculine assertiveness. The experience of slavery left as its most serious heritage a steady weakness in the black family (Glazer, 1963). What slavery began, prejudice and discrimination have continued to keep alive. The high rate of black unemployment is as current a source of psychological trauma as it was in the past. Work is more than income, it is an indication of worth. Not having a job is more than not having money, it is a sign that one is not worth much. The black male was not allowed to be a consistent wage earner. He could not present himself to his family as a person who had the opportunity or the ability to compete successfully in business or industry (Clark, 1965). This continued post-slavery relegation of the black male to menial and subservient states has made the female appear to be the dominant person in the black family. She has been required to hold the family together, to set goals, stimulate, encourage, and protect both the boys as well as the girls. Her compensatory strength tended to perpetuate the weaker role of the black male. Consequently, both the male and female are often struggling with ambivalent feelings about their own self-concept and self-worth. It is extremely difficult to engage in an intimate, fulfilling relationship with another person and to identify and clarify roles within the family when there is uncertainty about one's own identity, individuality, and worth. The struggle to discover "who I am" and to reinforce that "I am a good and worthwhile person" almost inevitably conflicts with the perception of "who I ought to be" as defined by the role in the relationship, i.e., husband and/or wife and "how I ought to feel about myself" as defined by society. The black female, as previously mentioned, has been identified traditionally as the predominant force in the black family and as a strong person who holds the family together by making all sorts of sacrifices in spite of insurmountable obstacles. Black females are no longer willing to accept and attempt to conform to this stereotyped definition of their roles as "super-woman" (Jackson, 1975). Their attempts at re-defining their roles often clash with their husband's expectation of what their wives' roles "ought to be." The black male, on the other hand, has traditionally been identified as the weaker link in the black family. Black males are also beginning to assert themselves and reject this stereotyped definition. Here again, this self-assertiveness might conflict with the wife's expectation of what his role "ought to be." More often, however, the conflict is a result of one or both individuals' newly defined roles and the vigor with which each attempts to play his or her role. All too often, the result is an unwillingness to be flexible and to compromise for fear of losing some of the recently discovered individuality sought after for so long.

Communication and compromise are crucial focal areas in marital therapy. Compromise is only possible if both spouses sit down and share information, ideas, and feelings with each other. In other words, verbal communication is extremely important. Many of the black couples with whom I have worked were raised in families, and thus came from backgrounds, in which verbal communication was at a minimum. Explanations, other than "do it because I said so," were not usually given by their parents, and verbal expression of one's thoughts and desires were often discouraged rather than encouraged. Consequently, one or both spouses have difficulty talking with each other because they have not learned to do so. In addition to being unfamiliar with talking to another person, many black couples are not used to listening to each other either. Listening to another person far surpasses just hearing because it includes synthesizing the input and analyzing it in an effort to sincerely understand. This, however, is a difficult task if it is not part of the couples' current repertoire of behaviors. For that reason, the partners are taught to listen by engaging in listening exercises. For example, the wife is requested to repeat accurately what her husband says before she is allowed to respond with her own thoughts and vice versa. Only when confirmation is received from the other spouse that what was said has been repeated accurately is the conversation allowed to proceed. Quite often what is expressed by one spouse is not what was actually said by the other. What happens is the listener hears what is said and then subjects it to personal modification and interpretation, thereby changing the message. Consequently, the response given will be inconsistent with the message that was actually communicated, and misunderstanding is perpetuated. In therapy the couple can learn to break these faulty patterns of communication by substituting more efficient methods, thereby facilitating better understanding. A marriage involves two people; and consequently, one person is not able to have his or her way all of the time. With improved communication skills and a workable level of understanding, the couple can learn to negotiate compromises that will be acceptable to both of them.

Emotional expression and sexual adjustment are frequently occurring issues or sources of conflict in marital therapy with black couples. The socialization process for black males is such that all too often they do not learn how to show affection or how to accept affection. Females are encouraged to play with dolls and to care for children (siblings); as a result, they learn how to give and receive love and affection. Males are taught that it is not "manly" to be interested in playing with female dolls and interacting with children. At an early age boys begin to get the subtle message that it is not acceptable or "manly" to show affection or emotions. For many black men, affection is correlated only with sex, thus the only time and reason to be openly affectionate is in preparation for intercourse. To display affection at other times is somehow associated with weakness, and it is the stereotype of being weak that the black male struggles to overcome. If the black male lived in a vacuum, this behavior might cause no difficulties. However, when he lives with a black female who has a desire for intimacy, i.e., hugging, kissing, and touching without it necessarily culminating in intercourse, conflict is inevitable. A typical homework assignment in this area is to ask the couple, male in particular, to engage only in affectionate, sensual experiences and to refrain from engaging in intercourse for one or two days. Assignments in this area serve a better purpose when they are small enough to avoid imposing a hardship on either spouse. In therapy, the black male can learn to feel good about himself and comfortable with his sexuality. He can learn that affection is a human quality that is not sex (gender) or strength/weakness linked. He can learn that it is not a sign of weakness to display affection, but rather a sign of uninhibited strength.

FAMILY THERAPY

In most instances, family therapy is considered when parents identify a child in the family as being problematic and want the child to be seen in therapy. A child, however, does not grow up in a vacuum; he or she grows up in a family setting and consequently becomes a product of that environment. My operating premise is that the problem exhibited by the child is a symptom of something amiss within the family setting. If this assumption proves to be factual, as a result of the interview, it then does very little good to see the child alone, in isolation of others who contribute to the difficulty. However, it has been my experience that a therapist must proceed with caution when attempting to involve the family in therapy. For most parents, the thought that they somehow contribute to their child's difficulties is far too threatening to deal with. A natural response to a threatening situation is retreat or withdrawal, i.e., refusing family therapy and withdrawing the child from individual therapy. In an effort not to lose a child or a family in need of help, I have developed, through experience, a gentle coercion approach because I find families are more receptive to and accepting of this method. I explain to the parents that while I will see the child individually as they wish, it will also be necessary to see them as a family on a regular basis (for example, once every two sessions or every other session, whichever is less threatening for the parents). I further explain that the purpose of the family sessions is to share information and to solicit their cooperation and involvement in homework assignments. Once the parents become comfortable with these sessions they are less defensive and more receptive to explorations of their behavior and interactions with their child. They also become more willing to increase the regularity of the family sessions.

In family therapy, I initially conduct a series of exploratory sessions with the entire family (Ackerman, 1970). After these sessions, my procedure is similar to that previously described, in that goals are established, a contract is written, and the therapy sessions begin. While any material is "fair game" for discussion, it is sometimes counter-productive and anti-therapeutic to deal with everything and anything in the family sessions. For that reason, there are times when I will see only the child or children to deal with specific problems they might be experiencing. Likewise, there are times when I will have separate sessions with the parents to focus on specific problems they have, for example, a marital or sexual problem. Some therapists are reluctant to include young children (under age five) in the family sessions. As Bloch (1976) explains, the reasons are understandable because some of these children are nonverbal, and they are distractions because they spill things, they make noise, and they need their diapers changed! On the other hand, I find it useful to observe how the family interacts with its younger member(s). Children usually occupy a powerless position, and it is important to observe how they express their needs and how the family deals with them. In many instances, the birth of a baby exacerbates already existing selfishness, jealousy, insecurity, or fear of rejection in one or both spouses. Observation of the familial interaction, if it does not prove to be anti-therapeutic and therefore contraindicated as a result of the distraction, can provide invaluable therapeutic material.

My experiences in family therapy have been exclusively with black families, and the majority of the children are referred because of acting-out behavior that most frequently occurs in the classroom, but in some cases also at home. Usually, the child exhibits observable behavior that is either overt or covert in form. Overt or active acting-out behavior may be manifested by talking in class, being inattentive, flirting, and fighting, to name a few. Covert or passive acting-out may be manifested by poor grades and withdrawn behavior, especially in a child who previously did well in school and was fairly outgoing. There is never any single cause of acting-out behavior, but the most frequently occurring factor is a lack of control by parents and a lack of consistent messages and appropriate discipline. In family therapy, many children express the belief that their parents do not care about them, do not take an interest in them or what they do, and surprising to many parents, the children complain that their parents are too lenient—"they let me do anything I want to do"! A major focus in therapy with black families, therefore, is usually parenting skills. Children have a need for structure and guidance, and that is what discipline entails. Discipline is not something negative, as many parents believe; it is really something positive that will help the child in the long run. Parents need to understand that children need to have a sense of belonging and need to feel worthwhile. They will attempt to get attention in any way they can. For many children the only time they are attended to is when they are acting-out. For them, negative attention is better than no attention. If the family will not provide the attention the child needs, he or she often turns to the peer group to provide this sense of belonging.

Most parents are not intentionally acting in a less-than-responsible manner with respect to discipline. For many it is as simple as a lack of knowledge—they do not know how to discipline their children or how to be a parent. They may lack appropriate models or they may not have been disciplined as children; and consequently, they proceed to raise their children the only way they know how—the way they were raised. For others, they believe that they were raised in an environment that was too strict; therefore, they make the decision to be more lenient with their children. Many of the parents are relatively young and are caught up in "doing their own thing," which may include going to parties, discotheques, and all sorts of social affairs with very little time remaining to be parents. Still others are overwhelmed by survival issues and problems of daily living, for example, earning enough money to make ends meet, pay the rent, or buy food, clothing, etc. The day-to-day survival requirements are so time and energy consuming that these individuals have very little, if any, time and energy remaining to devote to their children.

In therapy the focus is on helping the parents to realize that raising a child is a tremendous responsibility and not to be taken lightly. There has to be a re-emphasis on the importance of the black family unit as a focal point. Black parents must begin to put their children first, before everything else, including parties, the job, club meetings, etc. They must take an interest in what their children are doing and understand the importance of providing a good, healthy, stable home environment that fosters positive self-concepts in their children. Positive emotional development of children requires a positive family and home environment because children learn by observing and imitating the behavior of their parents. As stated earlier, the adults' model for marriage is that of their parents. Consequently, the way children relate on an interpersonal level will be an imitation, a reflection of how they have observed their parents relating to each other. Children are extremely perceptive, aware, and observant beings. They will be just as aware of a loving relationship between their parents as they are of a hostile, angry one. However, it is the latter that will leave a greater scar on their emotional development. Children will learn whatever behavior their parents exhibit. They will learn good or bad communication skills; they will learn that men and women relate as equals or that they relate as unequals (leading to chauvinistic attitudes); they will learn that both sexes share the responsibility; and they will learn that the relationship between a man and a woman is a beautiful experience of togetherness and loving or that it is a constant struggle that the man must always win because his manhood is at stake. The major goal in family therapy with black families is to help the parents learn how to provide a more positive home environment and model that will expose their children to a healthy male-female relationship, and consequently, will foster positive feelings about self.

NONTRADITIONAL APPROACHES WITH BLACK CLIENTS

Therapists who work with a predominantly black clientele must understand the reality of urban black life. They need to understand the cultural, economical, and environmental stresses, as well as the powerlessness that exists within the black community. They must begin to see black communities not as centers of pathology in and of themselves, as defined by traditional training programs (Bradshaw, 1978 and Mayfield, 1972), but as people affected by racism, manifested in numerous ways. Black people are troubled by environmental factors that affect their immediate survival, i.e., substandard, dilapidated, and overcrowded housing; poverty; inferior health care; and inadequate educational and employment opportunities (Hare, 1970).

Traditionally, textbooks on psychotherapy afford only brief attention to the problem of cultural barriers between therapist and client. Practically nothing is said about black American culture; and consequently, the conceptual frameworks and practical suggestions that a therapist can apply in the office remain few and far between (Flowers, 1972). As a black therapist, I do not totally disregard existing theories and methods; I modify these theories and techniques so that they are more applicable to black clients. It is a useless, self-defeating exercise to attempt to impose irrelevant theoretical concepts and obsolete methods on black clients. The style of the therapeutic intervention is very important when working with black clients. Consequently, I pull from different areas and various therapeutic approaches in an effort to develop a technique that I feel comfortable with, that fits my personality, and that works with my clients. I am an active, vibrant, outgoing person, and therefore, I come across that way in therapy. It has been my experience and it is documented in the literature (Calia, 1967 and Fanon, 1954) that sedentary talks as a medium for client-therapist interaction are not the most effective methodology. More action-oriented approaches seem to work better with black clients. Thus, I take an active, extremely vocal posture as opposed to a passive, nonverbal approach. Black people are, by culture, an emotional people. I feel perfectly comfortable exhibiting emotions in the sessions, i.e., laughing, getting excited; and I encourage my clients to do likewise. For that reason, I utilize methods and techniques that focus on feelings, emotions, and the here and now. Attempts are made to help clients focus on feeling levels. For example, when issues arise with couples, instead of allowing them to engage in a process debate, I require them to share with their spouse how the situation made them feel. It is often extremely revealing and therapeutic to incorporate role playing in situations like this. The couple is asked to switch roles, i.e., the husband takes the wife's role and vice versa.

I readily and frequently incorporate nontraditional forms of therapy in my sessions. Following a procedure described by Johnson (1974), I sometimes utilize music in my therapy sessions. Black music has always served a useful purpose in our lives. It served as a relief from psychological stress during slavery, and it was sung in the fields to assist in easing the pain of work and as a secret form of communication. This psychological relief can still be witnessed in many black churches today. While sitting and simply listening to music with a client may not be therapeutic, a black therapist, familiar with black music and the black experience, is able to select skillfully appropriate songs to assist the client in gaining insights. Music is used as an adjunct to traditional "talk therapy." Music dealing with interpersonal relationships and self-concept seems to be the most appropriate. Usually, I will play a song and then ask the client(s) to make associations, fantasize the experience, and discuss any feelings the song evokes.

I also utilize art as an adjunct to traditional "talk therapy." I have finger-paint, crayons, pastels (oil pastels are less messy), drawing paper, and drawing pencils readily available. The couple or family is encouraged to produce "group or family" pictures. In addition to the use of group or family drawings, I also incorporate the use of nontraditional assessment procedures with couples or families. The Rorschach, a projective technique traditionally administered to individuals, and the Wechsler, an individual intelligence test, can be used in marital and family therapy to reveal interactions around decision making, styles of thinking, problem-solving patterns, and domination patterns (Loveland et al., 1963 and Roman and Bauman, 1960). The ongoing interactions, as well as the finished product, provide a wealth of interpretative material.

Lastly, role playing is incorporated as an adjunct to traditional "talk therapy." Role playing with families is exceptionally fascinating and effective when the children switch roles with the parents or when the children play mother and father.

In family therapy with black families, it is not unusual for the family to consist of nontraditional members, for example: mother, boyfriend, and child; foster parents and children; or various combinations of the extended family whose members may or may not be related by blood. As a black therapist who is familiar with nontraditional family structures, I have no difficulty accepting nontraditional members in family therapy. Whenever possible, I make school visits and home visits to get a better understanding of other environments in which the members interact. I have also conducted sessions within the home in an effort to decrease missed appointments. In addition to observing and interpreting the family interaction and encouraging verbal communication, I also provide a collection of puzzles, games, construction paper, building sets, dolls, and other toys to serve as expressive vehicles for the children. What the child does with these items is interpreted according to play therapy theory.

In addition to these nontraditional approaches, I also find that brief psychotherapeutic intervention works best because, as I said before, most black clients are not motivated, regardless of the reasons, to participate in long-term psychotherapy. According to Guerin (1976), brief psychotherapy is most useful when it is highly structured, directive, and intensely focused. The goal of this type of therapy, necessarily, is to isolate and intervene rapidly in the presenting problem.

CONCLUSION

Black people are African people who come from a culture that primarily stresses the group (tribe, family, community) and secondarily stresses the individual as a member of that group. According to Luther X (1974), much of the emotional distress experienced by black people today is related to our attempt to do "our own thing." The problem is that "our own thing" is usually defined in terms of the Euro-American value system which, on the one hand, emphasizes the autonomy of the individual, while simultaneously attributing all blame to the individual, especially if that individual is black. Treatment of black clients, therefore, must rely on an elevation of individual consciousness. Consciousness is derived from the Latin phrase *con scio* which means *with knowledge*. Consequently, the therapist must concentrate on expanding the personal awareness and knowledge of the individual to appreciate better the aspects of himself or herself that are being denied in the attempts to follow faulty models. The traditional methods of increasing self-awareness must be supplemented by instruction about the nature and acceptance of self. The parroting of European values and behaviors must be replaced by the restoration of African consciousness (Luther X, 1974).

Therapy with black clients must, therefore, focus on knowing oneself, accepting the worth of self, developing positive self-concepts, and building self-esteem. A basic problem within the black community today is hatred of self. As black people, we realize that in the minds of white society we are associated with that which is thought to be inferior, less than, and not equal. In other words, the white value system attaches to black people a stigma of inferiority. One result of self-hatred is the projection of this hate onto other black people. Self-hatred divides and destroys our confidence in ourselves and others and it reinforces a lack of group solidarity. It causes us to fight, rob, and shoot each other, look down on each other, attempt to relieve the frustration we experience by using alcohol or drugs, and engage in the "crab in the barrel" phenomenon. This means that we are envious of other black people who get ahead and we try to pull them down. Therapy with black clients, therefore, must focus on ways to go from self-hatred to self-love. The key is that people who know themselves love themselves and, if permitted, will take excellent care of themselves. For example, the woman who recognizes and receives respect commensurate with the worth of a glorious black woman is incapable of being a prostitute, and the black person who believes in the essential beauty and worth of his or her body is unwilling to flood that body with alcohol or drugs (Luther X, 1974). Therapy often becomes a teaching/learning experience in which black clients are taught how to cope with the day-to-day reality of urban living, to understand and negotiate the system, and to institute problem-solving mechanisms within the family and the community. It is important to stress the need for collective and mutual support on the part of black people, particularly at the level of the family and the local community (Parsons, 1965). Destruction of the family constitutes destruction of the vehicle through which culture is transmitted. That we survived so cruel an ordeal as slavery is a miracle and a sign of tremendous strength; that we are ashamed of it is immoral (Fauntroy, 1979). The black family is strong, and solidarity within the family is the key to eradicating many of the problems plaguing the black community today. We must recognize this and begin to cement the black family. We must transcend self-hatred and engage in self-love. Love of self means acceptance of self. If we accept ourselves, we can accept others like us. Out of our common heritage of suffering, we can accept our past and feel proud when other black people become upwardly mobile because it indicates that we, too, can do the same thing.

REFERENCES

Ackerman, N. "Child Participation in Family Therapy," *Family Process*. New York: Basic Books, 1970, 9.

Adams, S., and M. Orgel. *Through the Mental Health Maze*. Washington, D.C.: Health Research Group, 1975.

Banks, G., et al. "The Effects of Counselor Race and Training upon Counseling Process with Negro Clients in Initial Interviews," *Journal of Clinical Psychology*, 1967, 23, 70–72.

Banks, W. "The Differential Effects of Race and Social Class," *Journal of Clinical Psychology*, 1972, 28(1), 90–92.

Bloch, D. A. "Including the Children in Family Therapy," In J. Guerin (ed) *Family Therapy*. New York: Gardner Press, 1976.

Bradshaw, W. H. "Training Psychiatrists for Working with Blacks in Basic Residency Programs," *American Journal of Psychiatry*, 1978, 135(12), 1520–1524.

Brannon, L. "Black Clients Perceptions of Empathy in Black Professional and Paraprofessional Therapists," Ph.D. diss., *Dissertation Abstracts*, 1976.

Bryson, S., and J. Cody. "Relationship of Race and Level of Understanding between Counselor and Client," *Journal of Counseling Psychology*, 1973, 20(6), 495–498.

Calia, V. F. "The Culturally Deprived Clients: A Reformulation of the Counselor's Role," *Journal of Counseling Psychology*, 1966, 13(1), 100–105.

Cameron, H. "A Review of Research and an Investigation of Emotional Dependency among Negro Youth," *Journal of Negro Education*, 1967, 36(2), 111–120.

Carkhuff, N., and R. Pierce. "The Differential Effects of Therapist Race and Social Class upon Depth of Self Exploration in the Initial Interview," *Journal of Counseling Psychology*, 1967, 19, 632–634.

Clark, K. B. *Dark Ghetto*. New York: Harper & Row Publishers, 1965.

Comer, J. P. "The Need is Now," *Mental Hygiene*, 1973, 57(1), 3–6.

Fagan, J., and I. Shepherd (eds). *Gestalt Therapy Now*. New York: Harper & Row Publishers, 1970.

Fanon, F., and J. Azaulay. "La Sociotherapie Dans Un Servial d'Hommes Musulmans," *L'Information Psychiatrique*, 1954, 9, 349–361.

Fauntroy, W. E. "Self-Hatred," A speech given at the 9th Annual United Negro College Fund Dinner, Detroit, Mich., 1979.

Fiman, B. G. *Special Report on Inequities in Mental Health Delivery*. McLean, Virginia: Human Services Research, Inc., 1975.

Fitzgerald, R. V. *Conjoint Marital Therapy*. New York: Aronson, 1973.

Flowers, L.R.B. "Psychotherapy: Black and White," *Journal of the National Medical Association*, 1972, 64(1), 19–22.

Glazer, N., and D. P. Moynihan. *Beyond the Melting Pot*. Cambridge, Mass.: The M.I.T. Press & Howard University Press, 1963.

Grier, W. H., and P. M. Cobbs. *Black Rage*. New York: Basic Books, 1968.

Gucrin, P. J. (ed) *Family Therapy*. New York: Gardner Press, 1976.

Haley, J. "Marriage Therapy," In H. Greenwald (ed) *Active Psychotherapy*. New York: Aronson, 1974.

Hare, N. "Black Ecology," *Black Scholar*, 1970, 1(6), 2–8.

Hollingshead, A., and F. Redlich. *Social Class and Mental Illness*. New York: John Wiley & Sons, 1958.

Jackson, L. B. "The Attitudes of Black Females Toward Upper and Lower Class Males," *Journal of Black Psychology*, February, 1975, 1, 53–64.

Jernberg, A. M. *Theraplay*. San Francisco: Jossey-Bass, Inc., 1979.

Johnson, S. "Black Music, Black Patients, and Psychotherapy," Paper presented at the 7th Annual Convention of the Association of Black Psychologists, August, Nashville, Tenn., August, 1974.

Jones, E. "Snapshot," *APA Monitor*. Washington, D.C.: APA, November, 1979.

Jourard, S. M. and P. Lasakow. "Some Factors in Self Disclosure," *Journal of Abnormal and Social Psychology*, 1958, 56, 91–98.

Krich, A. "Active Strategies in Marriage Counseling," In H. Greenwald (ed) *Active Therapy*. New York: Aronson, 1974.

Loveland, N. T., et al. "The Family Rorschach: A New Method for Studying Family Interaction," *Family Process*, 1963, 2, 187–215.

Mayfield, W. G. "Mental Health in The Black Community," *Social Work*, 1972, 17(3), 106–110.

McAdoo, H. "Family Therapy in The Black Community," *American Journal of Orthopsychiatry*, 1977, 47(1), 75-79.

Parsons, T. "Full Citizenship for the Negro American?," In T. Parsons and K. B. Clark (eds) *The Negro American*. Boston: Houghton Mifflin, 1965.

Roman, M., and G. Bauman. "Interaction Testing: A Technique for the Psychological Evaluation of Small Groups," In M. Harrower, et al. (eds) *Creative Variations in the Projective Techniques*. Springfield, Ill.: Charles C. Thomas, 1960.

Szasz, T. "The Myth of Mental Illness," In G. Stricker and M. Zax (eds) *The Study of Abnormal Behavior*. London: The Macmillan Co., 1969.

Vontress, C. E. "Counseling Blacks," *Personnel and Guidance Journal*, 1970, 48(9), 713-719.

X, Luther. "Awareness: The Key to Black Mental Health," *Journal of Black Psychology*, 1974, 1(1), 30-37.

12

WE ARE OUR PARENTS' CHILDREN

Adriaan T. Halfhide

As far back as I can remember, rumors have persisted about the black community that blacks are prone to believe in anything except reality. Furthermore, according to the rumors, blacks believe in religious cults as opposed to God; they embrace the concept of consumerism as opposed to postponing gratification; and they cherish the notion of promiscuity as opposed to that of fidelity in their sexual relations. The list goes on and on. As with all rumors, there is some basis in fact. Yet, when one examines the rumors carefully, one can see that their bases are grounded in certain perceptions of the black family unit. For the rumor perpetuator, these perceptions may have been fostered in experiences with the black family. However, rumors notwithstanding, I am confident that *most* blacks do not accept these descriptions of their reality and do not feel that they are indicative of black family life in general. Yet, what is disturbing is that some blacks do believe such rumors and that these rumors exist at all.

Because of these rumors and because of the premise held by many in our society that blacks do not have and do not want to have a stable and viable family experience, I was prompted to consider seriously the quality of black family life as it is presently manifested. Moreover, I wondered about the effects our families of origins, i.e., our grandparents, parents, and siblings, have had and continue to have on present-day black family life.

Acknowledging these things, I initiated a marital and family counseling service for blacks with the premise that a good many of the dysfunctions an individual observes in daily life have their ultimate origins in the family unit; and if one were to attempt to help alleviate these dysfunctions, even on a small scale, one might be able to demonstrate to blacks that the family experience is not all that negative. I also wanted to demonstrate that blacks, like any other ethnic group, were actively concerned with the quality of their family life as they attempted to raise their offspring to become both loving and productive adults in this society.

What I am saying about black family life is not new. The literature on this subject is voluminous. For example, Billingsley (1968), Hill (1972), and McAdoo (1975 and 1977), to name only a few authors, have highlighted the strengths of the black family. Conversely, the literature contains expositions of authors who have tended to view the black family life experience in a negative manner—for example, the well-known work by Daniel P. Moynihan (1965). Accordingly, it would be more than sufficient to state that black family life has been greatly researched and analyzed. Recent research has led to the negation of some of the older theories and to the conceptualization of more positive hypotheses regarding the black family. Yet, current research notwithstanding, the fact of the matter is that some of the same kinds of manifestations of black dysfunctional family units continue to be evidenced. Today in the black community there is drug abuse, religious cults, embracement of a consumerism concept, and acceptance of promiscuity. I realize that these problems are evidenced in other communities as well; however, my concern is with black family life, and I will limit my views to black people, while conceding that the black community does not hold exclusive rights to these problems.

The question is, what is to be done about these aspects of black family life? Are we to continue with our status quo methods of dealing with these issues, i.e., white scholars performing research on the black family and black scholars merely researching these very same family issues in order to gather data to dispute the findings of the white researchers? After this replicated research has been carried out, with its results celebrated as being contemporary, are we to continue observing still other black scholars researching the family, this time to negate their black predecessor's claims? This ongoing state of affairs is analagous to a classroom situation I once witnessed. The class was an introductory course in family therapy in which the professor was discussing the symptoms of a dysfunctional family unit. A number of the seemingly brighter students, in an attempt to impress the professor with their respective diagnostic skills, correctly identified the maladies the family presented; however, none of these students could respond effectively to the professor's query of how one would attempt to alleviate the symptoms therapeutically. Similarly, research is good when it helps pinpoint a family unit's dysfunctions, but it is better when it produces fresh methods of intervening in a family's dysfunctional interactional processes. Furthermore, research is even more praiseworthy when it helps to produce an intervention method that can be proven applicable and effective with black families, given their unique cultural experiences. As examples of these experiences, one asks the reader to consider a black couple living together in a consensual relationship, with or without offspring, sharing material possessions, whose relationship is based on the same kind of love and affection we, as traditional marrieds, experience. Should not this couple be considered married, that is, in the generic sense of the word?[1] Next, think of a single woman, one who has been left by her children's father to survive alone with her children. The woman and children are living together as a family unit with the woman evidencing nurturement as well as apprehensiveness over her children's welfare throughout their childhood and adolescence. Is it not a description of a family?[2] Whether this woman and her children are referred to as constituting an "attenuated nuclear family," as Billingsley (1968, p. 18) discusses, or as being a part of a "female-headed household," as Bernard (1966, p. 13) describes, or whether the former couple are part of a "consensual union," as offered by Liebow (1967, p. 105), I am confident that these people will experience the same kinds of problems and growth traumas as they grow as a couple or as a family unit that we traditionals experience in our marriages and family units. Therefore, the answers to these questions should be a resounding "yes." However, in the view of many social service agencies and of some marital and family psychotherapists as well, the couple is not married nor is the unit headed by one parent considered a legal family.[3] When this reality is conveyed to such individuals (that they are not legal entities per se), the result of these cognitions is, at least on some level, a diminished sense of self-worth.

These are some of the issues I considered when I conceptualized my marital and family counseling service, and these are the issues I will respond to presently. If we black professionals do not become actively concerned and involved on a meaningful level with these conspicuous, albeit semi-legal, aspects of our society as they exist in our community, who will do so? My experiences with these couples and family units in a clinical setting have more than supported my original impressions about present-day black family life. These experiences have also demonstrated to me that given a sincere and empathetic psychotherapeutic relationship between a counselor and his or her clients, black individuals will be receptive to psychological interventions in their marital and familial difficulties. Moreover, in working with these couples and family units, I have become very aware of both the saliency and the effects of our respective families of origin, i.e., the effect they have on an offspring's present-day perceptions of society in addition to the offspring's understanding of himself or herself and his or her personal independence. Yet, when this phenomenon is discussed with these couples or families, it is surprising to learn that many of them do not wish to or cannot consider sharing the fact of their achievement of autonomy or their current successes with their families of origin. They tend to feel that they alone achieved their autonomy, that they alone achieved their successes, not with their respective family of origin's assistance, but often in spite of it.

It should be clear (although unfortunately, it is not so apparent to many blacks today) that it was parents, grandparents, aunts, uncles, and all those within our families of origin who had an influence on us as youngsters and who guided us and helped make us the very individuals we presently consider ourselves to be. Furthermore, as they guided us in the past, in terms of assisting us in coping with the world as we experienced age-related difficulties and other problems, their influence, however slight it was felt to be, continues to guide us today as we interact with lovers, spouses, children, and the world. We are them.

There are several reasons why this connection is not so apparent to some blacks. For example, I have found that some blacks are ashamed of their parents' lack of formal education and feel that their parents' over-reliance on religion in times of stress interferes with their pragmatic and contemporary communication efforts. They cannot relate effectively to their parents' perceptions of the world. Still other blacks feel that they received no encouragement from their parents in their autonomy and risk-taking ventures. When they do succeed, they attribute their successes solely to themselves and choose to believe that they achieved their successes in spite of their parents. However, my experience and the therapeutic literature presents a different picture. A chief proponent of the role of early childhood experiences, Sigmund Freud, is well-known for his emphasis on the effects of parents on development. Freud (1924) felt that as a result of some inhibitory actions on the part of the parents, for instance, an individual may become stuck in any one of the developmental phases all individuals undergo and, as a result, may become distorted and underdeveloped in his or her emotional growth. In addition, Laing (1969 and 1972) felt that by looking at a client's family of origin, a therapist would be better able to understand the bases of dysfunctional behaviors. Moreover, Brown (1979) proposed that when specifically working with black families, a therapist should be flexible enough to include a family systems framework in the treatment repertoire to allow for the different ethnic variables that may change the presentation of the symptoms. I concur with these various observations, and I apply them in my therapeutic practice.

LISTENING FOR THE PAST

When a parent comes to me with a child who has a problem, after listening carefully to him or her, I often ask how this parent was raised and what the situation was like in his or her own family of origin. Once I have enough information to answer this question, it becomes apparent that it is not only a matter of a parent complaining about his or her offspring's behavior, but it is also a matter of the parent discussing his or her own childhood behaviors. The same is true of couples without children who are, for instance, having communication difficulties with each other. As soon as the history-taking is completed, it becomes apparent why this or that partner has the communication problem. He or she has learned to communicate in a particular manner from the family of origin, and unless these imitations are pointed out and frankly dealt with (in the case of the parent as well as the couple), there probably will be no amelioration of the dysfunctional behaviors.

At this juncture, let me make it clear that I am not proposing either a psychoanalytic or behavioral therapeutic approach,[4] when I emphasize the importance of understanding a client's family of origin. What I am advocating is that in any clinical setting it is pragmatic, if the counselor wishes to understand the client's present behaviors, to try to determine and comprehend the connection between these behaviors and those of the client's family of origin. This can be accomplished most readily using Bowen's (1971) approach. Taking this pragmatism further, when the counselor finally comprehends these connections, then this understanding can be shared with the client. This will assist the client in understanding the rationales for his or her present behaviors. Furthermore, the simple act of sharing these connections with the client will serve to lay the foundations for meaningful change and growth, both in marital and family problems. Assuming that this sharing is done in a noncondescending, intrinsic, and empathetic manner, the counselor/therapist is also demonstrating to the client that he or she is concerned and trusting of the client's ability to comprehend the generational connections. This empathetic sharing with the client of this recently understood connection between generational behaviors will, in turn, tend to foster a sincere receptiveness within the client, who perhaps for the first time, can begin to comprehend and appreciate the origins of his or her behaviors.

When I initially see a client who presents a marital problem, for instance, I tend to view the presentation as a "mirror-image" of his or her family of origin's behavior, while at the same time attempting not to negate the client's perception of the presenting problem. I feel that on some level, the client has incorporated the family of origin's methods of dealing with conflict, joy, trauma, and many other situations into his or her own behavioral repertoire. Assuming that the spouse has brought his or her own generational behavior patterns from the family of origin to the marriage as well, the couple is now faced with an interactional dilemma: which of the two behavioral repertoires should they follow in order to maintain both a viable and conflict-free relationship? Which one of the two makes the compromise, and to what degree is he or she expected to compromise? It has been my experience that both clients tend to view this potential compromise process as analagous to being "swallowed-up" in the process, i.e., a process that will eventually result in the loss of his or her identity as an individual. However, the direction I attempt to take is one that will somehow mesh these two behavioral repertoires into one that both clients will find mutually satisfying and functional. However, before this can be done effectively, it must be demonstrated to both clients that the act of effecting a compromise in perceptions does not in fact necessitate either one losing his or her individual identity.

In the course of ascertaining their respective family of origin's behavioral modalities, I do not attempt to dwell on the origins of personality formation, as is done with psychoanalysis. As with some of the more traditional psychotherapies, I feel that psychoanalysis is not applicable to most blacks, given their cultural background. Moreover, I am more concerned with the clients' present interactional processes with each other than with their personality formations. Rather, I focus on the client's post-adolescent perceptions of family life and how his or her family experienced and negotiated conflict, joy, and traumas. The rationale for this focus and emphasis is that clients, without much effort, are more likely to recall their family of origin's environment during the clients' older years and are likely to recognize what they have experienced now that they are beyond the adolescent period. This would not be the case should I focus upon a client's personality formation period and his or her family's interactional processes jointly. Also, the therapeutic process would indeed be much longer.

Once the generational behavioral connections are ascertained and understood, they can be cognitively shared with the clients. After this process is completed and after the clients are fully aware of their behavioral bases, the presenting problem (which is now viewed as a "mirror-image") can be dealt with effectively and hopefully ameliorated. The point stressed in this process is that we are our parents' children, and more often than not, will respond to the world and its stresses as they did.

CASE STUDIES

The following discussion contains excerpts from interviews with two cases I counseled—a single parent and a married couple. I feel that these excerpts highlight what I have been discussing in terms of the saliency of these clients' respective families of origin and the effects of their behaviors on the clients' behaviors.

Case 1

Delores, an attractive 26-year-old single parent, is living with Clifton, 30 years old, and her son Richard, a normal and active eight-year-old. Delores and Clifton have been living together for two years. During this time, they have represented themselves to the community as being a family unit. They have been accepted and admired by this community for their apparent intrinsic and viable relationship.

Delores, however, feels that she has a problem. She feels that her relationship is deteriorating, but cannot understand what is wrong. She is aware that the "sense of family" she had been experiencing is no longer there. She is also witnessing this lack of emotional security in her son's attitude. A friend of hers advises her to seek professional counseling.

When I first met Delores, I saw that she was on the verge of tears. As she struggled to hold them back, she managed to inform me of her perceptions of her present relationship. Specifically, she indicated that Clifton, who had until six months ago acted as the perfect "husband" and the perfect "father," now increasingly had decided to absent himself from their residence without explanation, for days at a time.

Delores said that her attempts to secure an explanation from Clifton had resulted in his belittling her concern for the relationship and often evolved into altercations. He had also begun criticizing her appearance. This caused her to wonder whether or not she was attractive. Delores also informed me that she wanted to maintain the relationship, but if this were not possible, she would attempt to manage on her own. At this point Delores began to cry uncontrollably. Afterwards, she regained her composure, and the following dialogue took place:

DELORES: I don't really know if I want to remain in this relationship, or attempt to manage on my own. Richard... he is so hungry for the "father" relationship that Clifton provides... whenever he wants to. Richard, he is fully aware of the tension. Maybe I am afraid of starting out all over again?

THERAPIST: I don't know at this point.

D: When I was weighing 160 pounds, it seemed that Clifton and I didn't argue as often. We seemed to do things as a family then. I changed my diet, lost some weight, and now all he seems to do is criticize me and my dress. It is as though he is afraid of my being too attractive. I wonder if I am or not?

T: I would say that you are.

D: I have even thought of having an affair. That way, I would be able to feel good about myself again... feel like a woman!

T: I don't think that this is the way you should look at things, I mean, after all...

D: I need some help in getting myself together. Then, maybe I could better understand what to do with my life. Am I secure or do I really want out?

T: At this point, I do not really know. I cannot answer that question.

There was a long silence as Delores pondered her own question. Then, because I was still unsure what it was that Delores wanted from me in terms of assistance, I asked her two questions:

T: Are you asking me to assist you in solidifying your relationship with Clifton or are you asking me to assist you with your ability to cope with life in general?

D: I want you to help me. I do not feel good about myself. Maybe afterwards I will be better able to make up my mind in deciding to stay in the relationship or to leave.

T: What about Clifton? Is he aware of your being here, and if so, do you feel that he would respond to an invitation to come here with you the next time?

> *D:* I have discussed counseling with him before, and he feels that he doesn't need anyone to help him. He is in his "macho bag." No, he isn't aware of my being here.
>
> *T:* Perhaps when he became aware that you thought it necessary to seek outside assistance, he might change his mind. Or, perhaps should he witness a change in you he may, out of curiosity, decide to accompany you here some time.
>
> *D:* I doubt that.

At this point we agreed that we should continue these sessions on a weekly basis and leave open the possibility of having Clifton join us in the future. When the session was over, I considered the interaction we had just completed. It was difficult for me to formulate even a tentative interpretation of the kinds of emotional impasses she had been experiencing. Delores seemed to be expressing a number of issues, and the one that seemed the most salient to me was the reference to her son's hunger for fatherly love. Thinking about this issue, I wondered whether or not Delores felt helplessly trapped in her situation solely because of Richard and whether or not she might take her frustration out on him. I was concerned that perhaps Richard's need for affection from Clifton may have been Clifton's rationale for staying away from the residence. However, experience had demonstrated to me that when a counselor gives in to the natural impulse to make a decision too early in the counseling process, he or she runs the risk of rendering an extreme disservice to the client. So I decided to wait for other kinds of information from Delores before I made any decision. Therefore, at our second session, I attempted to secure some specific background information from her including religious attitudes; friendship patterns; "in-law" liaisons; activities; budget; and sexual interaction.[5] Responding to my queries, Delores informed me that she had been raised a Roman Catholic, but had recently switched to an Eastern creed because Clifton was involved in it. She also stated that she had changed her devotion not out of conviction, but out of love for him. Discussing her "in-laws," Delores informed me that Clifton's mother seemed to like and accept her, while his father, who appeared very conservative and moralistic to her, did not appear to approve of her or the relationship. This fact seemed to bother her, but as she had been secure in her relationship initially with Clifton, she indicated that she tried to overlook his objections.

Asked about her parents, Delores informed me that hers was a long story, but that she would try to relate it to me:

> *T:* Tell me about your side, your parents, and how you get along with them, given your present life-style.
>
> *D:* Well . . . My mother and father separated when I was very young, and my mother moved us girls to another state. My parents didn't keep in contact, and when I was a teenager, I found out that my father had died when I had

been thirteen years old! (Remembering this, Delores attempted to hold back the tears)...My mother...she now lives in another state, and we don't keep in contact. My mother seems to accept my present life-style, but she doesn't visit often.

The remainder of this session dealt with other matters of concern, e.g., Clifton's type of employment, their joint household budget and expenses, etc. However, even as we discussed these matters, my mind kept returning to Delores' family of origin. At this point, I had not comprehended fully her present behaviors or the connection between them and those of her family of origin. However, I felt that this area would be explored further, once we had established a firmer rapport with one another. It was also apparent that continued discussion about her family at this point was too troublesome for her.

The third session was uneventful. Delores indicated that matters had not really changed that much between her and Clifton. We seemed to be getting nowhere, with the slight exception that Delores indicated that the sessions were helpful to her. However, between this one and the next session, Delores telephoned and requested that she be allowed to bring Clifton with her to the next session. She and he had been discussing the matter, and Clifton had expressed that, perhaps, he himself needed some counseling. Personally, I was elated. Perhaps now, I thought, some real progress might be made, for it was apparent that he was a very central figure in her life; and unless he instituted some movement, there would be no movement in her.

At the fourth session, after exchanging the usual pleasantries, Delores excused herself and went to the restroom. As Clifton and I were left alone, it seemed natural to strike up a general conversation until she returned. Clifton, however, was not prepared to interact with me yet. He looked around the office without saying a word. Afterwards, he sat down and said:

CLIFTON: What exactly are your qualifications to sit there and present yourself as a marital and family counselor?

(Taken aback momentarily by such frankness and also uncertain as to what he was asking, I asked for some clarification.)

THERAPIST: I am not sure that I understand your question. Is it possible that perhaps you could clarify what you mean?

(Visibly annoyed that I had not comprehended his initial query, he decided to re-phrase his question.)

C: Are you married?
T: Yes.

(He began to smile.)

C: That's what I wanted to hear! For I, as a man, can't seem to maintain any sort of long-term relationship...

At this point, Delores returned to the office, and Clifton reverted to his former stoical posture. It was as though he was not prepared to allow Delores to observe him in a feeling response set. Unfortunately, what had been about to unfold from Clifton never did. The session then focused around their respective perceptions of the relationship and the possibility that some different explanations might be applicable to their respective views of the relationship. Clifton expressed some ambivalence at being committed to additional sessions, though he admitted that this experience had not quite been what he had imagined. We then decided that perhaps it would be best if they themselves discussed the probabilities of continuing and that they should inform me of their joint decision during the following week. A few days later, Clifton telephoned and indicated that he wanted to see me alone. After he arrived, he took this opportunity to discuss some general matters, but resisted my efforts to deal specifically with issues between him and Delores. Clifton informed me that once he got to know me better, then he would feel more comfortable in discussing specific things. This, however, was the last time I would see Clifton. He cancelled his next two appointments (it had been decided that I would see them on a tandem basis, i.e., individual, individual, conjoint, etc.).[6] Yet, he chose not to interfere with Delores' attendance at subsequent sessions, which by now were changed structurally to individual and on a weekly basis.

Delores continued faithfully to attend her scheduled sessions and, in doing so, became an emotionally stronger individual. In time, she became able to formulate her priorities, and she informed me rather decisively that she did indeed want to remain in the relationship with Clifton, but would do so only if she could remain there on an equal basis.

Unfortunately, this was not to be so. Two months later Clifton decided to leave Delores and Richard, and his separation from the relationship had its predictable effects on Delores. She experienced the normal feelings of loss, hurt, self-doubt, and anger—the kinds of feelings anyone would experience in a similar situation. Delores' progress in therapy at this point was almost nonexistent as she struggled through each experiential phase of adjustment. Although, however, she had good reason to, Delores did not regress to her former emotional state. Instead, she seemed to make a concentrated effort to learn more about herself and the possible reasons for her present behaviors. It was as though she reasoned that if she understood herself more, perhaps she would be less inclined to repeat her present behaviors in the future. For me, it was this decision of hers that facilitated the therapeutic process; this decision that ultimately allowed me to understand her as an individual in her own right. Now, it became possible for me to begin to understand the connection between her present behaviors and those of her family of origin.

Together, we explored aspects of her past including her family composition, the presence of emotional feelings apparent to her within her family (nuclear and extended) and how they have been resolved, and her perceptions of her parents' interactions with each other. These discussions lasted for a few sessions as their content tended to evoke both powerful and warm memories.

THERAPIST: Tell me about your family life as you remember it. Describe for me, if you will, your immediate family composition.

DELORES: Well, there are two of us girls, my mother and father. What I should say is that it is just my mother now because my father is dead, although he left us when I was five or six... I really can't remember when.

T: Two girls? How did you two get along with each other?

D: Not too good. And even now we don't quite get along... although I wish that we did... that we could be closer than we are. She lives near me, but we seldom see one another. She's got her life and I have mine.

T: What did you mean when you said that the two of you did not get along too good?

D: Well, we just seemed to get on each other's nerves. We really didn't have any friends, so all we had was each other, and I guess that this was the cause of the friction between us.

T: No friends?

D: Yeah, no friends. Well, when my father left us, his leaving seemed to have a real bad effect upon my mother... so bad that she was hospitalized for her nerves. And afterwards, she seemed to feel that there was a conspiracy against us, so she wouldn't allow us to have any friends or even to visit them. We were only allowed to go to school and come directly back home. So, we often wound up playing with each other a lot.

T: It sounds as if your childhood was not all that pleasant.

D: No, it wasn't... (long pause)... I guess that I feel that I really never had a family life. I guess this is why I am so concerned that Richard has a good family life. (Her last statement was made more like a question).

T: Perhaps so. What about your mother now? Do you keep in contact with her?

D: No, not really. She doesn't seem herself. I often wished that we did keep in contact much more than we do now, but she doesn't seem to take care of herself... and, she is such a young woman! We should be closer, and she ought to do something with her life! She's just wasting away!

(Tears are now coming uncontrollably down Delores' face.)

D: If she would only settle down... then, the children would have a place to visit their grandmother like other children do! (Delores is also referring to her sister's children.)

> *T:* Tell me about your father. What do you remember about him?

(Wiping her eyes with a tissue and now smiling)

> *D:* He was big and gentle, so long as he wasn't drinking. He was nice.

> *T:* It sounds as if you have some good memories about him.

> *D:* I really didn't know him too well, but I do remember the drinking part. I guess that's why I do not like men today who cannot hold their drinking. And this feeling applies to Clifton when he drinks.

Considering our discussion, it became clear to me that Delores did not have many pleasant memories about her formative years, and even as she thought about this time frame, she experienced an "emotional void." Her adolescent years were also not particularly enjoyable, as her mother increased her control over the two girls as they relocated from city to city to avoid the possible manifestations of the "conspiracy" that the mother continued to believe existed.

Delores often wondered whether or not she would ever be happy. Moreover, she wished more than anything else to have a good family life for herself and for her son Richard. As we continued with our discussion of her family of origin, the connection between its behavioral modality and Delores' present life-style became clear. Delores' mother and father had separated when she was a child, and as she was not fully aware of the actual reasons for the separation, Delores perceived this separation as being abandoned by her father. Her mother, because of her emotional difficulties, was not really a mother to Delores; and as a result, Delores felt that she really did not have an adequate family life. This basic feeling was aggravated further by the fact that she and her family were continually on the move, never having a chance to establish security in any one community and the fact that Delores and her sister had not been allowed to interact with any peers outside of the family.

Eventually, it became possible for me to share my perceptions of this connection between her past experiences and her present life-style and behaviors. Delores finally arrived at the understanding of her sense of imperativeness in seeking to establish and maintain a viable family life—the one that she had often referred to as being a "void." She also understood how those previous experiences manifested themselves (in perhaps a negative manner) in her present relationship with Clifton. This sharing, as I commented on elsewhere in this discussion, thus became the vehicle for the meaningful change and growth I was to witness later.

By the start of our eleventh session, Delores had begun to evidence the beginnings of this change. She had become more interested in her employment, her apartment, and more importantly, in her son. However, it became necessary for me to caution her against being too involved with her son, as she was beginning to show signs of being too protective of Richard. It was as though she was afraid of losing him, too. Ultimately, however, it became clear to me that my concerns were in vain, as she accepted my comments. They developed a healthy mother-son relationship. Today, Delores has changed and grown, and has demonstrated to me that she is in full charge of her life. Richard has progressed normally in school, and it is apparent that he is enjoying his life as an eight-year-old. A follow-up telephone conversation with Delores had revealed that matters for her are generally much better than before. She informed me that Richard was excitedly looking forward to beginning his first camp experience, but that she had some ambivalence toward his leaving her for two months. She also informed me that she had recently encountered Clifton in a public building and was surprised to learn that he was now living with another friend. She seemed surprised also at her own reaction which indicated to her that she was obviously much stronger now. She stated: "I guess I am stronger now, stronger than I thought I was." Continuing, she intimated: "You know that I am afraid of allowing Richard to go away from me for such a long time, but when I realized that I would be doing the same thing my mother did with me, I decided that he has to go.... He should go! After all, he *needs* to be with his friends."

Case 2

Roxanne and Donald initially informed me that they had been having some difficulty in understanding each other. They have been married for 10 years, and now it seems that they have been experiencing communication problems with one another, much more than they had been previously. Neither one could offer an explanation for this present situation, and both feared that they were drifting apart. Roxanne, a 40-year-old housewife, and Donald, 35 years old, presented themselves as a loving couple and parents of four "beautiful" children. The clients felt that they were somehow the "victims" of some strange maturational process. However, together, we were able to identify this process as not being a maturational one, but rather a manifestation of the behavioral patterns of their families of origin present in their marriage.

During the initial interview with this couple, the following interchange took place:

THERAPIST: To start, I would like to state that I only seem to have some general information about both of you, as a couple and as individuals. So, if one of you would like to begin telling me some more about your problem, I think that this would be a good way to start.

ROXANNE: Well, we have been married for some 10 years now, and we have four beautiful children. Donald has a fairly good job, and we don't seem to have any problems financially. Also, we do not have any problems with the children to speak of. What we do have is a problem with each other. It seems that all we do lately is argue. I mean, it could be over something small...and we wind up arguing! I must say that so far . . . there has been no violence . . . any hitting. I don't know what is happening to us. But, I do know that it simply has to stop! My nerves can't take it anymore!

(She is addressing the husband, who seemed annoyed at his spouse's presentation of the problem.)

THERAPIST: Tell me, do you view the problem in a similar fashion as your wife?

DONALD: Well, yes and no. What she said about the arguing is correct. We do seem to argue a lot. But, I am not so sure that it is as great a problem as she says it is. All people have arguments! But, she seems to think that it . . . that is, when we argue our marriage is at stake. I don't quite feel that way. When there is something to discuss which I feel is important, I believe that it ought to be talked about. That's the way I was raised, and this is the way I try to teach my children. I don't believe in holding things in, as she does.

(A small disagreement arises, and the clients ignore the therapist.)

T: Let me interrupt this now. . . . Perhaps, if we could begin to listen carefully to one another, then we may begin to understand the problem. Now, why don't you, Roxanne, tell me how long this has been going on?

R: Well, it really has been going on . . . not to the degree that it is now, for some time. But, I was always able to work around it, being involved with the children and all. But, now that the children seem to be getting bigger and more interested in their friends, I find that I am more sensitive to it now. When he wakes, he starts arguing, and when he comes home, there is usually an argument. It seems that the only time there is any peace anymore is when he is working. . . .

D: That's not true! To hear you tell it, I am all bad! . . . Well, if I am all that bad, how do you explain all that you have? How would you explain the type of life that you lead? The house, the clothes you wear, and the private schools which your children had to attend, who gave them to you?

R: Donald, you did of course. . . . But, this is not what I am talking about. . . . I am talking about us and our marriage!

D: See what I mean?

T: This is what I was referring to when I said a moment ago that we should listen to one another. It seems to me, if I am hearing you both correctly, that you both seem to be saying something important to each other. The problem is that you both are not actually listening to one another. Obviously, there are some issues which have to be addressed, some historical issues which have to be dealt with before this problem can be corrected. Perhaps, these issues can best be dealt with in a series of tandem interviews. It is up to you. However, what you both have to realize is that I am not a judge, and I have no

intention of judging the correctness of either one's perceptions. I wish
to help both of you with your present difficulty, if you will let me.

At this point, I explained to them the term *tandem interviews*, and they
agreed to participate in them. Both clients felt that the tandem series of
interviews would be beneficial, for it would allow them the opportunity to
express individually their respective perceptions of the marriage to me without the other interrupting. Donald indicated: "Yes, this is what I would like.
This way, perhaps, I could say what I feel without constantly feeling like my
marriage was in jeopardy." The remainder of this session continued as it had
begun—accusation and defense.

At the next session, Roxanne was able to inform me that she felt that her
husband was not really interested in her as an individual. True, he was
responsible, and he had provided her with a fairly comfortable life. However,
in terms of their interpersonal activities, she felt that there was a lot to be
desired, and she had often thought of leaving him because at times he was
simply unbearable to live with. We discussed her consideration of separation
and divorce and the probable effects such actions would have on the children.
Resolving to give counseling efforts a try, but yet not fully convinced that
these efforts would bring about a change in their interactions, Roxanne
indicated that she would remain with these sessions as long as she felt that
Donald was sincere in his efforts, too. Listening to her, I was struck by the
metaphor of two children discussing a task to be performed: "I will try it if you
do!"

A subsequent session with Donald proved to be more fruitful when he
informed me that he had been raised in a very poor environment. Often, he
indicated, there had not been enough food for his family to eat, and he had to
leave school at a very early age to assist his father on their tenant farm. Donald
stated that he had then resolved that he would never attempt to raise his own
family as he had been raised. He viewed himself as a self-taught individual,
one who had overcome quite a lot of economic hardships and one who should
be respected by his spouse for his endeavors. Instead, he felt that she did not
respect him for his previous and present efforts and always seemed to want
more and more from him. He continued to say that he had obtained for her all
the things that she wished for, and yet, she still wanted more of him. Lately,
she expressed to him that she wanted more attention from him. Donald was at
a loss as to how this could be accomplished, since he was now working two
jobs in order to pay for some of the things they had purchased. Whenever he
stated his feelings about matters in the household, it inevitably resulted in an
argument. He did not think that he could do anymore than he was already
doing.

Once again the saliency of the family of origin became apparent. Here was
an individual who had been raised in almost squalid conditions, often not
having adequate food to eat, but who had bettered himself. He was overem-

ployed and making a more-than-adequate living for himself and for his family. Moreover, he had done all of this without the benefit of completing his formal education. He was self-taught, and he was responsible. He could indeed be proud of all he had accomplished. However, this connection between his family of origin's environment and his present difficulty with his spouse had manifested itself in a somewhat negative manner. He was too concerned with materialistic things to even consider the dysfunctional emotional aspects of his marriage. We frankly discussed this connection, and he began to understand the effect it was having on his spouse. Also, we agreed that these matters would again be discussed in the following session, which would be a conjoint one.

At the next session, both clients arrived at the office together in an apparently better mood with each other than before. When one discussed something, the other listened intently and without the obvious annoyance displayed before. It seemed as if they had decided actually to listen to one another. When we did discuss the connection between Donald's original family environment and his present attitude about material items, Roxanne was understanding and even supportive. Her response seemed to surprise Donald. Evidently, although they had been communicating with one another between sessions, he had not discussed these matters with her and had chosen instead to bring them up in this therapeutic setting. Once these matters had been discussed and accepted by both clients as being the bases for Donald's present attitude and behaviors, Donald then sought a more concrete answer to their present difficulties:

> *D*: Although I can accept the basic reason for my present concern with material things and that I do want to provide them for my wife and family, what do you suggest that we do to stop these arguments... these heated arguments?
>
> *T*: Well, specifically, I do not really know what to tell you. If, however, it seems that you find yourself in a rut, having to work continually to make ends meet, which in turn causes you to not have enough time to interact positively with Roxanne, which in turn causes her to feel neglected and not appreciated and results in arguments between you both; then, it would seem to me logically, that you should attempt to alleviate the basis for all of this—your having to work as you do....
>
> *R*: Yes.
>
> *T*: Perhaps, the two of you could come to some agreement regarding the necessity of working as you do? Perhaps it would be possible if Roxanne were to obtain a part-time job to assist you with the finances...a small, part-time job in the neighborhood, so that she would not have to be that far away from the children. This would seem to alleviate some of the tension and pressure on you, Donald, What do you think?
>
> *R*: Yes...I discussed this with him some time ago.

> *D*: I don't know.... Well, maybe it is possible....
>
> *T*: Well, whatever decision is made, it should be made together. Why don't the both of you return home and discuss it? Perhaps you will accept my suggestion, perhaps not. However, it is a start in the right direction.
>
> *R*: Yes, let's do that, Donald.

This couple's problem was solvable, again after the generational connection had been ascertained and understood by both myself and the clients. Unfortunately, attempts to determine any long-term results of my intervention proved to be unsuccessful, as the clients changed residences since I last saw them. However, if not immediately hearing from them could be construed as an indication of a successful intervention, then this intervention was indeed successful.

As with these two examples, a number of interventions might also be termed successful if the therapist/counselor were to seek out the generational connections between behavioral patterns, and once they are identified and comprehended, utilize them as a basis for meaningful change and growth in the individual, as well as in the relationship. However, a therapist/counselor must also be cautious enough not to perceive a client as a mere replica of his or her parents; but, rather view the client as an unique personality in his or her own right who is very similar, but at the same time different from his or her parents. For, as our perceptions of the world have essentially been formed as a result of our interactions with our parents and other family members, so too will our children's perceptions be formed as a consequence of their interactions with us. For, they are us. Our respective families of origin are and will continue to be a very powerful influence on all of our behaviors, notwithstanding our desires and our perceived states of independence. Hence, our family of origin's influence, however subtle it may seem, should not be underestimated; for, we are our parents' children.

NOTES

1. According to New York County Family Court Lawyers Association (475 Fifth Avenue, New York, New York), consensual relationships in New York State are not recognized as constituting a legal union. However, if a consensual relationship between two persons originated in a state that recognized it as a legal marriage, and the couple now resides in New York State, then New York State would also recognize it as constituting a legal marriage.

2. New York City Family Court does not recognize either a consensual relationship or a consensual family unit (except under the aforementioned conditions). Hence, domestic disturbances involving assaults are usually adjudicated in the Criminal Court system.

3. New York City Department of Social Services, which administers the Public Assistance Funds (Aid to Dependent Children and Income Maintenance Programs), does not recognize consensual family units. Yet, according to a recent article in *The New York Times*, June 27, 1979, by Robert Reinhold, the U.S. Census Bureau reported that the number of unmarried couples living together has more than doubled in the first eight years of this decade and has increased more than eightfold among persons under 25 years old. A corollary trend is the family headed by a woman. The numbers of families in which no man is present rose from 5.6 million in 1970 to 8 million in 1978—a 43 percent increase nationally. Unfortunately, this article offers no ethnic percentage breakdown.

4. *Psychoanalysis*: a psychotherapy, conceptualized by Sigmund Freud, wherein a client's intrapsychic past interactions with his or her parents when the client was a child are emphasized and explored to foster insight and change in his or her personality.

Behavior Therapy: based on the laboratory work of both B. F. Skinner and J. Wolpe, a psychotherapy emphasizing learned behavior and that re-learning of the present maladaptive behaviors is necessary in order to produce change and growth in a client.

5. This interview format is termed a Reality-Oriented Method of a conjoint diagnostic interview, originated by A. R. Williams (1974).

6. This format of marital counseling was originated by James M. Murphy (1976) and combines individual and conjoint sessions alternately with the same therapist.

REFERENCES

Bernard, J. *Marriage and Family among Negroes*. Englewood Cliffs, N.J.: Prentice-Hall, 1966.

Billingsley, A. *Black Families in White America*. Englewood Cliffs, N.J.: Prentice-Hall, 1968.

Bowen, M. "The Use of Family Theory in Clinical Practice," In J. Haley (ed) *Changing Families*. New York: Grune and Stratton, 1971.

Brown, A. "Understanding and Treating Black Families," *The Family*, 1979, 7(1), 38–40.

Freud, S. *A General Introduction to Psychoanalysis*. Boston: Boni-Liverwright, 1924.

Hill, R. *The Strengths of Black Families*. New York: Emerson Hall, 1972.

Laing, R. D. *The Politics of the Family*. New York: Pantheon Books, 1969.

———, and A. Esterson. *Sanity, Madness and the Family*. Baltimore, Md.: Penguin Books, Ltd. 1972.

Liebow, E. *Tally's Corner*. Boston: Little, Brown & Co., 1967.

Moynihan, D. P. *The Negro Family: The Case for National Action*. Prepared for the Office of Policy Planning and Research, 1965.

Murphy, J. M. "A Tandem Approach: Marriage Counseling as a Process in Tandem with Individual Psychotherapy," *Journal of Marriage and Family Counseling*, 1976, 2, 13–22.

McAdoo, H. "The Extended Family," *Journal of Afro-American Issues*, 1975, 3 & 4(1), 15–19.

_____ . "A Review of the Literature Related to Family Therapy in the Black
    Community," *Journal of Contemporary Psychotherapy*, 1977, 9(1), 15–19.
Williams, A. R. "The Initial Conjoint Marital Interview: One Procedure," *The Family
    Coordinator*, 1974, 23(4), 391–397.
Wolpe, J. "Reciprocal Inhibition as the Main Basis of Psychotherapeutic Effects,"
    American Medical Association's Archives of Neurological Psychiatry, 1954,
    72, 250–276.

13

STYLISTIC COUNSELING OF THE BLACK FAMILY

Johnnie McFadden

> The family is the most basic institution of any people, the center and source of its civilization .... (Black) families have shown an amazing ability to survive in the face of impossible conditions. They have also shown remarkable ability to take the barest shreds of opportunity and turn them into the social capital of stability and achievement.
>
> (Andrew Billingsley, 1968, p. iii)

Counseling the black family requires thorough knowledge of the components in the three dimensions to counseling blacks: cultural-historical, psychosocial, and scientific-ideological (McFadden, 1976). These dimensions, which will be discussed in full later, are germane to the diverse stylisms of blacks as a people. However, before discussing the processes of counseling black families, some background needs to be given about these entities.

The black family is a unit of special interest. It constitutes broad forms, from nuclear to extended, and various unique characteristics. Because of the varied adaptations with which blacks as individuals have identified, to group black families under a single description is to deny them their varying abilities to adapt to an array of economic, social, and political institutions. For the purpose of this discourse, the author refers to the majority of black families in America. A word of caution would indicate to the reader that there are black families in this country who would be grouped outside both ends of the author's continuum.

Andrew Billingsley (1968) has suggested that historically, many studies on the black family have failed to realize the diversity of the family structures and have focused on a limited number of functions. Although these family structures and functions differ from those of the dominant society, they are all viable and should not be expected to conform to the norm of any other group.

Since they do not deviate from a norm, then they are not inherently pathological. "Whatever ails the Negro family is a reflection of ailments in the society at large" (p. 32).

Robert Staples (1971) echoes the condemnation of the white middle-class norms that have been used as the barometer of what is regarded as desirable family structure and behavior. "As a separate sub-culture . . . the Black family may be depicted as an autonomous social system with mores and folkways that diverge from the larger society" (p. 120). "With its own values, norms, and sanctions, the black family 'represents a unit of considerable variety and complexity'" (p. 127).

Other works attest to the stability of the black family in a historical perspective. Herbert Gutman (1976) explains how, from the days of slavery, blacks maintained powerful familial and kin associations which sustained the developing Afro-American culture. The author attributes his book to the controversy between Moynihan and his critics, which sparked Gutman's preliminary study in 1967–1968. Providing additional witness to Gutman's findings is the widely acclaimed *Roots* by Alex Haley (1976). This book is compelling evidence of the power of the black family tradition as the author traces his ancestry over seven generations to the African, born in Gambia, named Kunta Kinte.

The black family is no longer being perceived as a "tangle of pathology" (Moynihan, 1965). William Ryan (1965) made public the serious shortcomings of the Moynihan Report, based on careful analysis. He considers the report a new form of subtle racism since it seduces the reader into believing that it is not racism and discrimination, but the weaknesses and defects of blacks themselves, that account for the present status of inequality between black and white.

Warren D. TenHouten (1970) discusses various myths associated with the black family and refutes them. For example, he does not consider matriarchy as dysfunctional because it is not in line with American society. "Female dominance in any role cannot be assumed to be dysfunctional for the particular group to which it refers. Since groups differ in their relations to important systems in society, especially the economy, it may be that different social contexts" must exist (p. 149). On the question of female-led households, TenHouten is of the opinion that there is little, if any, justification for defining black families as pathological on the ground that there is no husband present. The important criterion is the functioning capacity of the family. "Family units in which the husband is present may be unhappy and disorganized, and family units in which the husband is absent may be happy and well organized" (p. 154).

TenHouten also gives several reasons for the assumed high illegitimacy rates for blacks. Black "illegitimate births" are more apt to be recorded as such than are similar births for members of the dominant society. Statistics might show that a child is illegitimate simply because the mother, if she admits the presence of the father in the home, will risk her eligibility for welfare benefits. Finally, the poor have limited access to contraceptive devices. Moreover, "illegitimate black babies" are generally incorporated into the family unit rather than being concealed and expelled from the family and community. "In the black community there are norms that the entire family will take responsibility for a child" who becomes a regular member of the parent's family (p. 152).

CHARACTERISTICS AND FORMS OF THE BLACK FAMILY

The black family is a symbol of unity and strength. It represents a foundation on which the black community builds and generates a viable force for substance and progress. The black family is an entity that contains variable patterns. It is a mutually definable unit which is goal-oriented and embedded with internal commitment and mutual trust. To relate to the black family as a counselor is to understand the cultural world of this group and to know its history, psychology, sociology, and ideology.

Emerging models of the black family are among the variety of family forms representing various cultural and ethnic groups. These distinctive family life-styles are a product of black culture and exhibit such characteristics as strong kinship bonds; strong work, religious, and achievement orientation; and adaptability of family roles (Hill, 1972; Lieberman, 1973; and Nobles, 1974). Members of this cultural group have found these characteristics to be compatible with their life-styles. For example, unique child-rearing practices and differing parental roles and functions typify the black family. Lewis (1975) states that both male and female children are encouraged to be assertive and initiating. They are highly stimulated and supported for exhibiting strength and courage. Lewis further states that strong individuality is paired with strong connectedness. Black children are not "inculcated with standards which polarize behavioral expectations according to sex" (p. 228). Role separation is not amplified among black children. Behaviors appropriate for one sex are equally as appropriate for the opposite sex. Nobles (1974) states that it is not at all uncommon to discover that among adults black men engage in domestic or emotional functions generally assigned to women in the United States and for black women to be engaged in economic or support functions generally assigned to men. "Even children participate fully and integrally in family affairs" (p. 14). Black children learn at an early age that the primary object is to get the task done and that this requires a cooperative effort. Distinct separation of roles for the sexes, then, does not expedite this. The process in black family life is characterized by an "egalitarian pattern of relationships" (p. 14). Thus, child-rearing practices are uniquely geared toward equipping black children with a form of cultural sustentation that will enable them to exist in a hostile environment. They are prepared to assume roles germane to their being, roles that are flexible, interchangeable, and fluid by historical and philosophical definition in America.

Another characteristic of black families is that they consist of elements of the extended family. This extension invariably encompasses one or more grandparents. Hence, it is not uncommon for black youngsters to assume the moral and ethical characteristics of their elders. The concept of child-rearing had its linkage on the African soil and was transcended and ingrained on the American soil. Therefore, the black elderly have been traditionally an integral part of the total family structure. Institutional caring for black senior citizens has received minimal attention from the black community. Close association with one's children and grandchildren is natural. This is best maintained by physical proximity. It is not only expected by one's family and confidants, but it is generally accepted by blacks themselves that it is one phase of their life mission to house and/or care for older persons in their family. Even if the elder ones live in separate quarters, their children maintain a close relationship and contact. If there happens to be no blood children in the immediate vicinity, the black elderly interact with nearby neighbors or members of their extended family.

Concerning family forms, in order to counsel the black family, one must have a vivid awareness of the viability and variety of family forms and functions as well as the characteristics and strengths inherent in these forms. Billingsley (1968) suggests that many studies have neglected to recognize the large variety of black family structures. In order to correct this distorted image, Billingsley outlines a typology of family structures and a number of family functions that should be taken into consideration:

Nuclear Families
   Incipient - husband and wife
   Simple - husband, wife, children
   Attenuated - single parent, children

Extended Families
   Incipient - husband, wife, other relatives
   Simple - husband, wife, children, other relatives
   Attenuated - single parent, children, other relatives

Augmented Families
   Incipient - husband, wife, nonrelatives
   Incipient Extended - husband, wife, other relatives, nonrelatives
   Nuclear - husband, wife, children, nonrelatives
   Nuclear Extended - husband, wife, children, other relatives, nonrelatives

Attenuated - single parent, children, nonrelatives

Attenuated Extended - single parent, children, other relatives, nonrelatives

Billingsley's topology provided a start, and Williams and Stockton (1973) recommended some modifications in the foregoing descriptions. The topology by Billingsley requires that a household head must either have a spouse and/or be a parent. There are groups of related individuals living together who meet neither of these criteria, i.e., siblings living together, a child living with an aunt or grandparent. Thus, for example, Williams and Stockton suggest that consideration might be given to changing the heading "single parent" in the typology to "single parent or surrogate." Children living with individuals other than a parent could then be included. Individuals living alone and individuals living with unrelated individuals should also be categorized and included. Some consideration might be given to adding another category under household head where the head is neither married nor a parent or surrogate parent. Billingsley's (1968) topology and the modifications suggested by Williams and Stockton (1973) indicate some of the varieties of black family forms.

Black Americans "actually developed a resilient, family-based culture as early as the mid-18th century. That 'culture'—a network of extensive kin relationships held together by a shared commitment to familial values and norms—permitted American blacks to withstand the hostilities and humiliations they confronted both during and after slavery" (Fox, 1976, p. 15). "The patterns of black families which have been interpreted as problems are in fact solutions to problems" (Lieberman, 1973, p. 10). When intrafamilial and external troubles arise, black families tend to refrain from seeking individual or group therapy; instead, they use resources from within their own familial group. To explore strengths and fortitude that exist among themselves is traditionally a trait on which the black family capitalizes. Members of this group do not only display innate companionship for each other, they oversee brothers and sisters who comprise the extended family. What this implies is that mother or father may be present continuously in some form to help to shepherd the flock. However, Western society has established conditions by which survival for the black family becomes a matter of hard work, mistrust, and goal orientation. Unfortunately, the qualities, then, lead to physical, psychological, social, or emotional problems that place a strain on family relationships. The outcome of such strain is often the impetus of the emergence of problems which require attention from relatives, confidants, or counselors.

The black family far surpasses the numerous deficits that certain writers have projected. Scholars such as Billingsley (1968), Gutman (1976), Hill (1972), Peters (1974), Staples (1971), and TenHouten (1970) have competently

rejected familial myths associated with blacks. Matriarchy, pathology, illegitimacy, emasculation, etc. are not characteristics that depict this cultural group.

LANGUAGE PATTERNS

After counselors understand the general background and structure of the
families with whom they deal, they must come to know and understand
something about the individuals who make up these families. One of the first
issues to master in the client-counselor relationship is communication. Since
there is a variation in the language patterns within the black community, it,
therefore, behooves the counselor/therapist to become familiar with these
patterns so as to be able to communicate effectively with members of a black
family and to interpret their "messages" correctly. These "messages" could be
verbal or nonverbal and appear coded especially for the counselor/therapist
who is only slightly familiar with black life. The counselor needs to understand a broad range of idioms and modes of communication. Accompanying
gestures and other nonverbal cues must be noticed also and correctly grasped
by the counselor.

Each black family also develops its own means of internal communication.
The intra-family language pattern and channels of communication may also
differ due to age, sex, and occupation of the members. The counselor needs to
realize these facts. However, even after the counselor realizes the language
variation, many blacks are unwilling to reveal themselves to outsiders and
may appear to be quasi-verbal in a counseling interview. However, "quasi-
verbal communications sometimes say something that is just the opposite of
the words spoken" (Milloy, 1971, p. 44). The counselor should be extremely
observant of nonverbal communications, their timing, and their sequence. To
go a step further, the counselor should help the client become aware of
nonverbal communication and help him or her to express it in words so that
the whole family will know what he or she is saying and feeling. Communication then becomes more straightforward (Milloy, 1971).

"By watching nonverbal behavior, a counselor can learn many useful things
about the dynamics of a family. It can be important to him to note what the
family avoids doing as well as what it does. Sometimes nonverbal behavior
takes place in a way that obviously overshadows verbal behavior" (Fullmer
and Bernard, 1964, p. 211). It is mandatory that the counselor who works with
black families recognize the importance of "multilingualism." Counselors
must, figuratively speaking, know several "languages." This simply means
that the successful counselor has to master the competency of interpreting
both coded and decoded messages which members of the black family send.
The status and quality of a relationship between a family and the helper/coun-
selor determine the ease with which communication flows. The stage and state

of disclosure are correlated directly with the level of identification and trust between the black family and the counselor.

Listed below are some "Dos and Don'ts" pertinent to language patterns among blacks which the counselor should use as guidelines:

DOS	DON'TS
Do listen to the words used by the speaker.	Don't prejudge messages from the speaker.
Do wait until the speaker completes his or her points.	Don't impose your values on the client.
Do raise helping questions for clarity if you do not understand.	Don't force your points of view on the client.
Do avoid communicating value judgments to the speaker.	Don't relate any forms of unethical character.
Do hear the "music" behind words and phrases.	Don't use language unacceptable to the client.
Do establish eye contact with each speaker.	Don't direct all of your dialogue to one person in the group.
Do relate to experiences described in the dialogue.	Don't speak without thinking.
Do maintain open lines of communication.	Don't talk with clients void of affect.
Do expect messages of uncertainty about the helper to surface.	Don't use messages from clients for your personal gain.
Do appreciate cultural variations in language patterns by the speaker.	Don't operate behind a facade.
Do remain conscious of the tone of your responses to the client.	Don't transmit the message that you are the "one-missionary."
Do maintain an acceptable level of sensitivity to the clients as individuals and as a group.	Don't expect revolutionary changes to occur in your presence.

It is hoped that if these guidelines are followed, a more successful counseling process will occur.

FACILITATION IN THE EXPRESSION OF FEELINGS

Once counselors have opened the lines of communication and have obtained some general understanding of the clients' modes of communication, they must help the clients express their true feelings. Race and social class are among the cultural factors that affect the transmission of information in a counseling session. Both the interviewer and the interviewee approach the counseling setting with a range of social and cultural factors. "Different cultural values . . . could intrude into the interview situation by creating expectations among the participants which are not 'shared'" (Cross, 1974, p. 51). In a counseling interview the roles of helper and helpee may undergo change, communicators becoming recipients and vice versa. Learning becomes a shared phenomenon. Communication is reciprocal and involves a feedback element by which the person transmitting a message knows it is understood accurately.

A limitation that influences communication is the linguistic codes, the framework within which emotions are transformed into words, as well as the vocabulary, values, and ideas that blacks apply in interpersonal settings. The information in the interview may be problematic for both client and counselor, and the possibility of a breakdown in communication is real because the codes have a unique cultural and historical meaning for each. While the skilled interviewer must be able to interpret gestural and other nonverbal forms of communication, at the same time, he or she "must avoid the temptation to overgeneralize the true states of feeling of his [or her] clients from particular elements of behavior" (Cross, 1974, p. 84). Counselors must also avoid forming preconceived models of personality and applying them to black clients in an attempt to penetrate their alleged masks.

If hostility and anger are the issue, they can be directed skillfully by the therapist to elicit the family's true feelings and emotions. One of the challenges facing the therapist in working with the black family is to ensure that hostilities, if detected, are managed contructively. A prerequisite to accomplishing this is to avoid being defensive. If the ventilated frustration appears to be directed toward the therapist, he or she should raise self-searching, objective, and open-ended questions which will assist the family in analyzing its frustration in terms of source, purpose, alternative, and outcome. Being knowledgeable and experienced in history, culture, and motivation of the black family, in addition to having mastered basic skills of communication, afford one the insight of knowing how to proceed effectively through a counseling interview with blacks.

The pattern of black family interaction is designed to fulfill a protective and cohesive function. It has evolved over time as a result of the emotional balance between the needs of the family members. "Such norms represent the sum total of all the years of conflict, compromise, and concern for each other through which the family have built up all they have in the way of happiness, security and mutual support and protected themselves against the potential miseries and uncertainties of life together" (Jordan, 1972, p. 15). The counselor, therefore, must take into account "the strong forces in families by which they defend themselves against change" (p. 16). If the counselor is incongruent with the black family, he or she may represent a potentially dangerous and destructive force on offsetting the family's equilibrium established over the years through a pattern of interaction. Therefore, although it is important to help black clients express their feelings, caution must be taken by the therapist in how this revelation and expression is accomplished.

CONCEPTUALIZATION OF COUNSELING

The conceptualization of the stages of counseling, *relationship development, psychological investigation,* and *disclosure-insight/orientation*, might be applied effectively in the counseling of black families only when the therapist understands the "stylistic dimensions of counseling blacks" (McFadden, 1976). Those dimensions are cultural-historical, psychosocial, and scientific-ideological.

The Cultural-Historical Dimension

The cultural-historical dimension represents the most fundamental prerequisite to acquiring essential insight into the functioning of the black family. It is absolutely essential for the therapist to understand levels of racially discriminatory practices and the nature of oppression to which black people have been historically subjected (Figure 13:1, Cube One). A mere understanding, of course, is not to be all-encompassing. An identification with the feeling of pain, cruelty, stress, and debasement represents an avenue through which the helper sets a tone for the development of a relationship with the black family.

The institution of slavery has had a profound effect on the evolution of the black family. Contingencies considered to be dormant by the dominant society continue to prevail in the minds and hearts of blacks in America. The bonds within black families, the strength of black men, the tendering love of black mothers, the yearning determination of black youth, and the legacy of black ancestry thrive among these people even today. The role of the therapist becomes one of keeping abreast of the historical impact that the "dynamics of slavery" has on black culture (Figure 13:1, Cube Two). Equally as important,

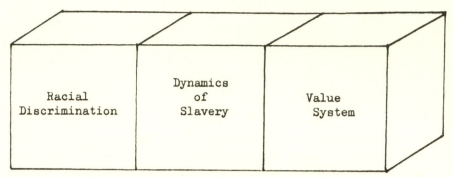

Figure 13:1.   The Cultural-Historical Dimension

the therapist recognizes a probable state of dichotomy that may exist between helpee and helper, dependent on racial differences or similarities. This cubical rests at the core of perceived crises occurring within a black family. In order to get in touch with this component, the helper finds himself or herself being submersed by authentic literature on the slave institution.

A "value system" (Figure 13:1, Cube Three) that emerges among members of a black family may greatly contribute to the formation of a relationship between therapist and client(s). The determining variable, of course, is that of attitude and state of readiness by the therapist. Blacks bring their own set of values to a counseling interview. Such values frequently may not be in concert with those of the helper. To illustrate the point, blacks in therapy perceive individuals on their own merit and not in relationship with relatives of these individuals. Furthermore, blacks have formulated a firm but useful value system based on association with their African heritage and survival in a hostile and debasing Western environment. In order for a family therapist to effect change with the client(s), he or she must intuitively know the interrelationship among racial discrimination, dynamics of slavery, and value system of black people.

The Psychosocial Dimension

A major part of exploring a second stage of counseling, psychological investigation, when counseling black families, is to have a firm grasp on the psychosocial dimension of the "stylistic dimensions of counseling blacks." Among the psychosocial cubicals are Racial Identity, Psychological Security, and Self-Inspection (Figure 13:2).

It becomes necessary for anyone performing functions of a counselor to recognize that black people in the United States may undergo a transitional period of "racial identity" (Figure 13:2, Cube One). They do, in fact, recall significant aspects of their background and are cognizant of a perpetual need

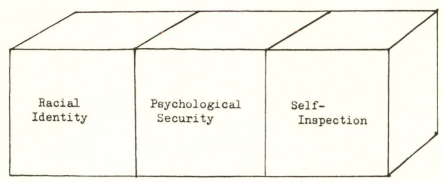

Figure 13:2.   The Psychosocial Dimension

to form a unified effort within themselves and their familial group, i.e., introspection in the form of racial identity which fosters self-maintenance. The hypothesis concerning black identity by Hall and Cross (1970) states that there exists a series of definitive stages through which blacks in the United States pass as they encounter blackness in themselves. Hall and Cross speculate that, as an outcome of such encounter and resolution, the individual defines himself or herself as black, adequate, and non-inferior. The stages are pre-encounter, encounter, immersion, and internalization. Hall and Cross hypothesize each stage as follows:

Pre-encounter
An individual is programed to view and think of the world as being opposite to black. A person's attitudes toward self are determined by "oppressor's" logic.

Encounter
An individual's present feelings about self and his or her people are shattered by a series of experiences.

Immersion
An individual's value of everything is in relationship to its relevance to blackness.

Internalization
An individual concentrates on things other than self and his or her own racial or ethnic group.

Relative to the black family, the hypotheses of Hall and Cross (1970) are germane. Adults provide experiences and conditions under which children learn concepts and form their own racial identity which transfers itself from one generation to another. When a therapist encounters a black family, he or she may discover that the group is operating from either of the stages of black identity as outlined by Hall and Cross. While it is not easy to determine in which stage the family is functioning, it is well to remember that variance in stages could well exist among differing age groups and personality types. The onus to master the competencies for engaging in productive dialogue with all members of the black family is on the therapist.

"Psychological security" (Figure 13:2, Cube Two) is a function of the total sum of experiences and the level of psychological encouragement that the black family receives within its own racial group. The family therapist should enter the stage of psychological investigation with the black family realizing that one's state of psychological security, indeed, contributes significantly to the formation of logic-behavioral chains which are indicative of the family's action dimension.

An exploration of both the subjective and objective situations of the black family will reveal problems they are encountering, perhaps, in coded form. Seeking the source of problems is advisable, not merely in the immediate family, but also in extended family relationships. Moreover, the counselor should be aware that the social environment of the black family may create more problems for the family itself than intra-family conflict. The social environment traditionally imposed on the black family from external forces has begun to diminish in impact as a result of the resurgence of social self-determination. Many issues within the black family stem from the stress of coping with the wider dominant community and from attempts to compensate for such stress within the fold of the family. The therapist should draw a distinction between varying forms of family conflict, as some are transitory and healthy in that they may enhance family unity. Also, the therapist should not assume personal disorganization but rather societal or institutional malfunctioning as causes of problems in black families. Despite the source of such issues, blacks in their familial grouping have been able to withstand the hostile environment by virtue of the family's many strengths.

"Self-inspection" (Figure 13:2, Cube Three) is the psychosocial cubical that emerges from the cultural-historical cubical labeled "value system." Some social scientists use the term *self-concept* because it tends to be more communicative for the listener. However, for purposes of this discourse, self-inspection is being used because of the diverse levels of intra-activity that comprise an individual's visions of self. Do you understand as a helper how members of the black family form images of themselves? Do you as a helper support the building of self-inspections or do you destroy self-inspection formation? This area is particularly applicable for the therapist who practices family counseling. Self-inspection formation for black people needs to be supported and encouraged by counselors, mental health workers, social workers, psychologists, and psychotherapists, since they are individuals who are likely to have a primary impact on the expansion of self-inspection for blacks.

The Scientific-Ideological Dimension

The scientific-ideological dimension of counseling black families is represented via nine cubes (Figure 13:3). For the purposes here, only the cubical of Race Relations, Logic-Behavioral Chains, and Individual Goals are discussed. Each depicts an area easily comprehensible to the observer. Each is indicative of activity among people and is also measurable. The base line for cubicals on the scientific-ideological plan is cultural-historical via psychosocial.

"Race relations" becomes a vital factor when the black family is being counseled by a white therapist. Timing of disclosure is correlated with race differences to the extent that the helper is able to effect a smooth relationship with the client(s). Mutual trust and confidence are variables that members of the black family demand in determining when and how they will share information pertinent to their cause. Upon initial disclosure, the manner in which the therapist responds influences succeeding levels of disclosure from the family. The solidarity of a black person's racial identity is reflected in his or her style of disclosure.

"Logic-behavioral chains" (Figure 13:3, Cube Two) provide the helper with basic insight therapeutically reflective of the black family members. What is logical for the black family may appear illogical to the helper if he or she neglects to develop thorough comprehension of stylistic dimensions of counseling blacks. Behavior determined to be useful in the life-style of blacks has roots in the cultural-historical origin of a people. By resolving issues with the black family that yield beneficial consequences, the helper gains additional personal insight in a therapeutic relationship.

Black family members demonstrate their "individual goals" (Figure 13:3, Cube Three) through observable behavior. While blacks are deeply affected by nature, they are also action-oriented. What they ideologically believe is reflected in their behaviors in or out of therapy. The helper will be wise to

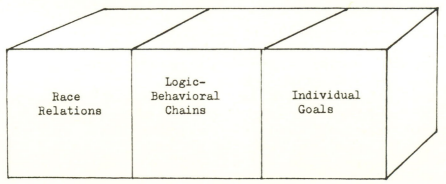

Figure 13:3. The Scientific-Ideological Dimension

remember that individual goals for black family members are augmented by group goals for the relatives themselves. Success for one is success for all. Disappointment for one is disappointment for all. Therefore, individual goals for reorientation are symbolic not of one person, but of the black family itself.

Understanding the stylistic dimensions of counseling blacks may enable the counselor/therapist successfully to effect the various stages of counseling. Following are some goals to be accomplished when counseling black families, and like the dimensions, they provide guides for helping the counseling process meet with success.

GOALS AND TECHNIQUES IN COUNSELING THE BLACK FAMILY

Counseling techniques are quite varied in intensity and form. The diversity accounts for the range of counseling approaches applied during an interview. Regardless of the technique, the therapist should understand the following set of mission goals in working with the black family (See also Appendix A):

To facilitate an understanding of the family constellation and how this affects functions within the family

To clarify the scope of roles and role definitions among family members

To enhance the valuing of one's self, one's family, and one's culture

To encourage the honoring and respect of each member of the unit and his or her contribution to family interaction

To demonstrate and support open communication with the family

To assist family members in clearly identifying familiar issues to be resolved

To help individuals acquire a broader perception of their social and psychological needs and those of others in their immediate life space

To analyze behaviors of family members and assist them in understanding how their behavior affects others

To process defense mechanisms detected within the family and demonstrate the importance of flexibility toward enhancing interpersonal relationships

To foster the emergence and continuation of self-disclosure among family members

To coordinate the formulation of relevant and reasonable objectives toward cohesively developing the family as goals are fulfilled

> To establish an environment conducive to changing behaviors deemed
> to be undesirable and incompatible with the goals of the family unit

To reiterate, it is hoped these goals can be achieved and, with that achievement, the counseling process may be a success. To facilitate this counseling
process, specific objectives and actions need to be considered for the black
family in therapy. The counselor also needs to be aware of certain cautions
during the counseling stages. Such applications are presented in Table 13:1.

SUMMARY

The effectively functioning black family is one with a substantive grasp on
its identity, definition, and self-determination. It is composed of members
who accept and value themselves, who communicate openly with the family,
who support each other in personal-social-career planning, and who recognize the meaning of life. External factors, which represent social, political, and
economic pressures, are managed successfully by black families that engage
regularly in family consultation. Members of these families comprise their
own consulting group and provide each other with support and clarity on
establishing mutual goals to accomplish. This methodology has historical
significance to blacks in that a direct relationship exists between what counselors and therapists define as "family consultation" and what black parents
referred to as " family gatherings" or what black teachers defined as "fireside
chats." In spite of the terminology, however, the importance of family interaction is a requisite to building unification and continuity.

Thorough knowledge of the black family is a prerequisite to understanding
black parents and children. Differences in elements of socialization, as experienced by blacks, may significantly influence future interpersonal relationships that black children may encounter as they develop. Such areas of
concern include formation of self-image, peer relationships, inner motivation,
self-determination, career aspirations, and familial commitment. Knowing
basic family patterns among blacks, family resources, potential for self-
management, family roles and goals, need response patterns, communication
patterns, supporting family structures, black family energy levels and toler-
ance, interactional patterns, and family flexibility is the genesis of acquiring
essential data for diagnosing issues germane to the black family.

Clarifying compounding tangents that impinge on problems experienced
by the black family in therapy can be simplified only to the extent that the
therapist has a valid and self-assuring grasp on black life and what it means to
survive in the United States. The Family Service Association of America
offers the following suggestion in identifying family problems:

Focus on understanding the main area(s) of difficulty that are interfering presently
with the family's self-management. Such focus should result in an understandable

TABLE 13:1

The Black Family in Therapy

Objective	Action	Caution
To expand modes of communication	Apply variety of active communication approaches in enhancing verbal and nonverbal openness.	Remain flexible in altering communication modes
	Demonstrate relationships between family issues and interaction within the entire group.	Accent strengths of the family and coping skills. Avoid generalizations.
To acquire independent perceptions of problems in the family	Codify interviews with individuals and interrelate with the presenting problem in the family.	Maintain openness and objectivity throughout individual interviews.
To determine levels of familial hierarchy	Provide incentive for everyone to express feelings germane to family issues.	Note order and frequency with which members speak for hierarchial clues.
To analyze nonverbal behavior	Observe facial expressions, intonations, body language, and physical proximity.	Recognize that the counselor's nonverbal behavior also sends signals
	Check out messages communicated through the above with communicants.	Permit inferred messages to remain open-ended.
To build support systems within the family	Determine positive contributions toward unification of each member and offer encouragement.	Avoid contributing to isolation and divisiveness
To assist family in being proactive	Explore with family the exhaustion incurred through reactionary behavior toward the system.	Define the system as related to the family in therapy
	Indicate to the family ways to conserve human energy for usage in	Retain alertness to the conservation of human energy for family

224

TABLE 13:1   Continued

The Black Family in Therapy

Objective	Action	Caution
		construction and unity.
To reassure a sense of positive identity	Plan with the family varied approaches to being pro-active as a group.	
	Support the establishment of an internal frame of reference toward the entire process of socialization which is self-sustaining.	Understand implication of the process of socialization and its impact.
To study social psychological, political, and economic pressures	Direct family members toward assertiveness in acquiring and retaining social, political, and economic justice.	Avoid analyzing all problems in relationship to psychological deficiencies.
	Reflect on the value of group and community action as a resource in solving social problems.	
To attain soluable directions in which the family can go	Assess options previously attempted by the family.	Utilize insights from the family in assessment.
	Attain consensus on a positive action plan for family implementation.	Refrain from mandating plans to the groups.
To arrive at closure in a counseling session.	Ask family to express and agree on positive points accomplished during the interview.	Encourage individual and group expressions of positive areas.

definition of the problem with the family and agreement about purpose, method, and goal of treatment (Family Service Association of America, 1965, p. 2).

Treating the black family requires a vision to perceive emotional conflict within the context of a Western culture. It is imperative that the counselor has the skills to help the black family discover that emotional constraints generally must be quelled among the members of the family themselves and that the counselor's role is one of clarifying, supporting, confronting, and posing alternatives. Jordan (1972) recommends that the counselor should treat the family as a unit. He or she should recognize that the ways in which the parents and children behave toward each other "reflect shared attitudes about how they can all pool their resources for their mutual benefit and protection" (p. 104). Such shared family norms contribute to family cohesion. While it is not necessary to work with the entire family as a group in each counseling session, it is useful to remember that the black family must be considered as a nucleus in therapy.

Counselors/therapists who participate in consultation with the black family can assist the members more efficiently when they have a clear perception of intra-family relationships and when they are able to focus these relationships in perspective so that behavioral changes for the family may be encouraged. To be in tune with the melody of the black family is to understand and appreciate its characteristics, ideology, and culture.

APPENDIX A

FAMILY CONSTELLATION

The structure of the black family represents a high level of interrelatedness with an intensity of independence among family members. Such interrelatedness can be understood more clearly by analyzing the family's constellation. An outline, adaptable to the black family, is herewith provided. The author recommends that it should be used only as one of the tools in collecting data toward the treatment of the black family.

DESCRIPTION

List names of members of the immediate family, including parents and children, in chronological sequence.

Beside the respective names list a few of the personality characteristics for each individual.

Identify members of the immediate family who are most similar in personality characteristics.

Identify those family members who are least similar.

RATINGS

Most	Attribute:	Least
_____	Creative	_____
_____	Oppressed	_____
_____	Critical	_____
_____	Wise	_____
_____	Political	_____
_____	Helping	_____
_____	Aggressive	_____
_____	Intelligent	_____
_____	Diligent	_____
_____	Industrious	_____

	Conforming	
_____	Selfish	_____
_____	Sensitive	_____
_____	Humorous	_____
_____	Realistic	_____
_____	Moral	_____
_____	Convincing	_____
_____	Strong	_____
_____	Charismatic	_____
_____	Achieving	_____
_____	Gregarious	_____

INTERRELATIONSHIP

Who most enjoys being with whom?
Who most cooperates with whom?
Who most disagrees with whom?
Who is the leader in the family? Describe this leadership. How does the leadership affect you?

PARENTAL DESCRIPTION

Describe your mother.
Describe your father.
Who does mother seem to like most? How do you know?
Who does father seem to like most? How do you know?
What do your parents do in order to earn a living?
Describe the relationship between your parents and their children.
    What values do they emphasize?
    What do they do to encourage their children?
    With whom do your parents usually interact?
How do your parents help each other?
What career expectations do your parents have for you?
What other adults share your household? How do you react to this? What relationship do you have with these adults?

EARLY RECOLLECTIONS

List some of your earliest recollections by completing the chart below:

Age	Significant experience	Key person	Meaning to you
___	_____	_____	_____
___	_____	_____	_____

_____

REFERENCES

Ackerman, N. W. *The Psychodynamics of Family Life*. New York: Basic Books, 1958.
_____ . *Treating the Troubled Family*. New York: Basic Books, 1966.
_____ (ed) *Family Process*. New York: Basic Books, 1970.
_____ , et al. (eds) *Exploring the Base for Family Therapy*. New York: Family Service Association, 1961.
Anderson, R. E., and I. E. Carter. *Human Behavior in the Social Environment: A Social Systems Approach*. Chicago: Aldine Publishing Co., 1974.
Bell, N. W., and E. F. Vogel (eds) *A Modern Introduction to the Family*. Glencoe, Ill.: The Free Press of Glencoe, 1960.
Billingsley, A. *Black Families in White America*. Englewood Cliffs, N.J.: Prentice-Hall, 1968.
_____ . "Black Families and White Social Science," *Journal of Social Issues*, 1970, 26(3), 137-142.
Committee on the Family Group for the Advancement of Psychiatry. *Treatment of Families in Conflict—The Clinical Study of Family Process*. New York: Science House, 1970.
Cross, C. P. (ed) *Interviewing and Communication in Social Work*. London & Boston: Routledge & Kegan Paul, Ltd, 1974.
Cummings, S., and R. Carrere. "Black Culture, Negroes, and Colored People: Racial Image and Self-Esteem among Black Adolescents," *Phylon*, 1975, 36(3), 238-248.
Dreikus, R., et al. (eds) *Adlerian Family Counseling: A Manual for Counseling Centers*. Oregon: University of Oregon Press, 1959.
_____ , et al. *Family Council*. Chicago: Henry Regnery Co., 1974.
Family Service Association of America. *Casebook on Family Diagnosis and Treatment*. New York, 1965.
Fooks, G. M. "Dilemmas of Black Therapists," *Journal of Non-White Concerns in Personnel and Guidance*, 1973, 1(4), 181-191.
Fox, R. W. "The Search for Roots," Review of *The Black Family in Slavery and Freedom: 1750-1925* by H. Gutman and *Roots* by A. Haley. In *Chronicle of Higher Education*, 1976, 13(10), 15.
Frazier, E. F. *The Negro Family in the United States*. Chicago: University of Chicago Press, 1939.
Freeman, D. S. "Phases of Family Treatment," *The Family Coordinator*, 1976, 25(3), 265-269.

Fullmer, D. W., and H. W. Bernard. *Counseling: Content and Process*. Chicago: Science Research Associates, Inc., 1974.

Gutman, H. *The Black Family in Slavery and Freedom: 1750–1925*. New York: Pantheon Books, 1976.

Haley, A. *Roots*. Garden City, N.Y.: Doubleday & Co., Inc., 1976.

Hall, W. S., and W. E. Cross, Jr. "The Formation of an Ego Identity in Black Americans: Toward a Conceptualization of Stages in Coming to Terms with Self," Paper presented at the Annual Meeting of the National Association of Black Psychologists, Miami Beach, Florida, 1970.

Hays, W. C., and C. H. Mindel. "Extended Kinship Relations in Black and White Families," *Journal of Marriage and the Family*, 1973, 35(1), 51–55.

Herzog, E. "Is There a Breakdown of the Negro Family?," *Social Work*, 1966, 11(1), 3–10.

Hill, R. B. "The Strengths of Black Families," In D. G. Bromley and C. F. Longino, Jr. (eds) *White Racism and Black Americans*. Cambridge, Mass.: Schenkman Publishing Co., Inc., 1972, 262–290.

Jones, R. L. (ed) *Black Psychology*. New York: Harper & Row Publishers, 1972.

Jordan, W. *The Social Worker in Family Situations*. London & Boston: Routledge & Kegan Paul, Ltd., 1972.

Koret, S. "Family Therapy in Residential Treatment," *Child Welfare*, 1973, 52(4), 234–242.

Lewis, D. K. "The Black Family: Socialization and Sex Roles," *Phylon*, 1975, 36(3), 221–237.

Lieberman, L. "The Emerging Model of the Black Family," *International Journal of Sociology of the Family*, 1973, 3(1), 10–22.

McFadden, J. (ed) *Counseling and Teaching-Identity vs Assimilation*. Atlanta: The College Board, 1978.

———— (ed) *Counseling-Parenting-Teaching*. Atlanta: The College Board, 1979.

————. "Stylistic Dimensions of Counseling Blacks," *Journal of Non-White Concerns in Personnel and Guidance*, 1976, 5(1), 23–28.

McNair, C. "The Black Family Is Not a Matriarchal Family Form," *Negro Educational Review*, 1975, 26(2&3), 93–100.

Milloy, M. "A Look at the Family and Family Interviewing," *Child Welfare*, 1971, 50(1), 40–46.

Moynihan, D. P. "The Tangle of Pathology," In D. G. Bromley and C. F. Longino, Jr. (eds) *White Racism and Black Americans*. Cambridge, Mass.: Schenkman Publishing Co., Inc., 1972, 197–218.

Nobles, W. W. "Africanity: Its Role in Black Families," *Black Scholar*, 1974, 5(9), 10–17.

Patterson, L. E. "The Strange Verbal World," *Journal of Non-White Concerns in Personnel and Guidance*, 1973, 1(2), 95–101.

Peters, M. F. "The Black Family-Perpetuating the Myths: An Analysis of Family Sociology Textbook Treatment of Black Families," *The Family Coordinator*, 1974, 23(4), 349–357.

Russell, R. D. "Black Perspectives on Guidance," *Personnel and Guidance Journal*, 1970, 48(9), 721–728.

Ryan, W. "Savage Discovery: The Moynihan Report," In D. G. Bromley and C. F. Longino, Jr. (eds) *White Racism and Black Americans*. Cambridge, Mass.: Schenkman Publishing Co., Inc. 1972, 219–227.

_____ . *Blaming the Victim*. New York: Vintage Books, 1971.

Sager, C. J., et al. *Black Ghetto Family in Therapy*. New York: Grove Press, Inc., 1970.

Satir, V. *Conjoint Family Therapy*. Palo Alto, Calif.: Science and Behavior Books, 1964.

Skolnick, A. S., and J. H. Skolnick (eds) *Family in Transition*. Boston: Little, Brown & Co., 1971.

_____ (eds) *Intimacy, Family and Society*. Boston: Little, Brown & Co., 1974.

Smith, P. M. "Counseling from the Past and Present with Blacks," *Journal of Negro Education*, 1974, 43(4), 489–493.

Smith, W. D. "Which Way Black Psychologists: Tradition, Modification, or Verification-Innovation," *Journal of Black Studies*, 1973, 4(1), 3–7.

Spaights, E. "Some Dynamics of the Black Family," *Negro Educational Review*, 1973, 24(3&4), 127–137.

_____ . "The Evolving Black Family in the United States; 1950–1974," *The Negro Educational Review*, 1976, 27(2), 113–128.

Staples, R. "The Myth of Black Matriarchy," *Black Scholar*, 1970, 1(3), 8–16.

_____ . "Towards a Sociology of the Black Family: A Theoretical and Methodological Assessment," *Journal of Marriage and the Family*, 1971, 33(1), 119–138.

_____ . "The Black Family in Evolutionary Perspective," *Black Scholar*, 1974, 5(9), 2–9.

Stein, J. W. *The Family as a Unit of Study and Treatment*. University of Washington, School of Social Work: Regional Rehabilitation Research Institute, 1969.

Stikes, C. S. "Culturally Specific Counseling—The Black Client," *Journal of Non-White Concerns in Personnel and Guidance*, 1972, 1(1), 15–23.

TenHouten, W. D. "The Black Family: Myth and Reality," *Psychiatry*, 1970, 33(2), 145–173.

Tucker, S. J. "Action Counseling: An Accountability Procedure for Counseling the Oppressed," *Journal of Non-White Concerns in Personnel and Guidance*, 1973, 2(1), 35–41.

Vontress, C. E. "Counseling Blacks," *Personnel and Guidance Journal*, 1970, 48(9), 713–719.

_____ . "Racial Differences: Impediments to Rapport," *Journal of Counseling Psychology*, 1971, 18(1), 7–13.

Williams, A. J., Jr., and R. Stockton. "Black Family Structures and Functions: An Empirical Examination of Some Suggestions Made by Billingsley," *Journal of Marriage and the Family*, 1973, 33(1), 39–49.

14

CAN A WHITE THERAPIST DEAL WITH BLACK FAMILIES?

Vincent D. Foley

Dr. John Spiegel (1959), former president of the American Psychiatric Association and a distinguished voice in the field of family therapy, wrote an article on the importance of recognizing cultural differences in the way in which a therapist proceeded. Addressing himself specifically to the question of whether a Jewish psychiatrist could be effective with an Irish and Catholic client, Spiegel answered, yes, if the therapist were sensitive to the value system of the client and also aware of the importance of transference in the therapeutic encounter.

This chapter is an attempt to flesh out the ideas articulated by Spiegel and to answer positively the question, "Can a white therapist deal with black families?" Perhaps the question should be rephrased since white therapists *must* deal with black families, given the number of black therapists who are presently available. Just as there are not enough black physicians who can care for black patients, so also is there a dearth of black therapists. This means clearly that white therapists are going to have to learn more about black families and how they operate if they are to do an effective job of therapy. These issues will be discussed fully later.

WHAT IS CONJOINT FAMILY THERAPY?

Conjoint family therapy is a technique of dealing with emotional problems in living that was first developed in the mid-1950s. Broadly defined, one can say that it is an attempt at modifying relationships between family members by seeing their behavior as interlocking parts of a system. This means that what is going on within one person in the family depends on the behavior of other members of the family. For example, in the Jones family how Mrs. Jones (All names have been changed to preserve anonymity.) is feeling (depressed) is related to how her husband is behaving (drinking heavily) and to how John, Jr., is doing in school (failing). In like manner, one must ask how the drinking pattern of Mr. Jones is related to the depression of his wife and the school problems of his son. Finally, how is John, Jr., affected by the marital relationship?

Seeing behavior from this point of view, called a *system concept*, is a departure from the more traditional manner of seeing behavior as the result of forces within an individual. Family therapy, therefore, is different from other modes of therapy not because more people are present at sessions, but because the family is seen as an interactional unit and not as a series of isolated individuals.

An important corollary of system thinking is that just as emotional stress can be attributed to the system, so also can emotional health. Families not only breed trouble, they also give strength. This fact is overlooked in many therapeutic approaches, but not in family therapy. In this approach, the family is seen both positively and negatively. In fact, family therapy emphasizes the positive, healing forces in a family by making open and clear what is often hidden and obscure. A goal of family therapy is to increase communication among family members because once problems are in the open they can be handled. Many family problems arise from the fact that things are hidden and concealed. A goal of family therapy then is to look at what is going on in the system and to change that system by new inputs so that members may function in a more satisfying manner.

Family therapy is a new way of looking at interaction. In the words of Thomas Kuhn (1962), it is a shift in the paradigm or model that is used. This shift brings new ways of seeing the reality being observed, in this case the family. In the previous paradigm used in therapy, the intrapsychic model (Levenson, 1972), the disturbance was located in an individual and, consequently, he or she was treated. In the paradigm used in family therapy, a system model, disturbance is located in the way in which the system functions and, consequently, the system is viewed as the client. This means that the individual is seen as a sympton and the system as the problem.

If the paradigm used in family therapy is the system, we must look at what a system is. A simple description of a system is that it is made up of sets of different parts having two things in common: (a) the parts are interconnected and interdependent, and (b) each part is related to the other over a stable period of time (Buckley, 1967). Clearly, a family fits this description in that each member is related by blood and this relationship lasts through time. A family, however, is what is called an *open system*, which means that it is constantly undergoing change as people are born, marry, and die. Because the family is an open system, it can be changed at any time by changing the way it now functions. It is not necessary to go back to the beginning of the system in order to accomplish change.

What seems to be a theoretical fact, namely, the family is an open system, has great practical significance. For example, if Mr. Jones is drinking excessively, this is a result of how the family system is presently functioning and not of some past cause. The behavior may have begun in the past because of a particular event, e.g., the birth of his son, but it continues now in the present because of other factors. A family therapist seeing the Jones family will not be concerned with the point at which Mr. Jones began to drink but with what causes him to drink presently. What is going on in the here and now is of more importance than what happened in the past. Furthermore, the family therapist would insist that digging into the past is not helpful to his drinking now, insisting that Mr. Jones may have begun drinking because of some past event but continues to drink now because of the way his family interacts at this time. According to the family therapist, what needs to be changed is not Mr. Jones, but the various relationships within the Jones family. This is accomplished by changing the feedback into the system. The reason why the Jones family is experiencing difficulty is that the members of it largely are unaware of their behavior. They do not see how they influence each other. Therefore, the role of the therapist is to make them aware of this influence.

However, the therapeutic process of helping people to change is made more difficult when the therapist is white and the clients are black because of the two critical issues raised by Dr. Spiegel of value systems and transference. By a value system we mean those attributes or qualities that are considered important in a family. These are determined largely by education, economic status, and national origin, as well as by personal choice.

By transference we mean the phenomenon that occurs in therapy whereby the therapist is seen by the client(s) as an authority figure and intense feelings of love and hate are evoked by this relationship, based, however, on past relationships with authority figures and not on the current one. In other words, feelings and emotions from the past are projected onto the therapist. Clearly, transference will be a critical issue when the authority figure, the therapist, is white and the client is black.

It is our contention, however, that a modification of conjoint family therapy, known as multiple family therapy, offers a way out of this twofold dilemma because it avoids clashes focusing on differences in value systems and it lessens the intensity of transference.

Twenty years' experience has shown that the most effective approach for a white therapist when confronted with a black family is to use multiple family therapy.

WHAT IS MULTIPLE FAMILY THERAPY?

Multiple family therapy (MFT) is an approach developed by Peter Laqueur (1973) in treating the families of hospitalized schizophrenic patients and was personally observed by me in 1961 in Creedmor State Hospital in Queens Village, New York. I was fascinated by the potential in MFT and became an observer of Dr. Laqueur's Sunday evening sessions. At that time I was seeing black clients on an individual basis and finding it a difficult experience. The idea of using MFT with black clients seemed to be one way of overcoming the white/black hostility I was experiencing. Since my client population was living in the Fort Greene Housing Project in Brooklyn, it was not difficult to assemble families. In addition, sessions at times were held in the homes of the various clients which also lessened the formal setting of an office. Clients were more comfortable on their "turf," and this lowering of anxiety made therapy more effective than using an office.

This therapist was white, middle-class, and had little experience in ghetto living. The clients were black, lower socioeconomic class, born in the urban North, but with roots in the rural South. There were no West Indians, Haitians, or black South Americans among this population. The historical roots of the client population was one of slavery, and this made it necessary to seek a way of lessening the barriers caused by slavery to effective therapy. Although I feel MFT can be used with a variety of clients, the comments made in this chapter are based on experience with a so-called ghetto population and not with middle-class American blacks or with blacks whose roots are not found in American slavery.

MFT is an adaptation of group therapy having the benefits of group therapy added to those of family therapy. Sessions are structured to last 90 minutes, and the therapist acts in the role of a conductor in that he or she guides or moves the families through themes. For example, if in the Jones family Mr. Jones is complaining about the poor school performance of his son John, Jr., the therapist might make a comment such as, "I guess issues about work in school concern all of us, Mr. Jones, and produce a lot of feelings on both sides. I noticed, Mr. White, you are nodding agreement. I wonder if you want to say something?"

MFT is concerned with problem solving, and this is best done by getting into themes familiar to all families rather than focusing on just one family. Adolescent behavior, for instance, is an issue for all families, and even though Mr. Jones may be the speaker, he is talking about matters of importance to Mr. Smith and Mr. White who also have adolescent children. The idea of introducing themes is helpful because it reduces the emotional heat in a given family system and allows people to discuss issues more calmly. As Thomas Fogarty (1978, p. 62), a family therapist, has commented, "The first task of the therapist is to reset the emotional barometer so that one person can listen to the other."

In any therapy, feelings run high but especially in family therapy when all members are present. If the feelings get out of control, no change will take place. It is a role of the therapist to move the system in a way so that people listen to each other. The therapist must monitor constantly the temperature of the family especially by lowering it when discussions become heated. MFT offers an effective way of doing this because the therapist can utilize material constantly from one family with another, pointing out the similarities among them. As time goes by, families begin to see that they are more similar than dissimilar.

ADVANTAGES OF MFT

There are three main reasons why a multiple family approach is of special value when a white therapist is dealing with black families: (1) transference feelings are diminished, (2) identification of one family member with a member of another family is enhanced, and (3) the advantages found in group and in conjoint family therapy are combined.

The first and most important reason for the value of MFT is that the transference is lessened because the process by which change takes place is not the relationship between the therapist and the family, but between one family and another. Transference is a critical element in any kind of therapy. It properly belongs in the process of psychoanalysis, but is found in all intense relationships. Sigmund Freud was the first to write about its importance and eventually made it the basis of his technique known as psychoanalysis. In one of his most famous cases, that of Dora, Freud (1905, p. 116) said that transferences "are new editions or facsimiles of the impulses and phantasies [sic] which are aroused and made conscious during the progress of analysis; but they have this peculiarity . . . that they replace some earlier person by the person of the physician." Therapy is an intense experience in which deep feelings are aroused. Therapy is a struggle between the client and the therapist around many issues, especially that of authority. The therapist is an authority figure. He or she represents one generation and the client another generation. This will produce feelings on both sides. Sometimes these feelings will be positive and sometimes negative. In all cases they will be intense.

Therapy can be likened to a fisherman stirring up muddy waters. The surface may appear calm and peaceful, but beneath there are many things hidden. When the fisherman sticks the pole into the mud, objects long hidden come to the surface. For example, fish appear from underneath pieces of wood, glass shines in the sun, and finally the long-sought-after treasure may appear. In a similar manner therapy breaks into a person's unconscious and feelings long dormant erupt. Memories of events long past emerge and, more importantly, the feelings attached to them once again surface.

It is clear that if a therapist—a parental figure—is white and the client is black, the feelings will be intensified. Blacks long accustomed to watching their words and to guarding their feelings will break forth with angry racial comments in therapy. In individual therapy this may be good, but in family therapy it is usually destructive because it moves the family off the issues of the session and into peripheral areas.

In family therapy, therefore, the aspect of transference is played down because the goal is not to change the feelings of an individual, but to change the way or manner a family interacts. Its focus is more on behavior than on feelings. Families are in pain because of behavior. Father drinks too much, mother is depressed and as a result neglects her children, who in turn perhaps do poorly in school. In family therapy the goal is not to change this or that person's behavior but to change the way various family members relate. Transference is not a help in accomplishing this goal because it focuses more on feelings than behavior and by doing this impedes the progress of therapy.

A white therapist seeing a black family has a potential for emotional explosion. They have feelings about the counselor and he or she about them. The therapist may deal with these feelings by getting a black co-therapist, if possible, or as an alternative utilizing additional black families as a way of lessening feelings and concentrating on problem solving. The white therapist is more of a catalyst than a center of attention in this approach and struggles with orchestrating the session rather than dominating it. Just as a good orchestra leader allows the listener to concentrate on the music and not on the performance, so also a good family therapist allows the participants to deal with their problems and not to become involved with him or her. The sessions are not designed to deal with intense feelings as such, but with problem solving, and the role of the therapist is to emphasize this aspect. Long experience has shown that MFT is a most effective means of doing this.

As noted earlier, the background of the stage on which the drama of family therapy with blacks is played is that of slavery. In slavery the white man was superior, he was the "boss," and the black man was the inferior, he was the "child." Therapy, regardless of the color of the participants, is a re-enactment of the superior-inferior positions. The therapist is in control. Anyone who has ever been in therapy recognizes the feelings of anger that well up inside the self in the role of client. When these roles include a white therapist and a black client, the issue is intensified, the stakes are raised. Only when such factors are dealt with can therapy proceed. Utilizing MFT is an effective way of lowering the emotional temperature so that therapy can proceed.

If MFT does not produce change by transference, then by what means does it operate? MFT uses the concept of *identification* as the medium of change. People and families coming for help see themselves as isolated from others. They feel different and as if their problems were unique. In MFT they quickly learn that the issues that trouble their family also disturb other families as well. They begin to see themselves to identify with members of other families. At times they can identify with another's anger or surliness but also with the strength and the compassion of another. When Mr. Jones, for example, complains about his son's indifference to school and how this upsets him, Mr. Smith can begin to feel less isolated than before. If Mrs. Jones can reach out to comfort her husband, Mrs. Smith can see something done that may help her reach her husband. Instead of being critical of him by saying, "Why don't you leave that boy alone!", she might put her arm around him and say, "Ed, how can I help you?" Seeing how other families act is much more effective than just talking about helping others.

Identification is the word given to the behavior of one person when he or she wishes to imitate or emulate that of another person. Laqueur (1973, p. 85) has said it best when he wrote about MFT, "The motto of the entire transaction is to teach families to help each other." The motto is important because it stresses two elements of therapeutic value: (1) the inherent strength of families and (2) the importance of indirect learning.

Sociologists and psychologists agree on very little, or so it seems, but they do agree that one of the major causes of what psychologists call *isolation* and sociologists *anomie* is a loss of family life. Individuals who are separated from others and likewise families suffer anxiety and disorientation. However, just as families can drive us "crazy," they can also give us strength. We in the field of mental health are too quick to emphasize the former and to de-emphasize the latter. Family therapy has been quick to recognize the importance of curative factors in the family and to utilize this strength. The strength of families rests in indirect learning. Most of what we know about social behavior we have learned in our family of origin. It has not been taught to us directly but indirectly. We have learned by observation and identification more than by having heard lectures on how to act or behave in public. In MFT the same process takes place. Family members who are puzzled about situations see how others act and so find new solutions to old problems.

One of the most effective ways of indirect learning is that of playing "family games." After several sessions in which various families get to know each other, the therapist can ask if the Jones family would like to play the Smiths for part of the session. This means that one member of the Jones family will act the way he or she sees a Smith act, i.e., Mr. Jones becomes Mr. Smith and John Jones, Jr., becomes Tommy Smith, etc. The therapist congratulates the Smiths for allowing the Joneses to act like them but stresses that the "game" is not for amusement but in order to learn about oneself.

The therapist can begin by asking the Joneses to play a recurring situation such as Tommy Smith's coming home late in the evening. He or she should choose a problem that, in fact, has been brought up in earlier sessions and that has not as yet been solved. As the re-enactment takes place, the Smiths become intensely concerned with how the Joneses see them. Mr. Smith may protest loudly saying, "No way do I sound like that," but others, e.g., the Whites, may shake their head in disagreement as Mr. White says quietly to Mr. Smith, "Sorry, Ed, but John there could get an Academy Award for his good acting." When such things are said, it is difficult for Mr. Smith to maintain his attitude that the sole problem in the family is Tommy's behavior.

Clearly, such play acting can be dangerous, but it is the role of the therapist to control such techniques and to use humor, if possible, as a way of lowering intense feelings. Again, the medium of change is not the feelings toward the therapist, but the relationship of family members. In fact, the therapist is present more in the role of commentator and outsider. It is easier for Mr. Smith to hear the observations of Mr. Jones and Mr. White than those of the therapist. Resistance is lessened and Mr. Jones may then think about what has been said. In the following session it is not unusual for Mr. Smith to ask Mr. White how he would have handled it. If Mr. White is not certain how to deal with the issue, the therapist might suggest something like, "It's a tough situation. Maybe we can all talk about how we'd handle it and then get the reactions of the kids." By making such a comment, the therapist moves the issue off feelings and onto the level of problem solving.

The third reason why MFT is of special value is that it combines the positive features of both group and family therapy. Group therapy is based on the idea that learning new ways of behaving can best be attempted in familiar surroundings. An individual can learn how to relate in new ways in the group and find support for his or her new behavior from the group. In brief, the group can give the needed support so that change becomes possible. In addition, groups are chosen for their diversification with different kinds of people comprising the group, so that it becomes a macrocosm of the outside world. MFT, too, has these features. The Smith, Jones, and White families contain a variety of personalities and, therefore, a range of possible people for members to identify with and emulate. New behaviors can be tried out in MFT just as in group, and support is always present for members.

A single family, on the other hand, offers only a limited world of possibility. John Jones, for example, may be scapegoated in his family and blamed for its ongoing problems, but it is likely that in MFT he will find some members of the Smith and White families who will be on his side. This is not possible in therapy on an individual or even conjoint family approach. This is absolutely critical during the stage of change when members are trying out new behaviors. It is a commonly observed fact that in families the system itself militates against change since this means that everyone has to make adjustments. Frequently, when the identified client attempts change, the rest of the system, sometimes consciously and sometimes unconsciously, pulls in the opposite direction. Change is painful and difficult and is usually resisted. In MFT, however, change is more likely because even if the Jones family is against a change in John, Jr., the other families will support his efforts and make it easier for him.

MFT is like group therapy in that it is made up of a wide variety of people. It is unlike group in that its members are united by blood ties and have a history together. MFT is like conjoint family therapy in that history is its common base, but it differs in that it allows individual family members firsthand observation on how other families behave. Family members are able to make their own decisions as to what is normal or abnormal and need not go outside of the group. In conjoint family therapy, on the other hand, John Jones does not know how other families behave except indirectly, but in MFT he sees and experiences how other adolescents are treated in their families. In summary, MFT offers a richer arena for experimentation and consequent change than either group therapy or conjoint family therapy.

THE IMPORTANCE OF CULTURAL FACTORS IN FAMILY THERAPY

Spiegel (1971, p. 201) writes, "I see the family in general as a system of reciprocal patterns and processes operating within a larger field of interpenetrating systems. Role and values are crucial in the workings of the system." I agree with these observations and feel we must apply them to black families. By role we mean: "What does it mean to be a husband/father or wife-/mother?"; "What does it mean to be a son or daughter?"; "How do grandparents fit into the nuclear family?" By value we mean those attributes or qualities that are prized or esteemed in a family. Clearly, all of these will vary from culture to culture. Indeed, within the black family, is one talking about American Southern black, Northern urban black, West Indian or Hispanic black? Certainly, all these families have different concepts of roles and adhere to different values. It is important for the family therapist to listen and learn how these various families see themselves or hope to accomplish their goals.

The wise therapist will not impose his or her concept of roles or values on clients. Such an approach is not helpful to the family nor in the long run is it effective. Although family therapists are bound by their own cultures and concepts of roles and values, nevertheless, they can be an instrument of change if they remember their role as therapist. No therapy is totally free of roles and values. However, in MFT the differences between the therapist and his or her families are minimized since the counselor is not the means by which change in the family takes place.

Although cultural differences are always important, this is even more critical when a white therapist meets an American black family. The overriding issue in such a meeting is that of the psychic trauma to both the white therapist and the black family as the result of slavery. Color, of course, will influence the relationship if the family is black regardless of national origin but not to the extent it does when the issue of slavery is in question. The ever-present fact of transference is intensified in such meetings as we have mentioned earlier.

The intense ambivalence experienced by a black family in the session with a white therapist cannot be ignored. Feelings on both sides are intense, appearances to the contrary. In particular, mention should be made of those families that either deny they have feelings toward the therapist or who appear overly polite. This denial of anger and hostility has been well described by Powdermaker (1950) in her classic article in which she discusses how blacks try to deal with their aggressive impulses toward whites.

More recently, the sociologist Robert Staples (1971, p. 38) commented, "...the black family had evolved a unique structure and style to cope with circumstances that it has confronted." The therapist must remember the unique experience of the black family. Although one may talk about the culture of poverty as a subculture, as does Oscar Lewis (1966), nevertheless, in the case of the black family, it is color and not poverty that is the critical issue. This is why the black experience is qualitatively different from that of Hispanics, Europeans, or Orientals who have been subjected to extreme instances of poverty. Slavery is not just something additional but something that has stripped the black of his or her identity and roots.

It is beyond the scope of this chapter to spell out in detail the ramifications of slavery except to highlight the transference occurring in the meeting of white therapist and black family. Although we agree with Spiegel's position that differences between people do not preclude effective therapy, nevertheless, we stress the need for the therapist to focus on slavery's impact on transference. Therapy of any type can be described as "working through the resistance." This means that even when people come looking for help they resist making the moves necessary to produce such change. Therapy is a power struggle between the therapist and the client(s). When played out against the background of the history of the American black family, the struggle intensifies and the family must question whether change means giving in to a white value system. It is important for the therapist to talk about this early in the initial sessions. He or she should make clear what is not mentioned or only hinted at in a vague manner.

Frequently, people do not use language to communicate openly but to suggest or hint at other things. This is why the nonverbal is so important in family therapy because the therapist learns more about the family by what is not said than by what is said. Feelings and attitudes, in particular resentments, are rarely articulated but must be surmised by the context of a session. The family therapist must become skilled at sensing what is lurking beneath the surface and quick to express it. It is our contention that feelings revolving around color are always present in such family sessions and need to be expressed. If the therapist is free enough to talk about his or her attitudes on color, this will help the family or families feel more comfortable so that they will express their attitudes.

MFT AND BLACK FAMILY VALUES

So far our focus has been largely on multiple family therapy and how it meets the needs of the therapist to dissipate the intense feelings generated by the interaction of therapeutic interaction. What of the black family? How does MFT fit into the pattern of black families?

To say the least, this is a question that is most complex and is one hotly argued among sociologists. There are right wing, left wing, and middle of the road positions about the structure and function of black families. Hill (1972) would seem to occupy a middle position, as Staples and Mirande (1980) point out, "he [Hill] stressed the more unique traits of strong kinship bonds and role flexibility" (p. 890). Hill in his 1972 study emphasizes a number of values important to black families. He cites among others: (1) strong kinships, (2) role flexibility, and (3) religion. Certainly, these values are congruent with MFT. Family therapy, in contrast to traditional individual approaches, is more consonant with black family cultural values in that it emphasizes kinship, examination of roles and education, whereas individual therapies put a major emphasis on self. In psychoanalysis, for example, only the individual is seen and never other members of the family. Such exclusivity is foreign to black values.

More specifically MFT fits into black cultural values by using each of the values cited by Hill. First, the use of kin is one that derives from the African roots of blacks. McAdoo (1978) in particular delineates the fact that middle-class black families keep their kinship patterns even after making it in the larger white society. There is no doubt this is even more true among the lower-class urban blacks mentioned in this chapter. The emphasis on self, the need to assert an "I," is one that is more attuned to the Anglo-Saxon white than to the African black, whose emphasis is on "us," the need to assert a "we." MFT with its use of others fits into the kinship pattern. It is not foreign to seek help from "brothers and sisters" for black families, whereas it is for white ones. Anglo-Saxon families do not talk to others about their problems, they do not "wash their linen in public." The Irish, for instance, have a saying that expresses this clearly: "What will the neighbors think?" (Greeley, 1979). To blacks, others are not neighbors or outsiders but family or extended kin. MFT would be strange and unacceptable to Irish families but more appropriate and acceptable to black families.

Hill's (1972) second observation concerns role flexibility. He points out that unlike individuals of other cultures, blacks do not have rigid ideas as to what men and women should do or say. Therefore, it is not considered wrong for women to work nor for men to watch children. Women can say things to men and vice versa. McAdoo (1977) confirms this and calls such flexibility "role reciprocity." Such reciprocity does not exist in many cultures such as Italian and Hispanic where the roles of men and women are more determined. Such flexibility is a great help in MFT in that it allows an equal right to talk for both men and women. MFT, as does any therapeutic system, has its implicit values. It espouses two values of special importance: equality between husband and wife and a strong bond between the generations. Both of these values are compatible with black family systems.

Hill's third value is that of religion. He suggests that his value has many implications especially in terms of child-rearing and as a way of dealing with racial oppression. It also has value for MFT in that religion is something that is taught and learned and MFT depends on this, too. As noted above, indirect learning is of the essence in this approach. Unlike more traditional therapies,

MFT is one that teaches people how to cope. The religious orientation of black families makes learning easier for them than for other families in which religion plays a lesser role. The value of family therapy as an approach to black families has been cited by a number of authorities, most notably McAdoo (1977).

MFT is a type of family therapy that utilizes the concept of identification as the medium of change, stressing the inherent strength of families and the value of indirect learning. Such an approach is most compatible with the values of black families, in that kinship bonds, role flexibility, and learning are special qualities for both black families and MFT. Culture is an important part of therapy and any therapeutic approach must take into account the cultural values of the client. All cultures are different and these differences are critical in producing change which is the essence of therapy. MFT is an approach in harmony with the basic values of the black family using the pathways common to its members, thus enhancing the possibility of change. MFT minimizes the problems between the therapist and the black family and maximizes its potential for change by being congruent with its cultural values.

AN ILLUSTRATION OF MFT

In using MFT with black families, we have found it best to have three families meet for 90 minutes on a weekly basis. Although others, e.g., Laqueur (1973), suggest using five or six families, we have found this too large a group to work with effectively. The groups are formed from current families being seen who exhibit specific kinds of issues. Problems of excessive drinking, adolescent acting-out, and the transition from single life to a married state are issues that have shown improvement through MFT.

The families chosen were the Jones, Smith, and White families. (The families are real, but the names fictitious.) Mr. John Jones (43) was drinking heavily, Mrs. Edna Jones (41) was depressed, and John, Jr., (16) was cutting classes and failing. The Smith family was composed of Mr. Ed Smith, a quiet, depressed man of 40; his wife Beverly (36), who coped with her husband's withdrawal by drinking large quantities of wine; and Tommy Smith (16), who frequently stayed out all night. The White family consisted of Mr. George White (38), who gambled excessively; his wife Leona (37), who suffered from migraine headaches; William (18), a college freshman; Tanya (17), a senior in high school; and Debra (15), a high school dropout and addicted to amphetamines.

The group members were chosen carefully because they had qualities in common. All were black, intact, lived in the Fort Greene Housing Project in Brooklyn, and were born in America. The parents were about the same age, had adolescent children, and presented problems of drinking, gambling, drug use, and depression. It was felt that the families were sufficiently homogeneous to be able to identify with each other while being sufficiently heterogeneous to allow for differences in family living.

The therapy sessions followed the phases of conjoint family therapy we have suggested elsewhere: (1) observation, (2) intervention, and (3) consolidation (Foley, 1979, p. 493). Phase one is an attempt at getting people to talk about their problems by way of themes that run in various families. It is an attempt at getting various family members to identify with members of other families. For example, Mr. Jones and Mrs. Smith each coped with life by drinking. Mrs. Jones and Mr. Smith, on the other hand, tended to withdraw and become depressed. John Jones, Jr., and Debra White had school problems and were "acting-out," whereas, William White and his sister Tanya were doing well in school and could serve as role models. Mr. White, a gambler, could identify with problems of alcohol as he, too, was addicted. His wife Leona could learn that depression and migraine headaches are ways of withdrawing and that by being more assertive in the family, symptoms tend to diminish and even disappear. In brief, there were many possible opportunities for identification.

The focus in these early sessions is to get the families to see that problems are not just isolated phenomena in a family system but maneuvers or strategies designed to help people cope with life. Getting the sequence of events in a family correct is a monumental task but one well worth the effort. When does Mr. Jones drink? When does his wife become depressed? When does John, Jr., start cutting classes? The pattern or sequence of events is important because the behavior of each family member reinforces that of the other members. When Mr. Jones states that he drinks because his wife nags and she says that she does so because he drinks, they are stating a principle of system functioning, namely, causality is not linear but circular. The therapist can then make the observation that the more Mr. Jones drinks, the more his wife will become depressed and vice versa. An obvious conclusion, perhaps, but one that neither has thought about before. By finding out that John, Jr., becomes disgusted when these events take place and he starts to cut class, one sees how he reinforces his father's drinking and his mother's depression. By placing these events in the context of the family, the therapist re-labels behavior and sees it not just as the property of this or that member but of the entire system. The therapist can then pick up on family themes by asking if similar patterns are found in other families. Debra White then makes a comment that when her father spends rent money on gambling and her mother goes to bed with a migraine headache, she gets so depressed that she needs to take uppers. The therapist can then ask if Mr. White or his wife ever thought of the way in which their behavior influences Debra. In like manner, he or she can make the observation that there are many similarities in families with drug and alcohol problems, especially "that alcohol abuse would be prevalent in both groups of families of origin" (Ziegler-Driscoll, 1979, p. 19). Mr. White then says, "My mother and sister drank and Debra is just like them." He then goes on to say that Debra is not a White like he is but a Johnson like his mother. Mrs. Smith, quiet until now, comments, "Maybe that's why you don't like Debra, 'cause she's like them." His son William and daughter Tanya, however, are Whites and very much admired by their father. With this knowledge, the therapist can suggest, "Maybe one reason why Debra finds life so tough is that she doesn't feel she belongs in the family." Such a comment then opens up the whole question of family of origin and how this influences current family life. Talking about roots introduces the issue of slavery in a natural way and leads to further investigation of white/black feelings.

Phase two is characterized by interventions designed to alleviate family problems. It is a natural outgrowth of phase one in that problems have to be known in order to be solved. Emphasis is placed on problem solving and less on dynamics of personality. A constant question raised by the therapist is "How does your behavior influence the behavior of others in the family?" In this way family members begin to think in terms of system rather than in terms of individual dynamics. A second question raised is "How do others handle such issues?" In this way the counselor utilizes the resources of the group emphasizing the importance of outside feedback for change. One of the main strengths of MFT is the ability of people to see conflict in others. Mr. and Mrs. Jones can tell you at length and with great accuracy the reasons why the Smiths are having trouble. However, they fail to see how they behave with each other. In MFT people are constantly saying, "But you do the same thing." In time, Mr. and Mrs. Jones begin to see that what is happening to Ed and Beverly Smith is similar to their interaction. When such a revelation occurs, change can take place.

When the themes have been elaborated sufficiently, the therapist suggests moving to resolution of problems. The bottom line is always change. *What* rather than *why* is the dominant theme of the group. Mr. Jones, for example, may have begun drinking 16 years ago when he had to face the responsibility of having a son, but he drinks now because of current family interaction. It is not necessary to go back 16 years to get him to stop drinking. The goal of the group is to help Mr. Jones find new and healthier ways of coping. This might mean calling up Mr. Smith when he feels like drinking. Mr. Smith may help Mr. Jones over his problem and begin to feel more helpful, and therefore, less depressed. Mr. Jones may then be able to tell his wife what Mr. Smith says, e.g., his attitude or nonjudgmental approach, which will enable her to act differently toward her husband. In this way, members of the group are seen as helping agents and not just as critics. Perhaps John Jones and Beverly Smith will give each other enough support so that they will join Alcoholics Anonymous. The point to remember is that instead of being critics of others, MFT members become allies. Having shared of themselves in phase one, each realizes that we all have problems in common and all need support.

Phase three, consolidation, is the most important one because it means that each family and each family member must face the fact that change is a difficult process. There are many things we would like to change in ourselves and in others but realistically only a few will take place. It is a phase of reality. It is a time of assessment and evaluation. It is also a time of saying goodbye to the group. It is an important phase because it allows people an opportunity of learning how to use other people in a way that is helpful. Most of us see the world outside our immediate family as hostile territory. MFT gives the members of the group a new experience of others as friends and colleagues instead of as indifferent or cold. It allows each person to feel that he or she was of benefit to someone else and could give support to another in words if not in deeds. In summary, then, phase three becomes a unique experience for each member in that it allows each one to see himself or herself in relation to another in an intimate way. It gives each family an insight into another family, and this is something that most people do not experience.

SUMMARY

This chapter describes one approach when a white therapist deals with black families. It is not the only or exclusive way of doing therapy, but it is one that has proven over the past 20 years to be effective.

Conjoint family therapy is an approach that sees problems as residing in the way in which a family system interacts rather than in this or that particular individual. The interactional system is the problem and the individual only a symptom. Multiple family therapy involves the use of more than one family in this process. It is considered particularly helpful when the therapeutic encounter involves a white therapist and black clients because the feelings of transference are lessened so that family problems become the focus of therapy and not the relationship of the therapist and the members of each family.

Change takes place by way of *identification* with other members in the group; indirect learning, i.e., by *analogy*, seeing how others handle similar problems; and by *mimicking*, i.e., imitating the effective behavior of others. The medium of change, therefore, is not the relationship of the therapist to the group but of one family to another. The therapist is seen as a conductor who weaves the various strands of the sessions together and develops themes that reoccur. MFT is seen to have the advantages found in group therapy especially in that it allows a family member to experience a variety of personalities with whom he or she can identify and those found in conjoint family therapy especially offering a safe atmosphere for new ways of behaving.

A case illustration of three families was given demonstrating the typical stages of MFT: observation, intervention, and consolidation. The similarities and differences among family members were noted, and suggestions on how a therapist might conduct such sessions were indicated, with special emphasis given to problem solving. A final comment regarding the realistic limitations of MFT was expressed, pointing out that its goal is to change behavior and not to solve intrapsychic conflict. In the final phase of MFT, consolidation, the therapist must make an effort at evaluating the gains made by the families as well as areas still to be examined. Doing this allows each family to disengage itself from the process of therapy without exaggeration of its benefits or disparagement of its limits.

MFT is still a relatively new approach to treatment, despite its presence on the therapeutic scene since 1951. In this chapter I am suggesting that it is most beneficial when a group of homogeneous black family members can be brought together for a limited time with specific goals because it mitigates the ever-present factor of transference and gives a white therapist his or her best chance of doing effective work with such families.

REFERENCES

Buckley, W. *Sociology and Modern Systems Theory*. Englewood Cliffs, N.J.: Prentice-Hall, 1967.

Fogarty, T. "Emotional Climate in the Family and Therapy." In E. Pendagast (ed) *The Family*. New Rochelle, N.Y.: The Center for Family Learning, 1978, 60–69.

Foley, V. "Family Therapy," In R. Corsini (ed) *Current Psychotherapies*. Itasca, Ill.: Peacock Publishing Co., 1979.

Freud, S. "A Case of Hysteria." In J. Strachey (ed) *The Standard Edition of the Complete Psychological Works of Sigmund Freud*, Vol. VII. London: Hogarth Press, 1955, 7–122.

Greeley, A. "Creativity in the Irish Family: The Cost of Immigration," *International Journal of Family Therapy*, 1979, 295–303.

Hill, R. *The Strengths of Black Families*. New York: Emerson-Hall, 1972.

Kuhn, T. *The Structure of Scientific Revolutions*. Chicago: University of Chicago Press, 1962.

Levinson, E. *The Fallacy of Understanding*. New York: Basic Books, 1972.

Laqueur, P. "Multiple Family Therapy: Questions and Answers," In D. Bloch (ed) *Techniques of Family Psychotherapy*. New York: Grune & Stratton, 1973, 75–85.

Lewis, O. "The Culture of Poverty," *Scientific American*, 1966, 215(4), 19–25.

McAdoo, H. "Family Therapy in the Black Community," *American Journal of Orthopsychiatry*, 1977, 47(1), 75–79.

———. "Factors Related to Stability in Upwardly Mobile Black Families," *Journal of Marriage and the Family*, 1978, 762–778.

Powdermaker, H. "The Channeling of Negro Aggression by the Cultural Process," In C. Kluckhohn and A. Murray (eds) *Personality in Nature, Society and Culture*. New York: Knopf, 1950, 47–84.

Spiegel, J. "Some Cultural Aspects of Transference and Countertransference," In *Science and Psychoanalysis, Vol. II, Individual and Familial Dynamics*. New York: Grune & Stratton, 1959, 160–182.

———. *Transactions—The Interplay between Individual Family and Society*. New York: Science House, 1971.

Staples, R. "Toward a Sociology of the Black Family: A Theoretical and Methodo-
logical Assessment," *Journal of Marriage and the Family*, 1971, 33(1), 33–38.
_____ , and A. Mirande. "Racial and Cultural Variations among American Families:
A Decennial Review of the Literature on Minority Families," *Journal of
Marriage and the Family*, 1980, 42(4), 887–903.
Ziegler-Driscoll, G. "The Similarities in Families of Drug Dependents and Alco-
holics," In E. Kaufmann and P. Kaufmann (eds) *Family Therapy of Drug and
Alcohol Abuse*. New York: Gardner Press, 1979, 19–39.

15

SOME FINAL COMMENTS

Constance E. Obudho

It appears from the various chapters that the marriages and family lives of black people are as diverse and substantive as those of any other people. No longer should we be viewed as simply a homogeneous group of people with a problematic nature. Our lives are characterized by loving relationships as well as jealousies. Some of our marriages end in divorce, but many remain intact. Our families include matriarchal forms in line with the long-studied stereotype, but there are also patriarchal and egalitarian situations which offset this trend. We have nuclearly aligned family structures, but may rely heavily on our extended families as well. Some black parents are warm and nurturing, while others are more rigid. Fertility is still a source of concern for us. Finally, while there are couples and families who are relatively free of conflict, there are, of course, those who have problems requiring therapeutic intervention and there are therapists who are attempting to deal with these problems.

Fortunately, we are at a time when efforts are being made to delve more fully into the innerworkings of the lives of black people in order to obtain a clearer picture of the circumstances and the attitudes and feelings we have about a variety of issues. It is no longer acceptable merely to compare our behaviors with those of other groups. What we do, think, feel, and have to say are important in their own rights. It is a time when we are emphasizing our strengths, and we hope this will continue. The various chapters in this book have presented some of the functionings of black lives in terms of marriages and family relationships. The contributors, who are educators, psychologists, sociologists, and therapists, have tried to present a view of black people that is consistent with the emphasis on the positive aspects of black lives and that recognizes their complexity. In Part I, we discovered various aspects of black family life and marriage. The following will be a review of the chapters, highlighting their purposes and findings.

The chapter by King and Griffin introduced Part I with a look at what black men and women felt were important factors for healthy and strong interpersonal relationships. King and Griffin found that blacks have learned that above all, to love others we must first love ourselves. They also found that such factors as trust, caring, and working together were considered important ingredients in a successful relationship. The writers noted that the experiential workshops they conducted have been successful in enlightening blacks to self-awareness, and they are being requested continually as training grounds: King and Griffin felt that their subjects were optimistic about the future of black marriages and other interpersonal relationships.

In the next chapter, Turner and Turner discussed the socialization process and its effect on the self-esteem of black people. They also presented the results of a study of their own on evaluations by black men and women of what "most men" and "most women" are like. These results were related to the information on socialization and self-esteem. Turner and Turner found, for example, that black men were evaluated by black women as being less responsible than they were by other black males. This seemingly stereotypic characterization was explained by suggesting that the women may have considered the men *not* responsible as opposed to *ir*responsible in terms of control over certain aspects of their own lives because of the effects of discrimination. Another finding was that black males were rated more positively by black females on expressive traits referring to the lively, gregarious male than were any other group. The effects of these perceptions on interpersonal relationships including marriage were discussed.

Noting that research was limited in the area of marital relations between black men and women, Rutledge (chapter 4) conducted a study describing aspects of interaction goals, marital happiness, and marital disagreements. She found that, for the most part, the marriages were solid and cohesive. Of course, disagreements were reported by her subjects, and often the goals established between husband and wife were not achieved; however, instability and weakness were not overriding qualities. Rutledge indicated in her introduction that her work was exploratory and that the results addressed only a small number of black men and women. Nevertheless, she felt they provided needed insights into the perceptions of husbands and wives about their marriages and material that might prompt further research.

Barnes (chapter 5) looked at family structure, spousal cooperation, spousal affection, and the influence of education, occupation, income, and sex on these variables using black middle-class men and women as subjects. One of her aims was to determine patterns of matriarchy, patriarchy, and egalitarianism within the 41 households she canvased. Barnes found that of the 32 households in which both spouses were present, matriarchy was the primary decision-making pattern in 16 and egalitarianism existed in the other 16. Patriarchy existed in the nine remaining households studied. Barnes concluded that there are numerous variables that enter into the determination of the type of interpersonal interaction that will exist between couples and also that while there are differences between how middle-class and lower and working-class couples behave, there are also similarities.

Allen (chapter 6) looked at the nature of marital systems by race and sex using a middle-class sample with individuals ranging in age from 35 to 55 years. His concern was with marital stability, satisfaction, and the distribution of power in the relationship. There were no racial differences in terms of length of time married, for example. However, there were differences in marital stability as measured by whether or not individuals had been married more than once, the presence of children from previous unions, age at first marriage, and whether or not the first marriage was earlier or later than the individual had expected it to be. Allen found that one-fourth of the black couples were in second or successive marriages, while 5 percent of the white couples fit this description. Furthermore, more black couples incorporated children from previous marriages than did white couples. Race did not affect the distribution of power, but it did affect satisfaction. Finally, socioeconomic factors and education reportedly affected the race by sex differences for marital adjustment.

In chapter 7, Addison discussed how the black wife views her husband and her perception of how he views her. Ratings on communication, behaviors, emotions, and attitudes were the types of perceptions sought. Addison found that husbands were felt to be easy to talk to as well as good listeners. They reportedly rarely lied or criticized their wives. However, they did not praise their wives very often. In terms of behaviors, husbands were generally not lazy, physically abusive, gamblers, or unfaithful. In addition, they were hard workers. The wives' perceptions of what their husbands thought about them were quite similar to those reported about the men with the exception that wives felt they would be viewed as giving more praise. Further research would be needed to determine whether or not husbands would describe their wives as the women expected.

Leggon (chapter 8) examined the views of middle-class black and white women on marriage, career, and motherhood. She was interested in similarities and differences between the races and the coping mechanisms used by black professional women, in particular, to deal with the conflicting demands of these three areas. Leggon discovered that many of the problems her subjects discussed came from the conflicting demands of marriage and career rather than motherhood and career, especially for black women. Furthermore, to alleviate the conflicts produced by career and motherhood, black women relied on relatives and paid babysitters. This reportedly removed some of the guilt experienced by mothers, and this support from outsiders was more acceptable to black mothers than to white mothers. Leggon also pointed out the differing experiences of working in a job and having a career. For instance, black women felt less guilt than white women over working in a job, while both had conflicts over having a career with its resulting demands on marriage and motherhood. Older women reduced the conflicts between career and marriage by deciding beforehand that their marriage would take precedence over their career. Most of the subjects noted that whether or not a mate shared the same profession, the greater his personal and occupational security, the more willing and able he was to accept his wife's professional status and encourage her. Finally, a self-fulfilling prophecy was usually met such that if an individual expected problems to arise over career, marriage, and mother-hood, they did.

In chapter 9, McAdoo reported the role of the black mother and its effect on the development and social competency (self-esteem) of her child. Nurturance and nonnurturance were the variables looked at in the mother-child interac-tional process. Verbal and nonverbal interaction patterns were observed among his upper and lower middle-class subjects. It was found that the mothers generally gave nurturing responses in terms of being supportive and warm. Limit-setting existed, however, and mothers explained why before it occurred. McAdoo also determined that the children had positive self-images, although there was no direct relationship between the child's perceptions and the frequency or type of verbal or nonverbal interaction between mother and child. Furthermore, there were no significant differences between the responses made by lower and middle-class mothers. Additionally, as dis-cussed by Leggon in the previous chapter, McAdoo addressed the issue of the roles engaged in by many of the mothers—wife, parent, and worker—and how the kinship network was used to alleviate strains produced by conflicts in these roles.

Finally, in chapter 10, Turner and Darity compared level of education, geographical region, and sex to determine the rates of ideal and actual fertility among black couples. They found that, as expected, for actual numbers of children, blacks with less education tended to have three or more children as opposed to blacks with more education. Geographical region results showed that black people who lived in the South had more children (three or more) than those living in the North, as was expected from past literature. The authors also looked at attitudes about the ideal and actual number of children as these feelings reflected race consciousness and genocide fear. They discov-ered that the individuals who had concerns about racial survival and who were threatened by birth control programs felt the ideal was to have more children, perhaps to counteract the threat or as a reaction against the norms of the majority population. However, when actual circumstances were investigated in relation to these attitudes, there was not much consistency between how the individuals felt and how they behaved.

The issues discussed in Part I were some of the features exhibited in black marriages and families. In Part II, various approaches to therapy with black clients were presented. The purpose was for the therapists to discuss some of the philosophies and techniques they have tried and which have been found to be successful when working with the population of clients noted. In chapter

11, Brannon provided a view of the process of entering therapy. She discussed how the stigma of being "crazy" and the resistance of the black male to seeking outside help were major obstacles to approaching the mental health professional in times of need. She also pointed out the tendency of black people to be less than assertive and self-aware in terms of choosing a therapist with whom they felt comfortable and confident. Once these areas have been reckoned with, however, the next important factor is that the individual knows what to expect from the experience. Here Brannon gave extensive examples of her own style as well as the approaches of some other therapists. She also discussed the differences between the black and the white client in therapy, pointing out how important it is that the therapist accurately judge the meaning of the different behaviors.

In chapter 12, Halfhide discussed his approach to marital and family therapy. He emphasized the role of the individual's family of origin in contributing to the manifestation of present behaviors, as well as providing strengths for coping with problems in his or her life. His method reportedly relies heavily on helping the client develop insight about this generational connection. Another aspect of the approach emphasized by Halfhide is to focus on the individual's post-adolescent feelings and perceptions of his or her familial experiences rather than early childhood experiences which may not be as clear or recognizable. He noted that one of the deficits to working with the earlier years may be that it will make the therapeutic process longer—a situation that may be counterproductive to therapy considering his experiences with his particular population of clients. As part of the description of his technique, Halfhide presented two case studies, a single mother and a married couple, and discussed their progress in therapy.

McFadden (chapter 13) discussed some basic issues in counseling the black family with its unique characteristics. He emphasized that in order for a counselor to relate to a black family, he or she must first understand the "stylistic dimensions of counseling blacks." The counselor must understand the culture of this group including its language patterns, values, history, sociology, psychology, and ideology. McFadden continually stressed in his chapter that merely because the practices within black families may not mirror those used in white families, this does not indicate pathology or instability within these units. Consequently, old myths should be re-evaluated and strengths should be accepted and valued.

In the final chapter, Foley addressed the issue of whether or not a white family therapist can work with black clients. Because of the relatively smaller number of black therapists, white professionals must deal with black families. However, Foley cautioned, as did McFadden, that to work effectively the white therapist must understand how black families operate. Speaking from his own experiences as a white family therapist, Foley discussed various aspects of family therapy and its emphasis. He noted that two major obstacles to helping clients were the differences in value systems that may exist between clients and therapist and the issue of transference. These issues may be particularly critical when the therapist is white and the clients are black. To handle these problems, Foley reportedly uses multiple family therapy (MFT). He discussed this method of treatment in detail and pointed out its advantages with black families.

In sum, we have seen that love is an important function for black people. This has implications for the future success and survival of our relationships. We have learned that indeed blacks and whites have different perceptions and may function somewhat differently within the marital relationship. This is an area that has raised many questions, and there are still many to be answered. We saw that as with working-class and lower-class couples, within middle-class families, age, sex, level of education, income, and occupation may also have an effect on marital relationships. In addition, we learned something about the attitudes of married working women concerning the possible strains of their circumstances on their marriages and family relationships. We also learned something about the relationship between working mothers and children, specifically in regard to the effective handling of discipline. We found that extended kinship networks are very important factors for working mothers who may need assistance in terms of custodial care for their children. In addition, a chapter on family planning informed us of the current status of the influence of education and ideology on fertility rates among black women.

In Part II we were given four views of marital and family therapy with black clients. We learned of some interesting approaches and cases. In general, we found that often the traditional approaches of psychotherapy are not applicable directly to black clients, but they have been modified creatively by many therapists.

We hope this book has been successful in providing useful information to those who are interested in knowing more about black marriages and families and who will continue to produce research that is both stimulating and useful.

AUTHOR INDEX

SUBJECT INDEX

ABOUT THE CONTRIBUTORS

Donald P. Addison did graduate study in sociology at Boston University, University of Missouri, and is presently a Ph.D. candidate at American University, Washington, D.C. He presently serves as a member of the faculty in the Department of Sociology and Anthropology, Howard University.

He formerly served as a staff member of the Urban League in Denver, Colorado and Kansas City, Missouri, and was Executive Director of the Urban League in Raine, Wisconsin. He has held faculty positions at North Carolina A & T State University, the University of Wisconsin-Milwaukee, and North Carolina Central University, Durham, North Carolina.

Walter R. Allen earned his Ph.D at the University of Chicago in sociology. Since 1979, he has been Assistant Professor of Sociology and the Center for Afro-American and African Studies at the University of Michigan. He has taught previously at the University of North Carolina, Chapel Hill, and has held visiting professorships at Duke University and Howard University. Currently, Professor Allen's research interests are in family and socialization, desegregation in higher education, and population studies. His articles have appeared in *Sociological Quarterly, Journal of Marriage and the Family*, and *Phylon*. In 1982, Professor Allen was awarded a Rockefeller Foundation Postdoctoral Research fellowship.

Annie S. Barnes received the Ph.D. degree at the University of Virginia in social anthropology in 1971. She is currently on the faculty at Norfolk State University in Norfolk, Virginia, where she teaches courses in anthropology, sociology, and social science research skills. She is Chair of the Blacks in Education Committee of the Council of Anthropology and Education and Vice President of the Virginia Social Science Association. Her publications are about American blacks in the areas of the beauty parlor, family, kinship systems, alternative family forms, women, voluntary association participation, retirement patterns, residential patterns, and the saga, *Roots*. She has also published a *Social Science Research Skills Handbook* and articles about adolescence in American society and the ceremonial, political, and familial systems in the Osudoku society, Ghana, West Africa.

Lorraine Brannon is a native Washingtonian who earned her Ph.D. in clinical psychology in 1975 from Southern Illinois University in Carbondale, Illinois. She earned her Masters degree in 1971 and her Bachelor's degree in 1968, both from Howard University. She belongs to numerous professional organizations, including the Association of Black Psychologists and the American Psychological Association. She has received numerous honors and has been cited in *Who's Who Among Black Americans* yearly since 1975 and in *Outstanding Young Women of America* since 1979. Dr. Brannon was recently re-appointed, by the Mayor, to serve on the D.C. Psychology Licensing Board. She has been a member of this board for the past four years and is currently the Vice Chairman. Dr. Brannon's career in psychology spans 14 years during which time she has worked in university settings, hospital settings, correctional facilities, and community mental health centers. Currently, in addition to her full-time private practice, Dr. Brannon consults to the D.C. CHARLEE Program for Abused and Neglected Children and conducts workshops on Stress Management; Parenting; and Communication Skills.

William A. Darity received his Ph.D. from the University of North Carolina (Chapel Hill) School of Public Health in the areas of Public Health and Health Education. He is presently Professor of Public Health and Dean of the School of Health Sciences at the University of Massachusetts. He has spent many years in international health in the Middle East and Africa. His paper in this volume with Castellano Turner relates to his major research interest in family planning attitudes with an emphasis on the black community.

Vincent D. Foley earned his Ph.D. degree at Boston University in psychology and counseling. He is the author of *An Introduction to Family Therapy* and the editor of the series *Family Therapy: Theory, Practice and Technique*. His special interests are in alcoholism and ethnic factors in family therapy, and he has presented on these issues in Israel, Ireland, and England. He is a former professor at St. John's University in Jamaica, New York, and is currently in private practice.

Jean T. Griffin earned her Ed.D. at Temple University in the area of educational psychology. She presently serves as a core faculty member of Union Graduate School and serves as Clinical Director of a drug program sponsored by Boston University. Dr. Griffin is one of the originators of the

Black Love Workshop. She has conducted research in the area of women in the labor force, especially women of color. She has presented papers and lectures on such topics as drugs, human relations, and women in the world of work for groups and organizations in the Eastern part of the United States.

Adriaan T. Halfhide earned his M.A. degree from New York University in psychology, specializing in personality and behavioral pathology. His Ed.M. degree was earned at Teachers College, Columbia University, Family and Community Education Department where he is currently preparing his dissertation for the Ed.D. degree.

Presently, he is the Supervising Counselor of the New York City Police Academy and has been engaged in private practice, on a part-time basis, working with couples and families since 1976.

As a result of his work with troubled couples and families, Mr. Halfhide has been cited in a number of publications and has also appeared as a consultant/guest on the popular television program, "Today's Black Woman," aired during March, 1981, whose theme was black marriages.

He has facilitated groups for the local Parents' Associations, and his current research interest is the effects of societal change on the structure of black families over time.

Dr. Ruth E. G. King has an extensive background with many varied experiences that led her to assist in the development of the Black Love Workshop. She is presently a family therapist for the Montgomery Health Department in Maryland. An experienced academician, Dr. King has taught from kindergarten to college and adult students. Her interactions with youth on the campuses of Howard University and Federal City College provided insights into current issues between black males and females. As a consultant/trainer, she has provided workshops and presented lectures for black female administrators, trained black men and women in economic development, and counseled young females in a Job Corps setting. These experiences sparked Dr. King's interest in providing a mechanism to improve black male/female relationships.

Cheryl B. Leggon earned her Ph.D. in sociology at the University of Chicago; she also earned a M.A. in sociology from the University of Chicago and a B.A. from Barnard College, Columbia University. She is a former Postdoctoral Research Fellow in the Sociology Department at the University of Chicago and a former Summer Fellow at the Center for Advanced Study in the Behavioral Sciences. She has been elected Secretary of the International Sociological Association's Research Committee on Ethnic, Race, and Minority Relations. Previously she taught at Mount Holyoke College. Presently, she is Director of Research at a business management consulting firm. She is co-editor of *Research in Race and Ethnic Relations*, an annual international journal published by JAI Press, and is writing a book on racism and sexism in the United States, which will be published by Wadsworth Publishing Co., Inc.

John Lewis McAdoo, Associate Professor, The University of Maryland, received his Ph.D. degree from the University of Michigan in 1970. He completed post-doctoral studies in mental health epidemiology in 1979 at Johns Hopkins University and post graduate courses at Harvard University. He has published several articles in the areas of patterns of racial attitudes and self-esteem in black children, parent-child interaction, fear of crime and well-being of urban minority elderly. He is currently involved in evaluating father-child interaction patterns and designing research related to the morale and well-being of older Americans living in urban and suburban communities.

Johnnie McFadden, Systems Vice President for Intercultural Affairs and Professional Development and Professor of Counselor Education, University of South Carolina, received his Ph.D. at the University of South Carolina in 1973. McFadden's teaching and research interests are in cultural and social dynamics of the Black family, cross-cultural counseling, international education, and leadership development. His recent research projects have included stylistic dimensions of counseling minorities, discipline and classroom management, and descriptors/stereotypes of black women. McFadden is 1982-83 President-Elect of the Association for Non-White Concerns, a division of the American Personnel and Guidance Association.

Constance E. Obudho received her Ph.D. from Rutgers University, New Brunswick, New Jersey (1978) in the area of social psychology. She is presently employed as a social worker-habilitation plan organizer at Johnstone Training Center, a facility for mentally retarded individuals. She has published two annotated bibliographies in the areas of racial attitudes and non-verbal behavior. She has also done research on racial preferences among young school children and implicit personality theories of parents and non-parents about children and other adults. She has worked as a Veterans Administration educational/vocational counselor and has taught undergraduate classes in black psychology. This is her first edited work.

Essie Manuel Rutledge earned her Ph.D. degree in sociology from the University of Michigan (1974). She presently serves as Chair and Associate Professor of the Department of Afro-American Studies, Western Illinois University. She has conducted research in the areas of role knowledge, marital and family relations of black women, socialization/aspirations and race relations, and is presently conducting a study of the quality of life in a Midwestern rural farming area. She has presented papers and lectures on such topics as black women, black families, black male-female relationships, and race relations. She has published articles in books and journals which include such topics as black women, black families, black separatism, role knowledge, and socialization and aspirations.

Barbara F. Turner received her Ph.D. from the Committee on Human Development at the University of Chicago with a specialization in adult development and aging. She is Professor of Education and Psychology and Director of the Center on Aging at the University of Massachusetts at Amherst. Her research and publications center on agism, racism, and sexism. With her husband, Castellano B. Turner, she has conducted an ongoing longitudinal study of socialization to careers, personality, and perceptions of occupational discrimination among black and white college students. The chapter in this volume represents one of many publications from this project. Dr. Turner's other publications focus on sex-related differences in aging.

Castellano B. Turner received his Ph.D. from the Psychology Department at the University of Chicago with a specialization in personality and psychopathology. He is Professor of Psychology at the University of Massachusetts at Amherst. Within the Clinical Psychology Training Program of the department, his specialty is community mental health. His two chapters in this volume represent aspects of his major research projects over the last 10 years: family planning attitudes among black Americans (with William A. Darity) and racial and gender differences in socialization (with Barbara F. Turner).

About The Editor

CONSTANCE E. OBUDHO received her Ph.D. in social psychology from Rutgers University. She is currently a Social Worker I at the E. R. Johnstone Training and Research Center in Bordentown, New Jersey. Her writings include *The Proxemic Behavior of Man and Animals, Black-White Racial Attitudes* (Greenwood Press, 1976), and *Human Nonverbal Behavior* (Greenwood Press, 1979).